Exh   ance

Exhausting Dance: Performance and the politics of movement examines the work of key contemporary choreographers who have transformed the dance scene since the early 1990s in Europe and the USA. Through their vivid and explicit dialogue with performance art, visual arts and critical theory from the past thirty years, this new generation of choreographers challenge our understanding of dance by exhausting the concept of movement. Their work demands to be read as performed extensions of the radical politics implied in performance art, in post-structuralist and critical theory, in postcolonial theory, and in critical race studies.

In this far-ranging and exceptional study, André Lepecki brilliantly analyzes the work of the choreographers:

- Jérôme Bel (France)
- Juan Dominguez (Spain)
- Trisha Brown (USA)
- La Ribot (Spain)
- Xavier Le Roy (France-Germany)
- Vera Mantero (Portugal)

and the visual and performance artists:

- Bruce Nauman (USA) and
- William Pope.L (USA)

This book offers a significant and radical revision of the way we think about dance, arguing for the necessity of a renewed engagement between dance studies and experimental artistic and philosophical practices.

André Lepecki is Assistant Professor at the Department of Performance Studies at New York University. He is an essayist and dramaturge. He edited *Of the Presence of the Body* (Wesleyan University Press, 2004) and is coeditor with Sally Banes of *The Senses in Performance* (Routledge, 2006).

D1614804

Exhausting Dance

Performance and the politics of movement

André Lepecki

Routledge
Taylor & Francis Group

NEW YORK AND LONDON

First published 2006
by Routledge
270 Madison Ave, New York, NY 10016

Simultaneously published in the UK
by Routledge
2 Park Square, Milton Park, Abingdon, Oxon OX14 4RN

Reprinted 2007 (twice)

Routledge is an imprint of the Taylor & Francis group, an informa business

© 2006 André Lepecki

Typeset in Baskerville
by Book Now Ltd
Printed and bound in Great Britain
by The Cromwell Press, Trowbridge, Wiltshire

British Library Cataloguing in Publication Data
A catalogue record for this book is available from the British Library

Library of Congress Cataloging in Publication Data
A catalog record has been requested

ISBN10: 0-415-36253-9 (cased)
ISBN10: 0-415-36254-7 (limp)

ISBN13: 978-0-415-36253-5 (cased)
ISBN13: 978-0-415-36254-2 (limp)

Contents

Illustrations

Acknowledgments

My deepest thanks to all that contributed so much with their ideas, comments, labor, friendship, mentorship, inspiration, intelligence, and art throughout the writing of this book. I would like to start with a very sincere thank you to the artists whose work this book addresses: Jérôme Bel, Trisha Brown, Juan Dominguez, Vera Mantero, Bruce Nauman, William Pope.L, La Ribot, and Xavier Le Roy. I also would like to thank their companies and their managers for their support in providing archival material, photographs, and videos, as well as for their always prompt and patient replies to my always urgent and almost endless questions. So, thank you Sandro Grando, Maria Carmela, Lydia Grey, and Rebecca Davis. I would like to thank Katrin Schoof and Luciana Fina for their gracious permission to print their beautiful photos. Alice Reagan proofread an early draft of the manuscript, and I thank her for her help at a delicate moment of this project. Chapter 6 was first published with a slightly different title in *Blackening Europe* (Routledge 2004), edited by Heike Raphael-Hernandez, and is reprinted here by permission. The ideas behind chapter 5 were first rehearsed in a short essay published in *Women and Performance*, issue 27, 2004. The final version of the manuscript was edited and proofread by Jenn Joy. To her dedicated attention to detail, to her critical insight, and to her research of some hard leads this book owes a lot. I am grateful to the anonymous readers who first evaluated for Routledge the project of this book. Their comments were invaluable for its development. My deepest thank you also to the two readers of the manuscript's complete first draft, Ramsay Burt and Mark Franko. Their scholarship has always been an inspiration and to have had the privilege to receive their insightful comments, suggestions, and pointed critiques made this a much better book. The support I received throughout the whole process from my two editors at Routledge, Talia Rodgers, Publisher, Theatre and Performance Studies, and Minh Ha Duong, Assistant Editor, was simply outstanding. My thanks to Richard Schechner and to Diana Taylor for their guidance in helping me prepare the initial project of this book. Thank you also José Muñoz and Tavia Nyongo for precious feedback on early drafts of some of the following chapters.

A warm thank you to three constituencies whose work and critical thinking inform much of my writing: the artists I have had the privilege to collaborate with in the past two decades either as a dramaturge or as a co-creator, my brilliant students, and my extraordinary colleagues at the Department of Performance Studies at New York University. In order then, my deepest thanks to Francisco Camacho, Vera Mantero, João Fiadeiro, Sérgio Pelágio, Meg Stuart, Rachael Swain, Eleonora Fabião, and Bruce Mau; to all my students, particularly Victoria

Anderson, Gillian Lipton, P. J. Novelli, Shani Shakur, Rodrigo Tisi, Jenn Joy, Sean Simon, Nikki Cesare-Bartnicki, Kim Jordan, Dorita Hanna, Fernando Calzadilla, Michel Minnick, and Sarah Cervenack; and to my colleagues Barbara Browning, Anna Deveare-Smith, Deborah Kapchan, Barbara Kirshenblatt-Gimblett, José Muñoz, Tavia Nyongo, Ann Pellegrini, Richard Schechner, Karen Shimakawa, Diana Taylor, and Allen Weiss for their ongoing support and true mentorship.

Thank you to my mother Maria Lúcia and to my father Witold for their support and love. Thanks to Manuel. Thanks to César. Thanks to Kika and Fernando, to Leo and Rê. Thank you Elsa and Tobias for your beautiful and intelligent becomings. Thanks to my friends Pedro and Teresa, Luis Pedro, Sérgio and Sissi, Vera, Scott, Myriam, Karmen and Matthew. Thank you Eleonora. This book is for you.

1 Introduction

The political ontology of movement

> One must introduce in the diagnostic of our times, a kinetic and kinesthetic dimension because, without such a dimension, all discourse about modernity will completely bypass that which in modernity is most real.
>
> (Sloterdijk 2000b: 27)

On 31 December 2000, the *New York Times* published an article by Senior Dance Editor Anna Kisselgoff titled "Partial to Balanchine, and a Lot of Built-In Down Time," a review of the New York dance scene for the year that had just ended. At a certain point in her text Kisselgoff writes: "Stop and Go. Call it a trend or a tic, the increasing frequency of hiccupping sequences in choreography is impossible to ignore. Viewers interested in flow or a continuum of movement have been finding slim pickings in many premieres." After listing some "hiccupping" choreographers, which ranged from New York-based David Dorfman to (then) Frankfurt-based William Forsythe, Kisselgoff concludes: "It is all very 'today.' What about tomorrow?" (Kisselgoff 2000: 6).

Perception of a hiccupping in choreographed movement produces critical anxiety; it is dance's very future that appears menaced by the eruption of kinesthetic stuttering. Before a purposeful choreographic interruption of "flow or a continuum of movement," the critic offers two possible readings: either those strategies can be dismissed as a "trend" – thus cast as a limited epiphenomenon, an annoying "tic" that does not deserve a too serious critical consideration; or they can be denounced, more seriously, as a threat – a threat to dance's "tomorrow," to dance's capacity to smoothly reproduce itself into the future within its familiar parameters. This last perception – that the intrusion of stilling hiccups in contemporary choreography threatens dance's own futurity – is of relevance to a discussion of some recent choreographic strategies where dance's relation to movement is being exhausted. I suggest the perception of the stilling of movement as a threat to dance's tomorrow indicates that any disrupting of dance's flow – any choreographic questioning of dance's identity as a *being-in-flow* – represents not just a localized disturbance of a critic's capacity to enjoy dance, but, more relevantly, it performs a critical act of deep ontological impact. No wonder some perceive such an ontological convulsion as a betrayal: the betrayal of dance's very essence and nature, of its signature, of its privileged domain. That is: the betrayal of the bind between dance and movement.

Any accusation of betrayal necessarily implies the reification and reaffirmation of certainties in regard to what constitutes the rules of the game, the right path, the correct posture, or the appropriate form of action. That is, any accusation of betrayal implies an ontological certainty charged with choreographic characteristics. In the case of contemporary dance's putative betrayal, the accusation describes, reifies, and reproduces a whole ontology of dance that can be summarized as follows: dance ontologically imbricates itself with, is isomorphic to, movement. Only after accepting such grounding of dance on movement can one accuse certain contemporary choreographic practices of betraying dance.

It should be noted that such accusations of betrayal (and their implicit ontological reifications) are not confined to the realm of North American dance reviews. They emerge also in European courtrooms. On 7 July 2004 the Circuit Court of Dublin heard a civil case against the International Dance Festival of Ireland (IDF). The Festival was being accused of display of nudity and alleged performance of lewd acts in a dance piece titled *Jérôme Bel* (1995) by contemporary French choreographer Jérôme Bel.[1] The piece had been presented by IDF in its 2002 edition. Due to technicalities, the presiding judge eventually dismissed the case. Apparently, the complaining party, Mr. Raymond Whitehead, had based his suit on a faulty mix of obscenity laws and false-advertisement laws seeking "damages for breach of contract and negligence" (Falvey 2004: 5). What is interesting in this case is that Mr. Whitehead supported his obscenity and false-advertisement case by claiming that *Jérôme Bel* could not be properly classified as a dance performance. In a statement to the *Irish Times* of 8 July 2004, Mr. Whitehead articulated a clear ontology of dance that was not at all dissimilar to Kisselgoff's. According to the *Irish Times:* "There was nothing in the performance [he] would describe as dance, which he defined as 'people moving rhythmically, jumping up and down, usually to music but not always' and conveying some emotion. He was refused a refund" (Holland 2004: 4).

Set side by side, these two discursive moments demand consideration. They reflect the fact that in the past decade some contemporary North American and European choreography has indeed engaged in dismantling a certain notion of dance – the notion that ontologically associates dance with "flow and a continuum of movement" and with "people jumping up and down" (with or without music . . .). But they also reflect a widespread inability, or even unwillingness, to critically account for recent choreographic practices as valid artistic experiments. Thus, the deflation of movement in recent experimental choreography is depicted only as a symptom of a general "down-time" in dance. But perhaps it is the depiction itself that should be seen as symptomatic of a "down-time" in dance's critical discourse, indicating a deep disjuncture between current choreographic practices and a mode of writing still very much attached to ideals of dancing as constant agitation and continuous mobility. It should be remembered that the operation of inextricably aligning dance's being with movement – as commonsensical as such an operation may sound today – is a fairly recent historical development. Dance historian Mark Franko showed how, in the Renaissance, choreography defined itself only secondarily in relationship to movement:

> the dancing body as such is barely a subject of treatises. As the dance scholar Rodocanachi put it, ' . . . *quant aux mouvements, c'est la danse en elle-même dont la*

connaissance semble avoir été la moindre des occupations du danseur' [. . . as for the
movements, it is the dance itself that seems to have been the least of the
dancer's concern].

(Franko 1986: 9)

Ann Kisselgoff's predecessor, *New York Times*'s first full-time dance critic John
Martin, would have agreed with Franko. In 1933, he affirmed: "When we first
find dancing assuming something of a theatrical form – that is, after the antique
days – we find it concerned little if at all with the movement of the body" (Martin
1972: 13). Why, then, this obsessive concern with the display of moving bodies,
this demand that dance be in a constant state of agitation? And why see in
choreographic practices that refuse that display and agitation a threat to dance's
being? These questions reflect how the development of dance as an autonomous
art form in the West, from the Renaissance on, increasingly aligns itself with an
ideal of ongoing motility. Dance's drive towards a spectacular display of
movement becomes its modernity, in the sense Peter Sloterdijk in the epigraph to
this chapter defines it: as an epoch and *a mode of being* where *the kinetic* corresponds
to "that which in modernity is *most real*" (2000b: 27, emphasis added). As the
kinetic project of modernity becomes modernity's ontology (its inescapable
reality, its foundational truth), so the project of Western dance becomes more and
more aligned with the production and display of a body and a subjectivity fit to
perform this unstoppable motility.

Thus, by the time when the Romantic *ballet d'action* is fully in place, we find
dance clearly performing itself as a spectacle of flowing mobility. As dance
scholars Susan Foster (1996), Lynn Garafola (1997), and Deborah Jowitt (1988)
have argued, the premise of Romantic ballet was to present dance as continuous
motion, a motion preferably aiming upwards, animating a body thriving lightly
in the air. Such an ideology shaped styles, prescribed techniques, and configured
bodies – just as much as it shaped critical standards for evaluating a dance's
esthetic value. Even though the first Romantic ballet is considered to be Filippo
Taglioni's 1832 production of *La Sylphide*, premiered at the Paris Opera, it is in
an 1810 text that we can find one of the earliest and certainly most densely
articulated theorizations of dance as clearly linked to a performance of
uninterrupted flow of movement. Heinrich von Kleist's classic parable "*Über das
Marionettentheater*" praises the superiority of the puppet over the human dancer
because the puppet need not stop its motions in order to regain momentum:

> Puppets, like elves, need the ground only so that they can touch it lightly and
> renew the momentum of their limbs through this momentary delay. We
> [humans] need it to rest on, to recover from the exertions of dance, *a moment
> which is clearly not part of the dance.*[2]
>
> (in Copeland and Cohen 1983: 179)

However, it is only in the 1930s that the strict ontological identification
between uninterrupted movement and dance's being was clearly articulated as an

inescapable demand for any choreographic project. John Martin, in his famous lectures at the New School in New York City in 1933, proposed that only with the advent of modern dance did dance finally find its true, ontologically grounded, beginning: "this beginning was the discovery of the actual substance of the dance, which it found to be movement" (Martin 1972: 6). For Martin, the choreographic explorations of Romantic and Classic ballet, and even the antiballetic freeing of the body's expressivity spearheaded by Isadora Duncan, had all missed dance's true being. None had understood that dance was to be founded on movement alone. For Martin, ballet was dramaturgically too tied up with narrative and choreographically too invested in the striking pose, while Duncan's dance was too subservient to music. According to Martin, it was not until Martha Graham and Doris Humphrey in the USA, and Mary Wigman and Rudolph von Laban in Europe, that modern dance discovered movement as its essence, and "became for the first time an independent art" (1972: 6).

The strict alignment of dance with movement that John Martin announced and celebrated is but the logical outcome of his modernist ideology, of his desire to theoretically secure for dance an autonomy that would make it an equal to other high art forms. Martin's modernism is a construct, a project that, as dance historian Mark Franko has shown, took place not only in his writings and reviews, but also in the contested space between the choreographic and the theoretical, the corporeal and the ideological, the kinetic and the political (Franko 1995). Dance scholar Randy Martin notes how the project of grounding the ontology of dance in pure movement leads to "a presumed autonomy for the aesthetic in the realm of theory, which is [. . .] what grounds, without needing to name or situate, the authority of the theorist or critic" (Martin 1998: 186). This struggle for critical and theoretical authority defines the discursive dynamics informing the production, circulation, and critical reception of dance; it defines how in journalistic dance reviews, in programming decisions, and in legal suits some dances are considered proper while others are dismissed as acts of ontological betrayal. To acknowledge that dance happens in this contested space clarifies how recent accusations of betrayal ventriloquize an ideological program of defining, fixing, and reproducing what should be valued as dance and what should be excluded from its realm as futureless, insignificant, or obscene.

Meanwhile, dance's ontological question remains open.

It is this open question, in its esthetic, political, economic, theoretical, kinetic, and performative implications that *Exhausting Dance* addresses. I dedicate each chapter of this book to a close reading of a few selected pieces by European and North American contemporary choreographers, visual artists, and performance artists whose work (regardless of whether that work properly falls into the category of theatrical dance) proposes, with particular intensity, a critique of some constitutive elements of Western theatrical dance. The critical elements that I highlight are, in order of appearance: solipsism, stillness, the linguistic materiality of the body, the toppling of the vertical plane of representation, the stumble on the racist terrain, the proposition of a politics of the ground, and the critique of the melancholic drive at the heart of choreography. The artists whose work sets in motion these critical elements are (also in order of appearance): Bruce Nauman, Juan Dominguez, Xavier Le Roy, Jérôme Bel, Trisha Brown, La Ribot, William Pope.L, and Vera Mantero.

The fact that two of these artists are not "properly" dancers, and do not describe themselves as choreographers, but have nevertheless explicitly experimented with choreographic exercises (Bruce Nauman) or explicitly addressed the politics of motility in contemporaneity (William Pope.L) is methodologically important for my argument. Their work allows for reframing choreography outside artificially self-contained disciplinary boundaries, and for identifying the political ontology of modernity's investment on its odd hyperkinetic being. To address the choreographic outside the proper limits of dance proposes for dance studies the expansion of its privileged object of analysis; it asks dance studies to step into other artistic fields and to create new possibilities for thinking relationships between bodies, subjectivities, politics, and movement.

One of the relationships this book privileges is that between dance, dance studies, and philosophy. This theoretical dialogue departs from the observation that the recent difficulties of critically assessing dances that refuse to be confined to a constant "flow or continuum of movement" indicate a reconfiguration of dance's relationship to its coming into presence. Now "presence" is not only a term referring to the dancer's negotiation between technical and artistic proficiency in the performance of choreography. It is also a fundamental philosophical concept, one of the main objects of Heidegger's *destruktion* of metaphysics and of Derrida's deconstruction.[3] Thus, any dance that probes and complicates how it comes into presence, and where it establishes its ground of being, suggests for critical dance studies the need to establish a renewed dialogue with contemporary philosophy. I am thinking in particular of those authors that follow Nietzsche's destruction of traditional philosophy through the proposition of a critique of the will to power – a project that informs the philosophical *and* political work of Michel Foucault, Jacques Derrida, and Gilles Deleuze and Félix Guattari; works and authors I invoke frequently throughout this book. For theirs is not only a philosophy of the body but a philosophy that creates concepts that allow for a political reframing of the body. Theirs is a philosophy that understands the body not as a self-contained and closed entity but as an open and dynamic system of exchange, constantly producing modes of subjection and control, as well as of resistance and becomings.[4] As feminist theorist Elizabeth Grosz explains, after

> Nietzsche [. . .] the body is the site for the emanation of the will to power (or several wills), an intensely energetic locus for all cultural production, a concept I believe may be more useful in rethinking the subject in terms of the body.
>
> (Grosz 1994: 147)

Rethinking the subject in terms of the body is precisely the task of choreography, a task that may not be always subservient to the imperative of the kinetic, a task that is always already in dialogue with critical theory and philosophy. Fredric Jameson, in a recent book, sees the return to philosophy in recent critical studies as a dangerous return to modernist and conservative ideals and ideologies (Jameson 2002: 1–5). I don't think one immediately follows the other. I see Jameson's position as a perfect example of Homi Bhabha's powerful opening words in his essay "The Commitment to Theory": "There is a damaging and self-defeating assumption that theory is necessarily the elite language of the socially and culturally privileged" (Bhabha 1994: 19). Bhabha reminds us that there is "a distinction to be made between the institutional history of critical theory and its conceptual potential for change and innovation" (1994: 31). This is precisely Deleuze's position in distinguishing the institutional history of philosophy and the political power of philosophy (Deleuze 1995: 135–55). If there is one contribution I would like to propose to dance studies it is to consider in which ways choreography and philosophy share that same fundamental political, ontological, physiological, and ethical question that Deleuze recuperates from Spinoza and from Nietzsche: what can a body do?

The work of the philosophers and critical theorists I engage with deploys this politically progressive power founded in this fundamental question; in the necessary dialogue this question proposes between critical theory, philosophy and all modes of performance, including dance. Thus, I invoke throughout the book Roland Barthes's and Michel Foucault's critique of the authority of the author, Jacques Derrida's critique of representation and general economy, Avery Gordon's notion of the sociological force of the spectral, Anne Anlin Cheng's reframing of the Freudian notion of melancholia, Deleuze and Guattari's concept of body without organs, Peter Sloterdijk's unveiling of a kinetic ontology of modernity, Frantz Fanon's critique of ontology in the colonial condition, and Judith Butler's recasting of the Austinian performative – in order to understand the choreographic deployments of these crucial concepts. Moreover, the dialogue with philosophy is one in which the artists I discuss are explicitly engaged. Indeed, it can be said that without their explicit commitment to philosophy and critical theory there would not be their artistic work. As I will show, Vera Mantero dialogues directly with Deleuze's notion of immanence, William Pope.L "talks" with Heidegger and Frantz Fanon, Jérôme Bel quotes the importance of Deleuze's notions of repetition and difference for his work, Bruce Nauman invokes Wittgenstein, while Xavier Le Roy explicitly acknowledges Elizabeth Grosz. Even when this dialogue is not directly made apparent, it is clear how Trisha Brown's converses with architectural theory and La Ribot is right in the midst of a debate with Heidegger's notion of *Verfallen*. Throughout this book, I do little more than to listen to each choreographer's proposals and then foreground the philosophy they deploy. And, in each chapter, I reiterate Bhabha's question: "In what hybrid forms, then, may a politics of the theoretical statement emerge?" (1994: 22).

Much of my argument in this book turns around the formation of choreography as a peculiar invention of early modernity, as a technology that creates a body disciplined to move according to the commands of writing. The first version of the word "choreography" was coined in 1589, and titles one of the most famous dance manuals of that period: *Orchesographie* by Jesuit priest Thoinot Arbeau (literally, the writing, *graphie*, of the dance, *orchesis*).[5] Compressed into one word, morphed into one another, dance and writing produced qualitatively unsuspected and charged relationalities between the subject who moves and the subject who writes. With Arbeau, these two subjects became one and the same. And through this not too obvious assimilation, the modern body revealed itself fully as a linguistic entity.

It is not by chance that the invention of this new art of codifying and displaying disciplined movement is historically coincidental with the unfolding and consolidation of the project of modernity. From the Renaissance on, as dance pursues its own autonomy as an art form, it does so in tandem with the consolidation of that major project of the West known as modernity. Dance and modernity intertwine in a kinetic mode of being-in-the-world. Cultural historian Harvie Ferguson writes, "the only changeless element in Modernity is the propensity to movement, which becomes, so to speak, its permanent emblem" (Ferguson 2000: 11). Thus, dance increasingly turns towards movement to look for its essence. German philosopher Peter Sloterdijk proposed that modernity's project is fundamentally kinetic: "ontologically, modernity is a pure being-toward-movement" (Sloterdijk 2000b: 36). Dance accesses modernity by its increased ontological alignment with movement as the spectacle of modernity's being. Writing on Baroque dance, particularly as performed by the body of the Sun King, Louis XIV, Mark Franko notes how the performance of choreography is first of all a performance centered on the display of a disciplined body performing the spectacle of its own capacity to be set into motion:

> Anyone who has studied baroque dance in the studio under the teacher's watchful eye can testify that it allows little or no place for spontaneity. The royal body dancing was made to *represent itself as if remachined* in the service of an exacting coordination between upper and lower limbs dictated by a strict musical frame. It was an early modern techno-body.
>
> (Franko 2000: 36, emphasis added)

If choreography emerges in early modernity to remachine the body so it can "represent itself" as a total "being-toward-movement," perhaps the recent exhaustion of the notion of dance as a pure display of uninterrupted movement participates of a general critique of this mode of disciplining subjectivity, of constitute being. If we agree with Ferguson's insight that movement is modernity's "permanent emblem," then this theoretical point of departure could allow for discursively reframing the current exhaustion of dance. If modernity's "only changeless element" (Ferguson 2000: 11) is, paradoxically, movement, then it could very well be that by disrupting the alliance between dance and movement, by critiquing the possibility of sustaining a mode of moving in a "flow and continuum of movement," some recent dance may be actually proposing political and theoretical challenges to the old alliance between the simultaneous invention of choreography and modernity as a "being-toward-movement" and the political ontology of movement in modernity. In that sense, to exhaust dance is to exhaust modernity's permanent emblem. It is to push modernity's mode of creating and privileging a kinetic subjectivity to its critical limit. It is to exhaust modernity, to use Teresa Brennan's powerful expression – an expression that could be read as synonymous to the title of this book (Brennan 1998).

Since "modernity" and "subjectivity" are two central terms in the following chapters, they deserve some immediate clarification. My use of "subjectivity" does not index a return to or a reappropriation of the notion of the "subject." The latter is usually associated with the reification of subjectivity in the legal figure of the person, with the assertion of the person as a self-enclosed, autonomous individual bound to a fixed identity, and with the identification of a full presence at the center of discourse (Dupré 1993: 13–17, Ferguson 2000: 38–44).[6] Throughout this book, subjectivity is not to be confounded with this conception of a fixed subject. Rather, it is to be understood as a dynamic concept, indexing modes of agency (political ones, desiring ones, affective ones, choreographic ones) that reveal "*a process of subjectification,* that is, the production of a way of existing [that] can't be equated with a subject" (Deleuze 1995: 98, emphasis added). Subjectivity is to be understood as a performative power, as the possibility for life to be constantly invented and reinvented, as "a mode of intensity, not a personal subject" (1995: 99). Deleuze's understanding of subjectivity is close to Foucault's "technologies of the self," which he defines as *operations.* Technologies of the self,

> permit individuals to effect by their own means [. . .] a certain number of operations on their own bodies and souls, thoughts, conduct and way of being so as to transform themselves in order to attain a certain state of happiness.
>
> (Foucault 1997: 225)

Thus, for Foucault as for Deleuze, subjectivities are always processes of *subjectification,* active becomings, the unleashing of potencies and forces in order to create for oneself the possibility of "existing as a work of art" (Deleuze 1995: 95).

In this dynamic, one cannot neglect the destructive effect of hegemonic forces that constantly try to dominate and prevent the creation of subjectivities by binding individuals into reproductive mechanisms of subjection, abjection, and domination. To account for this hegemonic effect, I would like to supplement Deleuze's and Foucault's notions of subjectivity by invoking a model of subjectification they explicitly rejected, but that I nevertheless believe is of use to critically account for the multiple forces at play in the constitution of subjectivities. This model is described by Louis Althusser in his essay "Ideology and Ideological State Apparatuses" (1994). Althusser proposed that hegemonic forces are permanently "interpellating individuals as subjects in the name of a Unique and Absolute Subject" (1994: 135). There is something uncannily choreographic in the way Althusser describes this mechanism:

The individual is interpellated as a (free) subject in order that he shall submit freely to the commandments of the Subject, i.e., in order that he shall (freely) accept his subjection, i.e., in order that he shall make the gestures and actions of his subjection "all by himself." There are no subjects except by and for their subjection. That is why they "work all by themselves".

(1994: 136)

We can see why Deleuze and Foucault would critique this mechanism, where there seems to be no place for agency and where reification is crucial. However, the relevance of Althusser's model for dance studies was highlighted recently by Mark Franko. Despite critiquing Althusser's location of centers of ideological power in specific institutions (Church, Police, State), Franko writes how "interpellation implies visceral address," and therefore remains a very useful notion for dance and performance studies, one that proposes that dance and "performance could also 'call' audiences to subject positions" (Franko 2002: 60). I agree with Franko's proposal that Althusser's model of how individuals are "recruited" into normative subjectivity is particularly useful to understand how choreography creates its process of subjectification. Choreography demands a yielding to commanding voices of masters (living and dead), it demands submitting body and desire to disciplining regimes (anatomical, dietary, gender, racial), all for the perfect fulfillment of a transcendental and preordained set of steps, postures, and gestures that nevertheless must appear "spontaneous". When Althusser writes that the individual "shall submit freely to the commandments of the Subject, i.e., in order that he shall (freely) accept his subjection, i.e., in order that he shall make the gestures and actions of his subjection 'all by himself'" (1994: 136), this sounds a lot like the fundamental mechanism choreography sets in place for its representational and reproductive success.

But there is another aspect of Althusser's model that is of critical import for my analysis. Judith Butler, in *Excitable Speech*, recuperates Althusser's notion of interpellation in order to demonstrate how subjectivity is constantly being constituted by a dialectics of resistance and subjection that is nothing more than "a mechanism of discourses whose efficacy is irreducible to their moment of enunciation" (Butler 1997b: 32). The notions of hailing and interpellation as discursive mechanisms will be particularly useful in Chapter 5, when I discuss William Pope.L's kinetic strategies of moving on the treacherous racist and neoimperial terrain of contemporaneity – a terrain informed by injurious utterances taking down bodies and shaping motions, gestures, postures.

I would like to turn now to the question of modernity. Harvie Ferguson writes, "modernity is a new form of subjectivity" (Ferguson 2000: 5). Given that, as we saw, Ferguson also affirms that modernity's permanent emblem is movement, it follows that modernity hails its subjects to constitute them as emblematic displays of its being: mobility. Modernity's subjectivity is its movement and modernity subjectivizes by interpellating bodies to a constant display of motion, to the ontological agitation Peter Sloterdijk identifies as modernity's "kinetic excess" (2000b: 29). It is within this overwhelming and ontopolitical imperative to move that subjectivities create their escape routes (their becomings) and negotiate their self-imprisonment (their subjection).

If modernity is a new form of subjectivity, what might be its historical scope? Can we use the term "modernity" to address contemporaneity? Here, consensus is hard to find. Recently, Fredric Jameson wrote on the "political dynamics of the word 'modernity,' which has been revived all over the world," and associated its dynamics and its recent revival with the (for him disturbing) demise of "post-modernity" (Jameson 2002: 10). Jameson sees all kinds of regressions taking place with the resurgence of the word "modernity." For Jameson, the demise of postmodernity and the return of modernity as concept indicate an undesirable return of philosophy, of esthetics, and of the "phallocentrism" of modernism in critical discourse (2002: 9–11).[7] As for identifying modernity's epoch, Jameson affirms, "the only satisfactory semantic meaning of modernity lies in its association with capitalism" (2002: 11). Thus, according to Jameson, one can talk of "modernity" only after two conditions are met: the emergence of Kant's critique of Enlightenment and the establishment of the modes of production of industrial capitalism (2002: 99). Jameson's views are close to Foucault's and Habermas's who tend to identify the formation of the political, epistemic, and affective conditions prevalent in contemporaneity in the eighteenth century, particularly with Kant's philosophy.

However, another mode of temporalizing modernity would be to follow Ferguson's formula and consider that modernity is indeed "a form of subjectivity." Thus, modernity's periodization would be predicated on identifying not a particular period, nor a particular geography, but processes of subjectification that produce and reproduce this particular form. Cultural historian Louis Dupré identifies a modern form of subjectivity clearly in place by the seventeenth century and extending to our moment (Dupré 1993: 3, 7). The epochal understanding of modernity I deploy in this book aligns with Dupré's and also with those outlined by Francis Barker (1995), Teresa Brennan (2000), Gerard Delanty (2000), Harvie Ferguson (2000), and Peter Sloterdijk (2000b). These authors identify the establishment of modernity with the subjectification set in place by the Cartesian division between *res cogita* and *res extensa*. Even Jameson, in his harsh critique of the revival of the word modernity states, "it is only by way of this newly achieved certainty [exposed by Descartes's method] that a new conception of truth as correctness can emerge historically; or in other words, that something like 'modernity' can make its appearance" (Jameson 2002: 47). Here, Jameson is explaining Heidegger's critique of representation (*Vorstellung*) in relation to the philosophy of Descartes and argues that Heidegger's critique is one that illustrates modernity as a mode of "subjectification" (2002: 47). Jameson concedes that such an understanding of modernity as subjectification "may well be preferred to any number of vapid humanist just-so stories" (2002: 49).

What characterizes this mode or form of subjectification? First and foremost, it locks subjectivity within an experience of being severed from the world. In modernity, subjectivity is trapped within a solipsistic experience of the "ego as the ultimate subject for and of representation" (Courtine 1991: 79) that views the "body as independently existing and governed by immanent laws" (Ferguson 2000: 7). Brennan is particularly insistent on the centrality of this subject experiencing his or her being as fully independent and ontologically severed from the world as constitutive of the modern process of subjectification. She identifies in the self-sufficient monadic subject the psychic work of a particularly alienating "foundational fantasy" (Brennan 2000: 36).[8] This fantasy must reproduce itself at all costs in order to keep in place the ecological and affective plundering that characterizes the modes of production unleashed by early capitalism and exacerbated to their paroxysm in our neoimperial contemporaneity. She writes:

> one can debate whether the birth of the interior consciousness marks modernity, a hard case to sustain because of the evident exceptions to it. I would submit that a better measure would be the uniform denial, in the West, of the transmission of affect that we find in effect from the seventeenth century onwards.
>
> (Brennan 2000: 10)

For modern subjectivity, the ethical, affective, and political challenges are of finding sustained modes of relationality. How can a putatively independent being establish a relation with things, world, or others while remaining at the same time a good representative of modernity's "emblem": movement? The inclusion of the kinetic into this political-ethical question of modern subjectivity brings us back to the problem of how to dance against the hegemonic fantasies of modernity, once those fantasies are linked to the imperative to constantly display mobility.

This is where analyses of choreographies and performances that directly address the impossibility of sustaining "flow or continuum movement" are of theoretical and political import. If the formation of what Randy Martin calls "critical dance studies" is to be taken seriously, then his proposition, developed in *Critical Moves*, for reexamining the notion of mobilization, understood "as mediating concept between dance and politics," seems particularly relevant for this discussion (Martin 1998: 14). Indeed, for Martin, mobilization is a key concept dance studies must probe in order to step out of its dubious political paralysis.[9] The formation of a political theory and a political practice based on the primacy of movement must depart from Martin's suggestion that "the relation of dance to political theory cannot usefully be taken as merely analogical or metaphorical" (1998: 6). Thus, considering literal or metonymical (as opposed to analogical and metaphorical) relations between dance and politics becomes a fundamental step for political and critical theory to address the choreographic dynamics of social movements and social change – regardless if those movements and changes manifest themselves on the stage or in the streets. Martin points out how

> theories of politics are full of ideas, but they have been less successful in articulating how the concrete labor of participation necessary to execute

those ideas is gathered through the movement of bodies in social time and space. Politics goes nowhere without movement.

(Martin 1998: 3)

Martin's project could be read not only as a critical-kinetic updating and rephrasing of Marx's famous eleventh thesis on Feuerbach,[10] but also as a challenging articulation that the perception and practice of dances through the viewpoint of political thought could indeed open up the possibility to mobilize not only theories but also otherwise politically passive bodies. The word "participation" in Martin's theory is important, since it contains a critique of representation. For Martin, mobilization is already participation, it is a moving-toward-the-world – in the sense that methexis proposes a participatory encountering that challenges the distancing forces of mimesis. Indeed, Martin's argument is predicated upon a progressive politics as "those forces mobilizing against the fixity of what is dominant in the social order" (1998: 10).

Martin's observation repeats a usually uncontested notion that associates the force of movement with a politically positive dynamics. Think for instance of Gilles Deleuze, when he defined two basic political positions: "embracing movement, or blocking it" (Deleuze 1995: 127). Deleuze associated the latter with a reactionary force. Think also of Deleuze and Guattari's notions of becoming, as forces and powers coalescing on a plane of consistency defined as a plane of immanence where intensities circulate unblocked, and of the body without organs (remember how, for Deleuze and Guattari, the body without organs can be successful or unsuccessful, the latter being defined always by a blocking of intensities).

In Randy Martin, in Deleuze, and in Guattari movement seems to be associated positively as that which will always apply its force towards a politics of progress, or at least towards a critical formation that could be considered progressive. We can think of many other examples of this association. But given that I have just posited that the condition of modernity is that of an emblematic motility, the question becomes of finding out where "the fixity of what is dominant" might be. The question is to know if and how the dominant moves. And to know when, what, and who is it that the dominant requires to be moving.

This is where the "critique of political kinetics" proposed by Peter Sloterdijk in his book *Eurotaoismus* becomes particularly relevant. Sloterdijk writes that the only way of fully assessing the political ontology of modernity is by critically addressing what he calls "the kinetic impulse of modernity" (Sloterdijk 2000b: 35).[11] Sloterdijk posits that "ontologically, modernity is a pure being-toward-movement" (2000b: 36). Therefore, "a philosophical discourse of modernity is not possible except as a critical theory of mobilization" (2000b: 126). Here, we could almost read in Sloterdijk's propositions Randy Martin's words in *Critical Moves*, since for both it is modernity's kinetic being that has been profoundly neglected by critical theory. But Sloterdijk's ideas could also be read as a cautionary argument that both disagrees with and at the same time supports and supplements Martin's insights. As opposed to Martin, Sloterdijk argues that critical theory and progressive politics must take into account the fact that *there is nothing fixed* in the dominant, or hegemonic, order. Rather, for Sloterdijk, it is precisely the *kinetic impulse* of modernity articulated as mobilization that displays the process of subjectificaton in contemporaneity as that of an idiotic militarization of subjectivity associated to widespread kinetic performances of tayloristic efficacy, efficiency, and effectiveness (to use Jon Mackenzie's terms [2000]). For Sloterdijk, the lack of a critical theory of the kinetic impulse of modernity is a fundamental flaw in Marxist theory, that theoretically neglected to engage in a critique of the kinetic due to its enthusiastic embrace of full industrialization. Although Randy Martin's proposals seem to have been articulated unaware of the political philosophy of Sloterdijk, and despite the fact that on occasion they may even be in direct disagreement with some of Sloterdijk's readings of Marx, the German philosopher's critique of modernity as "kinetic excess" supplements Martin's notions of the different uses of mobilization in political processes and in political thought. If Sloterdijk is much more critical of Marxist theory than Martin would probably allow, both are nevertheless attempting to articulate "if it's possible to imagine politics from within mobilization" (Martin 1998: 12). Sloterdijk, just as Martin, also looks for possibilities of countering hegemonic policies by thinking from within mobilization, if only to point out the conflicting problems such a term entails. Indeed, I believe Martin would agree with Sloterdijk when he writes:

> [U]p to the present, the two known versions of a critical theory (I am thinking mainly of the Marxist school and of the Frankfurt schools) have remained without an object, either because they cannot seize their object – *the kinetic reality of modernity as mobilization* – or because they cannot show a critical difference in relation to mobilization.
>
> (Sloterdijk 2000b: 26–7, emphasis in the original)

Sloterdijk's philosophy outlines a critique of mobilization by addressing modernity's "kinesthetic politics" as an exhausting and exhausted ontopolitical project of "being-toward-movement" (2000: 36). What Sloterdijk's and Martin's works show is that we have arrived at a moment in critical theory and in critical dance studies where the political problem of contemporary modernity, capitalism, and action have been theoretically cast as essentially belonging to the realm of the choreographic ontology of modernity. This is a fundamental development not only for critical theory, but also for the possible theoretical interventions critical dance studies may attempt in its analysis of subjectivities.

In short, modernity is understood throughout this book as a long durational project, metaphysically and historically producing and reproducing a "psycho-philosophical frame" (Phelan 1993: 5) where the privileged subject of discourse is always gendered as the heteronormative male, raced as white, and experiencing his truth as (and within) a ceaseless drive for autonomous, self-motivated, endless, spectacular movement. But how could a body move about so spectacularly, so effectively, and so self-sufficiently? What is the ground this kinetic subject moves about apparently without effort, apparently always energized, and never stumbling? This is where the inescapable topography fantasy of modernity informs its choreopolitical formation: for modernity imagines its topography as already abstracted from its grounding on a land previously occupied by other human bodies, other life forms, filled with other dynamics, gestures, steps, and temporalities. As Bhabha explains, "for the emergence of modernity – as an ideology of beginning, modernity as the new – the template of this 'non-place' becomes the colonial place" (1994: 246). Fundamental for the argument of this book is the fact that the ground of modernity is the colonized, flattened, bulldozed terrain where the fantasy of endless and self-sufficient motility takes place. Since there is no such thing as a self-sufficient living system, all mobilization, all subjectivity that finds itself as a total "being-toward-movement" must draw its energy from some source. The fantasy of the modern kinetic subject is that the spectacle of modernity as movement happens in innocence. The kinetic spectacle of modernity erases from the picture of movement all the ecological catastrophes, personal tragedies, and communal disruptions brought about by the colonial plundering of resources, bodies, and subjectivities that are needed in order to keep modernity's "most real" reality in place: its kinetic being. Given that all social and political creation today takes place within the frame of colonialism and its current metamorphoses, I foreground postcolonial theory and critical race theory as fundamental partners to critically assess how some contemporary dance and kinetic performance challenges colonialism and its new guises. I explore the colonialist force of modernity and its impact on contemporary choreographic practices in Chapters 4, 5, and 6 when I discuss works by Trisha Brown, La Ribot, William Pope.L and Vera Mantero, and invoke the critical theories of Homi Bhabha, Henri Lefebvre, Frantz Fanon, Paul Carter, Anne Anlin Cheng, José Muñoz, and Avery Gordon.

A final epistemological remark brought by Bhabha's identification of the colonialist condition as the condition of modernity is that the colonial project not only introduces a spatial blindness (of perceiving all space as an "empty space") but it introduces as well a fantastical temporality of which the concept "postmodern" participates. My hesitancy throughout the book in using this central term in dance studies derives not only from the inconclusive debate in the late 1980s on the pages of *The Drama Review* between Susan Manning and Sally Banes on what constitutes "postmodern dance,"[12] but also from the profound insight by Bhabha when he writes that "the project of modernity is itself rendered so contradictory and unresolved through the insertion of the 'time-lag' in which colonial and postcolonial moments emerge as sign and history, that I am skeptical of those transitions to postmodernity" that "Western academic writing" theorizes (Bhabha 1994: 238). Throughout this book, my use of the word "modernity" is a result of this same skepticism, opened up by postcolonial theory and reinforced by the recent hypervisibility of the same old colonialist and imperialist brutality proficiently deploying bodies and mobilizing death. Bhabha's insight reframes Habermas's depiction of modernity as an "incomplete project" (Habermas 1998) – as long as the colonial condition exists (no matter in what guise) there will be no closure of modernity.

During the time frame that Sloterdijk (in 1989) and Martin (in 1998) were independently attempting to call critical theory's attention towards the kinetic-political formations of contemporary modernity, some experimental dancers and choreographers in Europe and in the USA were refashioning dance's relationship to its own politics and its own ethics of movement. Thus, dancers were challenging dance's own political ontology by the enactments of stillness, by the practice of what Gaston Bachelard calls a "slower ontology" (Bachelard 1994: 215). As it will become clear in all the works discussed in this book, the insertion of stillness in dance, the deployment of different ways of slowing down movement and time, are particularly powerful propositions for other modes of rethinking action and mobility through the performance of still-acts, rather than continuous movement.[13]

The "still-act" is a concept proposed by anthropologist Nadia Seremetakis to describe moments when a subject interrupts historical flow and *practices* historical interrogation. Thus, while the still-act does not entail rigidity or morbidity it requires a performance of suspension, a corporeally based interruption of modes of imposing flow. The still *acts* because it interrogates economies of time, because it reveals the possibility of one's agency within controlling regimes of capital, subjectivity, labor, and mobility. "Against the flow of the present," Seremetakis writes,

> [T]here is a stillness in the material culture of historicity; those things, spaces, gestures, and tales that signify the perceptual capacity for elemental historical creation. Stillness is the moment when the buried, the discarded, and the forgotten escape to the social surface of awareness like life-supporting oxygen. It is the moment of exit from historical dust.
>
> (1994: 12)

To exit from historical dust is to refuse the sedimentation of history into neat layers. The still-act shows how the dust of history, in modernity, may be agitated in order to blur artificial divisions between the sensorial and the social, the somatic and the mnemonic, the linguistic and corporeal, the mobile and immobile. Historical dust is not simple metaphor. When taken literally, it reveals how historical forces penetrate deep into the inner layers of the body: dust sedimenting the body, operating to rigidify the smooth rotation of joints and articulations, fixing the subject within overly prescribed pathways and steps, fixating movement within a certain politics of time and of place. It is experimental choreography, through the paradoxical still-act, that charts the tensions in the subject, the tensions in subjectivity under the force of history's dusty sedimentation of the body. Against the brutality of historical dust literally falling onto bodies, the still-act reshapes the subject's stance regarding movement and the passing of time. As Homi Bhabha remarks, "it is the function of the *lag* to slow down the linear, progressive time of modernity to reveal its 'gesture,' its tempi, 'the pauses and stresses of the whole performance'" (1994: 253). My first encounter with dance's kinetic depletion as still-act, as a suspensive response to pressing political events, happened during the fall of 1992, when a series of still-acts were presented by a (very) diverse group of choreographers, musicians, critics, and artists gathered at Cité Universitaire in Paris, for a month-long choreographic laboratory titled SKITE curated by French dance critic and programmer Jean-Marc Adolphe. The insertion of the still-act had all to do with violent performances of colonialism and its racisms. This was the fall after the first Gulf War. The civil war in Bosnia-Herzegovina was raging. The Los Angeles uprisings had just happened. In SKITE, Portuguese choreographer Vera Mantero and Spanish choreographer Santiago Sempere both stated that the political events in the world were such that they could not dance. North American choreographer Meg Stuart choreographed a still dance for a man lying on the ground, reaching out carefully for his past memories;[14] Australian choreographer Paul Gazzola lay quietly in the night, naked in an improbable shelter, by a highway. I see this moment in SKITE as one where the sedimentary forces of historical dust were unveiled by choreographers through their rearrangements of the very notion of dance: not only of the position of dance in relation to politics, but of the ontological and political role of movement in the formation of those disturbing events. And the choreographic unveiling happened by the means of the still-act. At the time, I felt the pieces had a spontaneous quality – there had been no discussions to create work based on dramaturgies of stillness. But the series of still-acts performed then suggested a sudden crisis of the image of the dancer's presence (on the stage as well as in the world) as being one always serving movement. The still-act, dance's exhaustion, opens up the possibility of thinking contemporary experimental dance's self-critique as an ontological critique, moreover as a critique of dance's political ontology. The undoing of the unquestioned alignment of dance with movement initiated by the still-act refigures the dancer's participation in mobility – it initiates a performative critique of his or her participation in the general economy of mobility that informs, supports, and reproduces the ideological formations of late capitalist modernity.

The following chapters can be read in any order but I should outline their major thematic progression. Each chapter addresses a particular element that I believe is crucial for a critique of choreography's participation in the political ontology of modernity.

In the next chapter, I discuss some nonkinetic elements and forces that are intrinsic to choreography and that have haunted its conditions of possibility at least as powerfully as the desire to move. Those elements and forces are: the dead master's voice, the relation between choreography and what Jacques Derrida called the "illocutionary or perlocutionary force" at the core of law (Derrida 1990: 929), the solipsistic nature of the dance studio, and the masculine homosocial desire at the core of the choreographic. I identify those forces in a series of films created by visual artist Bruce Nauman in the late 1960s, where he appears alone in his empty studio performing rigorously predefined steps. My readings of these films account for the hauntological force of the choreographic, a force that disrupts linear time and that erupts whenever certain conditions of subjectification are met. I then analyze two recent pieces by contemporary European choreographers Juan Dominguez and Xavier Le Roy where solipsism and masculinity are deployed in a critique of the choreographic to reimage the male dancer's body in its relation to language (Juan Dominguez) and in its investment on becomings (Le Roy).

Chapter 3 expands some of the notions explored in Chapter 2 by analyzing several pieces by French choreographer Jérôme Bel in regard to his uses of repetition, stillness, and language. I propose that the linguistic materiality of the body proposed by Bel, when associated with the deflation of movement that also typifies his work, allows for the identification of paronomastic effects that recast choreography's relation to temporality, while approximating Bel's work to Derrida's and Heidegger's philosophy. I also propose that Bel's work operates temporally along the lines of what Gaston Bachelard defined as a "slower ontology" – one that distrusts the stability of forms, that refuses the esthetics of geometry, and instead privileges addressing phenomena as fields of forces and as systems of intensities.

My reading of Bel's work introduces the framework for the critique of representation that I pursue in Chapter 4 when I focus on two recent pieces by two very different choreographers, the North American Trisha Brown and the Spanish La Ribot. Here, I am interested in investigating how each choreographer engages in a direct dialogue with visual arts, in order to refigure what constitutes dance's ground. Brown's *It's a Draw/Live Feed* is read through its critique of verticality as a critique of the masculinist drive in Pollock's drip paints. I invoke Rosalind Krauss's readings of Georges Bataille's notion of formless, and I use Henri Lefebvre's disclosing of the "erectility" embedded in the architectural formation of "abstract spaces" in order to consider how Brown makes space by confounding normative and disciplinary relations between dancing and drawing. My reading of La Ribot's long duration performance *Panoramix* introduces a discussion of the oblique as a space of dismorphic challenges to the architectural privileging of the vertical. La Ribot's work, however, adds the phenomenological question of the weight of the gaze, which supplements Brown's attachment to the perspectival in her performance of *It's a Draw/Live Feed*.

Since modern subjectivity proposes a "being-toward-movement" roaming about on colonized and racialized fields, any critique of dance's political ontology inevitably implicates a critique of how to move on a ground ravaged by racist injuries and colonialist plundering. In Chapter 5, I locate how the stumble is a term mediating politics and kinetics by offering a choreopolitical reading of Frantz Fanon's "The Fact of Blackness" (1967) in relation to the parachoreographic practices of performance artist William Pope.L. I propose that Pope.L's crawls reveal their full choreopolitical force once read in relation to what Paul Carter called "a politics of the ground" (Carter 1996). And I advance that such a politics of the ground refigures Fanon's critique of ontology in "The Fact of Blackness". I propose the effort on the sagittal plane as performed by

Pope.L as a slowing down of the kinetic that answers directly and interpellates profoundly the neocolonial surrounding and traversing us.

Attending to the ways colonialism and choreography, as facets of the modern kinetic being-toward-movement, are predicated on a politics of the ground reveals those movements initiated by "improperly buried bodies of history" – those bodies Avery Gordon sees as haunting epistemology, as powerful ethical and critical forces (Gordon 1997). In Chapter 6, I read Vera Mantero's solo *uma misteriosa Coisa disse e.e. cummings* in order to rethink postcolonial melancholia. I pay particular attention to the ethics of remembering and of forgetting as it relates to recent critical race studies (particularly with José Muñoz) and to the ontological project of choreography. By focusing on the particularities of a solo piece created in the last European openly Imperial nation, Portugal, I attempt to show the centrality of the racialized Other as energetic source for choreographic mobility in general. The book ends with a short concluding note, where I address the "project of melancholia" in modernity (Agamben 1993) in order to map the impact of such a project in recent ontological framings of choreography by dance and performance studies, and where I propose an alternative modality of time and a different kind of affect for those two disciplines.

2 Masculinity, solipsism, choreography

Bruce Nauman, Juan Dominguez, Xavier Le Roy

> If we wish to understand and describe correctly this performance, and its temporality in particular, we need to put aside altogether the terminology of causation, memory and expectation, and representation.
>
> (Carr 1986: 36)

> The site of dance circulates through Time, it haunts both the real and the imaginary.
>
> (Louppe 1994: 13)

> To be haunted is to be tied to historical and social effects.
>
> (Gordon 1997: 190)

Haunting the temporally circulatory site of dance, defying logics of causation and representation, there moves a particular subjectivity, ontohistorically foundational to Western choreography: the solitary male dancer. This chapter crisscrosses dance's historical time to examine contemporary echoes of the coming into being of Western choreography – in Thoinot Arbeau's dance manual *Orchesographie* (1589) – as an early modern subjectivity-machine in which masculine solipsism is an essential element. Thus, the pieces analyzed in this chapter all feature men moving alone in explicitly enclosed and empty spaces – empty chambers, empty studios, empty rooms, somber voids where haunted solitude, concentration of will, and precision in execution all fuse to create what can only be described as a solipsistic excess. Such is the case with Bruce Nauman's parachoreographic experiments of the late 1960s, particularly *Walking in an Exaggerated Manner Around the Perimeter of a Square* (1967–8),[1] *Dance or Exercise on the Perimeter of a Square* (1967–8),[2] and the beautifully silly antigravitational exercise *Revolving Upside Down* (1969).[3] Such is the case with Juan Dominguez's overwhelmingly self-centered textual *AGSAMA* (2003), or with Xavier Le Roy's playful *Self Unfinished* (1999). My readings of these works make a case for how choreography's ontological, social, and historical effects haunt (and are haunted by) solipsistic masculinity.

Solipsism in choreography reflects its dubious status in philosophy. I will discuss solipsism's philosophical ambiguity by focusing particularly on Ludwig Wittgenstein's brief comments on solipsism in his *Tractatus Logico-Philosophicus* (propositions 5.6 to 5.6331, Wittgenstein 1961), when the Austrian philosopher finds solipsism at the core of the metaphysical subject's relation to experience, thus surprisingly opening solipsism up to the world. Wittgenstein's propositions in the *Tractatus* allow us to think that it is precisely at the critical point where solipsism binds subjectivity to the logic of language that the choreographic – that is, the technology that binds modernity's "being-toward-movement" to writing – decidedly aligns itself with philosophy to simultaneously generate *and* critique solitary masculinity.

Time to ground and expand these preliminary observations. Let me start by focusing on visual artist Bruce Nauman's parachoreographic experiments of the late 1960s, as he recorded them in a series of astonishing black and white videotapes and 16 mm films. After completing his graduate studies in painting and sculpture at the University of California at Davis in 1966, Nauman began to create photographs, sculptures, and films taking his body as central element. Art critic Coosje van Bruggen describes 1966 and 1967 as a period when "Nauman began to develop a strong body awareness" in his work (van Bruggen in Morgan 2002: 43). Nauman's "body awareness" generated three significantly divergent yet complementary series of works: body casts (the beautiful *From Hand to Mouth*, 1967); structures to be occupied by the audience's moving bodies (the uncanny *Performance Corridor*, 1969); and an intriguing, more elusive, and performative use "of his body as a standard for measuring his surroundings" (Bruggen in Morgan 2002: 43). Of this third series, some pieces were performed in galleries (such as *Performance (Slightly Crouched)*, 1968), while others were recorded in tapes and films. I am interested in the latter, Nauman's studio films (1967–9). For they reveal, in extraordinary ways, how choreography haunts whenever its ontohistorical elements are summoned.

Nauman's studio films, first shot in the artist's studio in California (1967–8) and later in New York (in the winter of 1968–9), depict Nauman moving in empty, derelict studios, performing a series of carefully obsessive and rigorous explorations of his self-consciously isolated body's relation to motion, sound, anatomy, language, balance, space, masculinity and dance. Nauman: "I thought of them as dance-problems without being a dancer" (interview with Willoughby Sharp, in Kraynak 2003: 142).

Some critics have recently posited Nauman's relationship to dance as deriving from his direct "indebtedness to experimental dance of the early to mid 1960s, in which the basic materials and meaning of dance were scrutinized" (Kraynak 2003: 15). Janet Kraynak refers specifically to the choreographers performing with the Judson Dance Theater in New York in the early 1960s – particularly Yvonne Rainer. In a recent catalogue, art critic and curator Susan Cross also affirms Judson's influence on Nauman (Cross 2003: 14). To place Nauman directly within 1960s postmodern dance is an intriguing historiographic move – but it is one that has been emerging recently and insistently in unexpected places. In an interview with Eric de Bruyn, visual artist Dan Graham remembers how "in San Francisco this was the time of La Monte Young, Terry Riley (who influenced Steve Reich), and *dancers like Simone Forti and Bruce Nauman*, all of whom were doing work in Anne [*sic*] Halprin's workshop" (Graham and de Bruyn 2004: 110, emphasis added). Graham's recent placing of Nauman in Halprin's workshop is quite remarkable. When I came upon his statement,[4] my research for this chapter had not revealed any other indication suggesting Nauman's participation in Halprin's famous (and even foundational, as far as the Judson Dance Theater is concerned) dance workshop.[5] Eventually, I received two independent confirmations that Nauman had *not* participated in Halprin's workshop – from Constance M. Lewallen, Senior Curator for Exhibitions at the University of California, Berkeley Art Museum, and directly from Bruce Nauman's studio through the Donald Young Gallery.[6] With these confirmations, Graham's recollection gains the contours of a quite indicative memory slip – that in turn becomes a symptom of the recent desire to recast Nauman's relationship to dance. By calling Nauman a dancer and by placing him at one of the major sources of Judson's movement esthetic, Graham's memory slip echoes Kraynak's desire to reframe Nauman's relationship to choreography and place him under a master narrative of postmodern North American dance. This a disturbing drive that attributes to Judson a totalitarian role in relation to any other forms of movement experiments in the USA in the 1960s. To "remember" Nauman where he was not, to call him a postmodern *dancer*, or to place him in a relation of "indebtedness" to Judson prevents alternative assessments of the very particular functions that the choreographic takes in his work.

Coosje van Bruggen, in a 1988 text, although emphasizing the pedestrian quality of Nauman's "dances" (pedestrianism is one of the defining characteristics of early Judson dance), does not extend Nauman's influences to any "indebtedness" to Judson. Rather, she describes Nauman's relationship to dance at the time of his studio films as deriving from his "awareness" of Merce Cunningham's uses of everyday movements and of nontrained dancers in the early 1950s at Brandeis University Creative Arts Festival (1952) (Bruggen in Morgan 2002: 50). But what does Nauman have to say about his relationship to dance? In a 1972 interview with Lorraine Sciarra, Nauman recalls his frame of mind while working on his studio films:

> I met Meredith Monk who was a dancer up in San Francisco. She had seen some of the work [Nauman's studio films] on the East Coast and we talked a little bit and that was really good to talk to someone about it. Because I guess I thought of what I was doing sort of as a dance because I was familiar with some of the things that Cunningham had done and some other dancers, where you can take any simple movement and make it into a dance, just by presenting it as a dance. I wasn't a dancer but I sort of thought if I took things that I didn't know how to do, but I was serious enough about them, then they would be taken serious.
>
> (interview with Lorraine Sciarra in Kraynak 2003: 166)

There is a clear relation to dance in Nauman's recall of his working process for the films: "I guess I thought of what I was doing sort of as a dance." But perhaps even clearer is his *hesitation* in defining what he thought he was doing, as well as in defining lines of esthetic transmission, influences, and authorial indebtedness. Nauman's hesitation asks at least for some tempering of recent statements affirming the direct influence of Judson on his work. Nauman does not mention by name those "some other dancers" that might have influenced him on the West

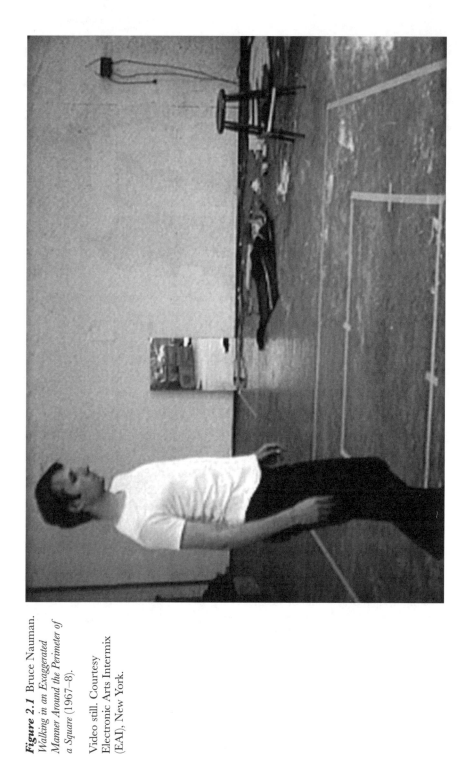

Figure 2.1 Bruce Nauman.
*Walking in an Exaggerated
Manner Around the Perimeter of
a Square* (1967–8).

Video still. Courtesy
Electronic Arts Intermix
(EAI), New York.

Coast. Confirming van Bruggen's more cautious phrasing, in a 1970 interview Nauman does refer to his awareness of Cunningham's experiments of the early 1950s (in 1969 Nauman would eventually design a stage set for Cunningham's *Tread*, which opened in 1970). But in the same interview he also states that "the first time I really talked with anybody about body awareness was in the summer of 1968" ("*Interview with Bruce Nauman*, 1971 (May 1970)," Willoughby Sharp in Kraynak 2003: 142). Nauman was referring to Meredith Monk, who was at the time in San Francisco.[7] Recent suggestions of Nauman's indebtedness to Judson rely on a historical synchronicity that nevertheless meets a curious silence in Nauman's own statements about his work's relation to dance in general and to the very vivid dance scene in the USA throughout the 1960s. Could it be that the whole problem comes from the uncritical usage of the word "dance"?

So, how to rephrase the problem? Regardless of who begat who (a question that dance historian Susan Manning has rightly discarded as unbearably Oedipal in its obsessive persistence within dance historiography [2004: 13]), the fact is that starting in the winter of 1967–8 Nauman began to work on a series of films and videos where he appears executing very precise movements in his empty studio. The hyperbolic quality of Nauman's solitary presence is remarkable in itself, and it becomes even more so as one watches successively the twenty-something films and videotapes created during the years of 1967–9. Truly remarkable in Nauman's studio films is the uncanny, yet quite explicit emergence not necessarily of dance, but of the *choreographic* – indexed by Nauman's rigorous, methodical, mono-maniacal execution of a set of previously established steps. Take for instance *Walking in an Exaggerated Manner Around the Perimeter of a Square* (black and white, 16 mm film, 1967–8).[8] Let's write its movements down. Let's choreograph it.

Find an empty room. Lock yourself up in it. Define a front, as in a theatre, and clear the floor at the center. Lean a not too small rectangular mirror against the back wall, its narrower side on the floor, facing the room, yet reflecting nobody. Trace a 10-foot square on the floor with white tape. Trace within that square another, smaller square with sides running parallel about a foot away from the outer square. Stand on top of one of the segments of the outer square, placing one foot right in front of the other, heel against toes, as if on a tightrope. Start pacing calmly, placing one foot always immediately in front of the other, making sure each foot stays on the white tape, while you undulate your hips in a very exaggerated manner with each step (it helps if your lower back is slightly arched, pushing your belly forward, looking silly). After completing one full perimeter, reverse, walking backwards in an exaggerated manner placing one foot right behind the other, heel next to toes. After completing one full perimeter again, reverse, walking forward. After completing one full perimeter again, reverse, walking backwards. After completing one full perimeter again, reverse, walking forwards. Repeat. Ad nauseam. (Note: Leave an empty stool next to the leaning mirror reflecting nothing by the wall just in case you're not so sure, despite appearances, whether you are really alone in the empty room.)

To describe Nauman's methodical choreography in this silent, 10-minute-long film is almost to suggest a dance that anyone could do. Or could you? As with much performance art of the late 1960s and early 1970s, the point was not so much whether anyone could do it, or whether "anything was possible" – to quote the subtitle of a recent book on 1960s dance (Banes and Baryshnikov 2003) – but rather to probe what could be produced physically, subjectively, temporally, politically, formally whenever someone decided to strictly and methodically follow a preestablished program to its ultimate consequences. In the case of Nauman's studio films, it is quite clear that, whatever that program might be, it must be strictly followed to the letter. Kraynak notes,

> all of Nauman's Studio Films, with their focused execution of the tasks outlined in their titles, *essentially constitute the display of a set of instructions.* In other words, they depict not simply the body but the choreographic score as well: what might be understood as the language of movement.
>
> (Kraynak 2003: 17, emphasis added)

Let's pause for a moment on the associative link Kraynak establishes between displaying a "set of instructions" and depicting a "choreographic score" as "the language of movement." To follow Kraynak's associative path is to understand choreography as a means by which instructions can be clearly displayed, thoroughly carried out, made visible. Kraynak binds choreography to the problem of obedience, to the question of the law, and to choreography's mysterious capacity for making visible and present otherwise absent forces and voices of command. Now, if this is indeed the case – that choreography displays and makes present a force of law – then the inclusion of the word "language" at the end of Kraynak's associative sequence complicates matters. For that inclusion does not logically or etymologically proceed, since choreography is not and could never be "the language" of movement[9] – rather, it is the writing of it (a writing that either precedes or comes after movement).[10] So, where does language fit with the choreographic, with the writing of movement? I suggest that, by invoking "language" after defining the choreographic as a careful and dutiful execution of a preestablished set of instructions, Kraynak's sentence reveals how language is akin to choreography only in those strict cases when utterances can be classified as performatives – particularly in those cases when the perlocutionary effect of the speech act sets bodies in motion (in the perlocutionary utterance "speech leads to effects, but it is not itself the effect" [Butler 1997b: 39]). Nauman's choreographic experiments disclose language acting on and through the body; they display how language mobilizes.

Kraynak notes how in the studio films "the entire process is generated from a linguistic statement: an instruction, so to speak" (Kraynak 2003: 23). This statement-instruction is always manifested in the title of each piece. Each of Nauman's studio films "perform" or "do" what its title enunciates. The title gains an authorial authority, defining a narrow space for behavior and being.[11] Kraynak insightfully suggests that Nauman's titles in his studio films operate precisely as what J. L. Austin called "perlocutionary performatives," thus bespeaking Nauman's concerns with the "doing" aspects of language, language's nonconstative function: "We must distinguish the illocutionary from the perlocutionary act: for example we must distinguish 'in saying it I was warning him' from 'by saying it I convinced him, or surprised him, or got him to stop'" (Austin 1980: 110). What I would like to add to Kraynak's insight is that by "saying it" (the title) Nauman "convinced himself" and "got himself to go" (irrecusably, as in a command), thus revealing at the core of the perlocutionary speech act an oddly choreographic nature.

Nauman's carefully executed actions – methodically and precisely embodying and mobilizing a set of pregiven instructions – reveal a commanding force in both language and choreography; better, they reveal how the relation between language and choreography is one mediated by force. When Nauman walks in an exaggerated manner around the perimeter of a square, dutifully following the title as an imperative organization of his mobility, he reveals the tensions and cracks in "the relation between force and form, force and signification, performative force, illocutionary or perlocutionary force," to use Jacques Derrida's reflections on the "differential character of force" (Derrida 1990: 929).

What does it mean to compulsively submit oneself to the force of a perlocutionary utterance, to follow a choreographic demand as an inescapable program? One answer would be: to subject oneself to a structure of command, to follow the rules of the game, to yield to the citational force of the speech act uttered under the sign of the law – a force that would always precede and determine one's own stepping into subjectivity. But perhaps there might be other ways of thinking about this desire to submit oneself so thoroughly to a perfect execution of the choreographic command. Jean-Charles Massera explicitly associates Nauman's programmatic law-abiding with the choreographic in his essay "Dance with the Law" (in Morgan 2002). But he proposes law-abiding as a mode through which the fulfillment of the choreographic demand becomes not a passive submission, a blind obedience, but the purposeful activation of a will, of a power: "the law is a cadence, a rhythm that circulates through bodies. The more your drives are synchronized with the rhythm of the law, the easier the execution of the task" (in Morgan 2002: 178). This lawful dance for the sake of ease of expression is the ideological cadence of the choreographic. Would there be a historical, even ontological, association between the choreographic, writing, and the law? An association, moreover, where solipsism and masculinity revolve around each other to establish choreography's ambiguity in regards to its project for subjectivity?

Let's circulate in dance's time to invoke the moment when Western dance alloyed writing with its being to create the neologism "*orchesographie*" (a writing, *graphie*, of the *orchesis*, dance), the title of Thoinot Arbeau's famous 1589 dance manual.[12] We find not only that the alloying of writing with dancing into a new word created a proper name for modernity's "being-toward-movement" (Sloterdijk 2000b: 36),[13] but also that this lexical act with corporeal implications was performed thanks to a lawyer's request. In *Orchesographie*, a young lawyer returns from Paris to Langres to visit his old master of "computation." But the lawyer's teacher, Thoinot Arbeau, is not only a mathematician but also a Jesuit priest and a dance master. Capriol, the lawyer, begs his dance master/priest/math teacher Arbeau to teach him the art of dance, so that Capriol may be able to live properly in society, or, as he puts it, so that he may "not be reproached for having the heart of a pig and the head of an ass" (Arbeau 1966: 17). At the critical point where dance finds its new destiny as choreography, we find the joint labors of a lawyer and a priest. Here is a powerful foundational duo to consider choreography's ontohistorical relationship to the force of law. A male couple, dancing within a psycho-philosophical, theological, and gendered space triangulated by hard discourses and disciplines: mathematics, religion, law. The young lawyer's desire for dance as a mode of socialization initiates a project that is as much kinetic as it is textual, as much social as it is subjective, as much corporeal as it is a writing project: orchesography. In the coming into being of orchesography as a new signifier, as practice, as a technological binding of writing and dancing, as a pedagogical bond between men, as an answer to a call from and for the law, some intriguing nonkinetic elements take on an important role: law, writing, the isolated studio, pedagogical homosociality, and paradoxically, given the dialogical couple, solipsism.

Capriol asks for dance lessons to attain what Erving Goffman called a socially acceptable "performance of the self" (Goffman 1959: 17–79) – a performance that would give the young lawyer admission into social theatrics, into society's normative heterosexual dancing. What is interesting in this concern is how *Orchesographie* grounds the possibility for heterosexual dancing and mating on a previous, pedagogical homosocialization. Moreover, a socialization with the same-other appears in *Orchesographie* as choreography's specific mode for accessing absent presences. This is no rhetorical turn. In *Orchesographie,* the project of dancing-writing, the nascent art of choreography, is cast as being pregnant with a spectral-technological promise: that of finding a means for the male subject to transcend presence as that which must always be present. The coining of the neologism "orchesography" unleashes the spectral force in the signifier and allows direct access to absent presences. Socialization with those who are not quite there is achieved whenever a dance book is read in a secluded chamber. Partnering with the spectral requires a peculiar form of masculine solipsism.

> ARBEAU: As regards ancient dances all I can tell you is that the passage of time, the indolence of man or the difficulty of describing them has robbed us of any knowledge thereof. [. . .]
>
> CAPRIOL: I foresee then that posterity will remain ignorant of all these new dances you have named for the same reason that we have been deprived of the knowledge of those of our ancestors.
>
> ARBEAU: One must assume so.
>
> CAPRIOL: Do not allow this to happen, Monsieur Arbeau, as it is within your power to prevent it. Set these things down in writing to enable me to learn this art, and in so doing *you will seem reunited to the companions of your youth* and take both mental and bodily exercise, for it will be difficult for you to refrain from using your limbs in order to demonstrate the correct movements. In truth, your method of writing is such that a pupil, by

following your theory and precepts, *even in your absence,* could teach himself in the *seclusion of his own chamber.*

(Arbeau 1966: 14, emphases added)

Thanks to the choreographic book, a student will dance with his master's ghost in the seclusion of an otherwise empty chamber. Thanks to the choreographic, a lawyer will wholeheartedly offer his body for a becoming spectral. Moreover, through this becoming, Capriol may channel his master's melancholic affect – all he needs to do is to grant his master one more dance as he becomes, through the effect of solitary reading-dancing, one of his master's long departed companions of youth. While *dance* is a technique for socializing, while dance is in itself a socialization, *choreography* appears as a solipsistic technology for socializing with the spectral, making present the force of the absent in the field of masculine desire. The choreographic effect can now be clarified as the spectral effect of writing in the field of masculine desire.[14]

In *Orchesographie,* writing becomes a technology of transportation, more precisely of tele-transportation. The dancing lawyer and the dancing priest anticipate Derrida's description of the type of telecommunicational effect writing produces. In "Signature Event Context," Derrida identified a "kind of machine" operating at the core of writing that he associated with the technology of telecommunication. For Derrida, writing's telecommunicational function profoundly disturbs the notion of presence:

> all writing [. . .] in order to be what it is, must be able to function in the radical absence of every empirically determined addressee in general. And this absence is not a continuous modification of presence; it is a break in presence, "death," or the possibility of "death" of the addressee, inscribed in the structure of the mark.
>
> (Derrida 1986: 315–16)

Derrida concludes: "What holds for the addressee holds also, for the same reasons, for the sender or the producer" (1986: 316). It is because the deaths of producer and addressee are constitutive of dance that the choreographic plea can be stated. "Set these things down in writing to enable me to learn this art, and in so doing *you will seem reunited to the companions of your youth,*" asks Capriol, who seems particularly able to identify in writing the possibility of a becoming spectral. The lawyer perceives in choreography a performance of melancholia, a mechanism that will prevent the loved object to depart forever, thus identifying a morbid core in dancing itself. The certainty of the future death of the choreographer, of the master, of the dancing writer-priest becomes central in the creation of the choreographic project: reading dances will allow Capriol to reunite himself again with his master once he is no longer among the living. Choreography becomes that which allows a lawyer to cite, to quote, to repeat the foundational gestures, the absent presence, and the cadence of a dance's originary force. We return to the deep connection between choreography and the performative speech act –

both can enforce themselves properly only under the condition of their citationality (Butler 1993: 12–16).[15]

Thus, to alloy dancing with writing is not just to create a new linguistic sign. For this creation is already a particular mobilization of the written mark towards its telecommunicational capacity to call the spectral. No wonder then that in the first edition of *Orchesographie*, right above the printer's coat of arms, we find as the book's epigraph an explicit acknowledgment that the new signifier alloying dance with writing can only remain whole as long as it relates directly to the melancholic core of the choreographic. *Orchesographie*'s epigraph reads: *tempus plangendi, & tempus saltandi* – time to mourn, & time to dance (Eccles. 3:4). Capriol's plaint in the opening pages of *Orchesographie* suggests that the function of the conjunctive "&" in the epigraph of a book whose title is already conjunctive is to plug the time of mourning directly to the time of men dancing each other's absent presence. This dancing happens, let's not forget, in an empty chamber.

In the haunted space of the choreographic chamber, what writing sets in motion, functioning even after the future disappearance of its author, or even of its addressee,[16] is a cadence and a productivity in the signifier that can simultaneously reiterate but also rewrite the already written. This continuous rewriting generates the haunting temporality of which choreography participates. My use of the term "haunting" has a double intent: one is to emphasize the function of specters in the choreographic "time to mourn &/as time to dance," to emphasize choreography's capacity to invoke absent presences; another intent is to propose an epistemological accounting of the particular circulatory temporality initiated by choreography's capacity for haunting history, as suggested by Laurence Louppe's epigraph for this chapter. For, "haunting is historical, to be sure, but it is not dated, it is never docilely given a date in the chain of presents, day after day, according to the instituted order of a calendar" (Derrida 1994: 4).[17] In other words: haunting messes up time and accounts for apparitions when we least expect them – for instance, the apparition of the choreographic in a series of films by a young sculptor in his empty studio in California.

What is the function of the (dance) studio in all this? With the dancer removed from the social field and confined to the haunted privacy of bookish reading, the solitary chamber operates as an accumulator of subjectivity. While analyzing the formation of modern subjectivity, Francis Barker writes that by the seventeenth century "the scene of writing and of reading is, like the grave, a private place" (Barker 1995: 2). The consolidation of this new private place for reading and writing is being set in place when Arbeau writes *Orchesographie* in the last years of the sixteenth century. Barker depicts the room that cocoons the modern subject as a sort of spectral echoing chamber – one where, literally, and by the means of that telecommunicational power of the book, "ghostly mutterings can indeed be heard, rustling among the feints and side-steps of the text's involuted speech" (1995: 2). Barker's description illustrates quite well how choreography as a technology of modern subjectivity needs the space of the chamber for modernity's spectral operations. In this new private chamber called the studio (by that time, in Europe, a place disturbingly evocative of the ones where the dead lie)[18] it is not only modern philosophy that will find itself, as in Descartes's proposition of a metaphysical foundation for subjectivity whose truth is to be found in soliloquy. With Arbeau, choreography as writing and as a subjectivity-machine mediating absence and presence finds its conditions of possibility by dwelling in studious privacy.

So, we go back to Nauman in his studio and note that, despite its seeming empty, the space of *Walking in an Exaggerated Manner around the Perimeter of a Square* is filled with choreographic elements: the mirror on the wall, the dance square on the floor, even the stool for the master. This is why I must disagree with van Bruggen, when she writes that in this piece, as well as in *Dance or Exercise on the Perimeter of a Square* (1967–8), "the use of the square on the floor is somewhat arbitrary – it could have been a circle or a triangle" (Bruggen in Morgan 2002: 48). Although van Bruggen acknowledges that the shape on the floor "serves to direct the movements and to formalize the exercises, giving them more importance as dances than they would have had if Nauman had just wandered aimlessly" (2002: 48), my point is that the formalization in itself marks the shift from dancing in general to the specifically choreographic. The square is a fundamental indexing of the haunting presence of the choreographic – not only of Capriol's chamber, but of Raoul-Auger Feuillet's depiction of the dance floor in his 1700 manual *Choréographie*, represented as an empty square on a white background.[19] Just as with Barker's description of the rustlings of the spectral in the philosopher's chamber, Nauman's studio is filled with the rustlings of choreography's specter, in the messed-up temporality of the hauntological.

Thus, we have to repeat for Nauman the question asked in relation to Arbeau: what might be the function of the studio in Nauman's choreographic experiments? Van Bruggen tells of an interesting incident that apparently preceded Nauman's secluded motions in his studio. According to van Bruggen, Nauman once told

> a friend who was a philosopher that he imagined him [the friend] spending most of his time at a desk, writing. But in fact his friend did his thinking while taking long walks during the day. This made Nauman conscious of the fact that he spent most of his time pacing around the studio drinking coffee. And so he decided to film that – just the pacing.
>
> (Bruggen in Morgan 2002: 47)

We have already seen how there is much more than just random pacing in Nauman's studio films, that Nauman formalizes pacing, and that this formalism is crucial for the impact of his pieces not as dances, but as choreographic exercises. But there is an irony in the telling of this anecdote that van Bruggen seems to miss. Nauman imagines the proper environment of philosophy to be that of the secluded room and the kinetics of philosophy as a thoughtful stance. He thinks of the philosopher as a lonely thinker-writer, a subject removed from the world, sitting quietly at his desk. But it turns out that the philosopher is actually a meanderer (like Socrates, like Rousseau, like Nietzsche, like Débord, like Deleuze and like Guattari). And not only is the philosopher's thinking happening thanks to his walking about, but the space for his walking-philosophizing happens to be in the open, outside the room and in the city or field. The irony is that after having heard all that from the friend philosopher, by an equivocal operation, Nauman transforms philosophical drifting in the publicly open into a private, and often[20] very methodically and very carefully choreographed pacing in his solitary studio. Instead of launching himself into the world, Nauman locks himself up in his empty studio for a series of self-contained, cloistered, choreographic solipsistic explorations – under the excuse of philosophy.

How does philosophy play in Nauman's choreographic solipsism in his studio films? In choosing for his experiments a confined space for choreography, which he thought equivalent to the space of philosophizing, Nauman recasts his studio as a cranial space. Robert Morgan writes:

> In the case of the earlier black and white tapes, such as *Revolving Upside Down* (1969), the sheer physicality of the body moving in the illimitable space of the artist's studio, with its properties so sparsely attenuated, gives over to a mental act, what Duchamp understood as *cervelle*, the 'brain-fact'.
>
> (Morgan 2002:13)

Nauman explicitly equates his "mental acts" with the private room in an extraordinary installation work contemporary to his studio films. In 1968, he created a sound installation for two loudspeakers in an empty room. Anytime someone walked into the room, the loudspeakers would blast the title of the piece: *Get Out of My Mind, Get Out of This Room.* So, for Nauman the mind is the room, just as the room is the mind: both intimately bound to language by the means of a commanding, mobilizing speech act. This is the solipsist thought-space Nauman builds when he starts not only to "pace in his studio" but to carefully execute extremely precise walks: around perimeters of squares, revolving on one foot, square-dancing in patterns. The choreographic happens in a space explicitly defined as solipsistic, choreographic, and philosophical: the space of thought moving.

If the chamber is an accumulator of subjectivity, what kind of subjectivity does it accumulate? In *Bouncing Two Balls between the Floor and the Ceiling with Changing Rhythms* (1967–8)[21] we find Nauman within the same square where he danced and walked around in an exaggerated manner – the choreographic square sheltered by the studio-accumulator. In this piece, Nauman engages in a high energy Newtonian experiment: he tries to keep two balls bouncing continuously between studio floor and ceiling. Choreographic precision is shattered by Nauman's inability to fully follow the title's command. The trajectories and speeds of the two balls escape his mastery. The whole scene becomes random, absurd, frustrating. The balls bounce around the studio in unforeseeable trajectories, despite the promises of Newton's laws of inertia and the putative predictability of ballistics. We find once again Nauman involved with solipsism, inside his space of nonrelation, performing a mental act on the choreographic square marked on the floor, all elements working in tandem to fuse physics with sports – playing fields of normative masculinity. It is not possible to think about this experiment as one in pace with a choreographic subjection to a commanding cadence. Here, there is no cadence. The world of physics is not docile, it does not yield easily to the perlocutionary force of the speech act, to the artist's desire to dutifully fulfill the command of a title.

> BRUCE NAUMAN: At a certain point I had two balls going and I was running around all the time trying to catch them. Sometimes they would hit something on the floor or the ceiling and go off into the corner and hit together. Finally I lost track of them both. I picked up one of the balls and just threw it against the wall. I was really mad.
>
> WILLOUGHBY SHARP: Why?
>
> BRUCE NAUMAN: Because I was losing control of the game. I was trying to keep the rhythm going, to have the balls bounce once on the floor and once on the ceiling and then catch them, or twice on the floor and once on the ceiling. There was a rhythm going and when I lost it I ended the film.
>
> ([1971] in Kraynak 2003: 147)

The lack of cadence and movement control in *Bouncing Two Balls* is striking when compared to Nauman's calm, chronometric, controlled pacing around the same white square marked by a metronome in his *Dance or Exercise on the Perimeter of a Square* (1967–8). In *Bouncing Two Balls* Nauman gets mad. We see that clearly in the videotape. No wonder then that a few months later he returns to the problem of control over bouncing balls. Only this time, he masters them by withdrawing even further from the world and deeper into the realm of masculine choreographic solipsism, deeper into a hyperbolic relation to self-sameness, to a hyper-homorelationality now approaching narcissism. In *Bouncing Balls* (1969)[22] Nauman recuperates the title of the piece that had maddened him so and uses a special high-speed camera to film a close up of his testicles, which he strokes. Here, in the space of masculine solitude, choreographic solipsism glides into the masturbatory. But something else is added at the level of temporality: the actual action of Nauman's fingers stroking his balls took only a few seconds, but by filming this action in high speed and then rendering the film at regular speed the result is an extremely slow-motion image: a 6- to 10-second original action now extends to a 10-minute film. With this effect, Nauman achieves "a suspension of time and gravity" (Bruggen 2002: 57) countering the Newtonian pull. Bouncing his balls, Nauman displays a weightless image of the self-sufficiency of male desire as solipsistic mastering of movement.

Rosalind Krauss observed that the question for Nauman in the 1960s was to exert critical and material pressure on the project of Western sculpture. By introducing not necessarily dance but the choreographic in the expanded field of the sculptural, Nauman "puts pressure on the viewer's notion of himself as 'axiomatically coordinated' – as stable and unchanging in and for himself"

Figure 2.2 Bruce Nauman. *Revolving Upside Down* (1969). Video still.

Courtesy Electronic Arts Intermix (EAI), New York.

(Krauss 1981: 240). In other words, when sculpture is produced choreo-graphically, it challenges the axiomatics of subjectivity's self-foundational myths: subjectivity as monadic masculinity, as being-toward-movement, as unchanging, locatable "self." Nauman's choreographic experiments are not only esthetic: their solipsism and maniacal abiding with law saturate masculine subjectivity to the point of absurdity. In 1969, this reaches an apex with the masturbatory *Bouncing Balls* and with the silly *Revolving Upside Down* (1969). In the latter, the antigravitational pull rehearsed in *Bouncing Balls* by the means of slow motion is now conveyed by an inversion of the camera – creating the illusion that Nauman is actually suspended from the ceiling. As Nauman methodically spins on one foot by alternating his supporting leg, he displays a choreographic pattern that perfectly blends technical difficulty (demanding a strong sense of balance and thigh and lower back strength) with a minimal performance of sheer, silly dizziness. In Nauman's solipsistic choreographies, and particularly with these two 1969 pieces where the masturbatory and the space of dizziness appear so literally, the masculine being-toward-movement as solipsistic subjectivity reaches a critical point of total saturation. This critical point is filled with potential, kinetic, and critical energies for much needed choreopolitical mutations. To pursue some of these mutations, I would like to turn now to some recent experiments in masculine choreographic solipsism, where the choreographic ontohistorical is pressured to its limits.

We saw how Western theatrical dance finds its primary (melancholic) energy and increased (modern) autonomy thanks to a particular figure occupying a particular place: a lawyer reading a book in "the privacy of his room" so he may dance with the ghost of his absent, departed master. I argued that the choreographic is ontohistorically hardwired to what Derrida called the telecommunication effect of writing. The reader-dancer might be alone in his chamber, but thanks to the choreographic book, he is always ready to invoke and dance with those who are not quite there, those who have already moved on. There is something in the imbrications between dance, writing, melancholy, solipsism, haunting, masculinity and the modern, kinetic, self-propulsive, self-sufficient being-toward-movement that can only be called idiotic – in the specific etymological sense Paola Mieli finds in the term "idiot": from the Greek *idiotes*, "a private person, individual, 'one in a private station' – from ideios, one's own, separate, removed from social responsibility" (Mieli *et al.* 1999: 181). This particular sense means the idiot is not necessarily stupid, or feeble of mind. Rather, this idiot is the isolated, self-contained *one* fantasizing subjectivity as an autonomously self-moving being. Choreography, as technology and expression of modernity's being-toward-movement, participates fully of this exhausting psychological, affective, and energetic project of modern subjectivation as the creation of a socially severed, energetically self-contained, emotionally self-propelled idiot experiencing the appearance of the other as unbearable crisis that initiates the symptom. The dynamics of this idiocy, and its deep relation to choreography, is explored by Spanish choreographer Juan Dominguez in his latest piece *All Good Spies Are My Age* (*AGSAMA*) (2003).

Figure 2.3 Juan
Domínguez. *All Good Spies
Are My Age* (2003).

Photo: Cuqui Jerez.
Courtesy Cuqui Jerez and
Juan Domínguez.

As opposed to Nauman's studio films, in *AGSAMA* Dominguez is unquestionably before an audience. Thus, in this piece, masculine choreographic solipsism appears as the representation of a condition. Choreography as writing is hyperbolically displayed: almost all the audience and the choreographer do throughout the 70 minutes of the piece's duration is to read a convoluted, obscure, self-centered narrative, whose pace is set by the choreographer's will. Silently sitting at a desk in a room,[23] Dominguez manipulates a series of small cards printed with sentences, paragraphs, or sometimes just one word, whose images he projects on a white screen next to him via a live feed from a small video camera on the desk. It is as if Dominguez can only face his audience, can only be before the other, because he has choreographed his mode of appearing as completely mediated by writing and by the ghostly "mutterings" of absent presences that writing evokes.

A series of ontohistorical hauntings can be identified intruding *AGSAMA*. *Intrusion of the ontohistorical choreographic number 1*:

> Where its status as a tool for communicating over a distance is concerned, one may cite, among other testimonies, the procedure detailed by a text from the Hardouin-Médor archive in Caen: the city's dancing masters are shut up in a room with paper, writing desk, "mathematics case, etc.," as if for a written examination; they compose choreographies for balls or ballets, which are sent to Paris to be judged and classified by the Academy; only afterwards comes the practical test, or "execution."
>
> (Laurenti 1994: 86)

Thus dance historian Jean-Noël Laurenti describes the procedures of choreographing in seventeenth-century France. Three centuries later, *AGSAMA* restages the scene: a male choreographer sits at his desk – which, by the way, looks suspiciously like a school desk – alone in a room to create a dance that exists only as a text to be read by a distanced audience. All we need to know is what kind of delayed test, or "execution," *AGSAMA* proposes.

AGSAMA's set is minimal: a small desk with a minute video camera, lens facing the desktop; a regular white screen on a tripod right next to the desk; a video projector placed before the screen; a vertical halogen lamp by the desk. All suggest that the piece could be experienced either as a semiprivate slide show or as a lecture in a large classroom. *Intrusion of the ontohistorical choreographic number 2*: The desk in *AGSAMA* is unusual – there is a stool physically attached to it where Dominguez sits, and there is another, identical stool directly across, on the side of the audience. This stool will remain empty throughout the piece. As in Nauman's *Walking in an Exaggerated Manner around the Perimeter of a Square*, the empty stool in the chamber where a man dances alone raises the question: for whom is this empty stool? Arbeau's ghost? *Intrusion of the ontohistorical choreographic number 3*: the stool attached to the desk, the desk's shape and scale, all suggest a school desk. Just as in *Orchesographie*, the space of the choreographic conflates with the pedagogical, and both are filled with forcefully present absences. Even before

AGSAMA properly starts, the piece already proposes the choreographic as always addressing itself to absence, always staging itself within the space of writing, always framing itself within the mark of the pedagogical, and always binding these aspects to a certain masculine solitude that remains nevertheless in tune with invisibilities. All the elements of the ontohistorical choreographic effect are in place in *AGSAMA*. How are they mobilized by Dominguez, how are they executed, and what do they execute, that is, destroy at the moment of their (ontohistorical, that is, hauntological) reiteration?

After the audience settles down, Dominguez, dressed in a white suit, enters the room. He turns on the video projector. He plugs in the power cord for the camera. He turns on a tall vertical halogen lamp standing by the desk to illuminate the room behind him in bright white light. Casually, Dominguez sits down and organizes several piles of note cards that were already set on the desk. He picks up one pile of cards and carefully places the top card of that pile under the camera lens. A projected image of the card fills the screen. We read in bold lettering, printed in English: "TTIM = The Taste Is Mine."[24] After about 3 seconds, another card is placed on top of the first one and we read:

> AGSAMA = All Good Spies Are My Age
> TTIM = The Taste is Mine
> SL = Swan Lake

Then consecutively, almost too fast to follow, three more cards, one on top of the other: "Do a show with ten people," then "Obsession with age," then "Exhibition in a Museum in Paris Theme: Memory." Then, a brief break, and another card: "How much time do you buy with an entrance ticket?"

It goes on, card after card, word after word, weaving a complicated series of narratives, lines of flight, obscure references, explicit references, detours, turns of phrase, turns of plot, loss of plot, plotless scenes, masturbatory dreams . . . for 70 minutes. The title of the piece, the program tells us, is *AGSAMA*. But right at the very beginning, a card with the single word "Title" appears on the screen – only to be followed and covered by another card that reads:

> In a hotel room in Oporto: My girlfriend asleep on a bed turned to the right. In front of her the wardrobe with mirror doors [*sic*]. I am awake on the same bed behind her, also turned to the right. I watch her body. I lift my head a little and see everything in the mirror. I hide myself behind her.

Could this be *AGSAMA*'s other title? A nonrelational title in the space of a chamber where a masculine I/eye hides from mirrors that reflect too much of the world and of a feminine other who happens not to be quite fully present. Moreover, in this dance that performs itself as literally choreographic, typography frames signification and semantics by a playful reference to the performative impact of writing. The words on the cards are all printed in multicolored capital letters (light blue, red, yellow, black, light green) in a font called **Impact**. *Intrusion of the ontohistorical choreographic number 4:* the choreographic effect as the typographic impact of the signifier within the space of solitary reading.

The next several cards tell the audience about women, beautiful women, excessive women, too many women, too desirable women – their collective existence contrasts sharply with the figure of the man at his desk. Later in the piece, we read that the narrator, instead of relating to these beautiful women that clearly excite him (so the cards tell us), shuts himself up in a public toilet and jerks off. Another solo performance of male desire within a secluded chamber. *Intrusion of the ontohistorical choreographic number 5:* Nauman's studio film *Bouncing Balls* (1969) where masculine solipsism meets desire, cadence, and will to control motions. It is by the careful accumulation of all these intrusions of the choreographic ontohistorical, that *AGSAMA* stages and masterfully reintroduces the foundational figure of the solitary male dancer in the masturbatory economy of modernity's exhausted energy, melancholic relation to time, and idiotic subjectivity.

What to do with *AGSAMA*'s propositions regarding the temporality of writing, the cadence of reading, and the impacting effect of solitary masculinity on the ontohistorical field of the choreographic? More specifically, what to do with this piece's propositions understood as choreographic ones? Because of its full participation in the formation of modernity's kinetic subjectivity-machine, the choreographic is informed by modernity's own structural incoherences: if it emphasizes presence, choreography discovers absence; if it emphasizes dancing, it finds mourning; if it desires socialization, it needs to abstract itself into a chamber. Coming from within the field of the choreographic effect, these incoherences are what *AGSAMA* so systematically identifies and dismantles by emphatically presenting their mechanisms and cadences in all their force.

Dominguez sets the cards on the table according to his own timing, arranging them carefully under the lens of the small video camera. The reading is exhausting. The audience is asked to fall into a cadence of reading that is imposed by another. At the edge of giving up on this pacing, on this reading, on this man, perhaps three-quarters of the way into the piece, the relentless flow of words shift to a relieving flow of images. Dominguez interrupts the procession of cards and words, showing us (always through the eye of the camera) a series of photographic portraits of himself. From babyhood to adulthood, the man carefully lays photograph of himself upon photograph of himself. This change is only momentary. The sedimentation of images one on top of the other repeats the pacing of the text cards, reinforcing the solipsistic self-production of subjectivity as secured by reiterative mechanisms of appearing. Unexpectedly, a disturbance in the accumulation of self-same images: one of the photos displays a second person. The unexpected eruption of the other is like a jolt. But before we can identify even the slightest contours of this other, Dominguez immediately covers his or her face with a card. The man at his desk, handling writing and images as a dance, remains the absolute and only center of all attention: ours and his. This repressed eruption of the other is the dramaturgical core of the piece.

The other's unexpected intrusion is *AGSAMA*'s trauma, and its symptom. It is the excessive gesture of withdrawing the other from the room of dancing that allows for the possibility of reading this piece choreographically.

But how could we read this piece in its relation to philosophy? Philosophically, solipsism is usually associated with the Cartesian project of a self-motivated, self-referential production of truth that places the solitary subject of discourse at the center and limit of that truth. No wonder then that solipsism has been the focus of serious objections raised against the Cartesian project. At the turn of the twentieth century, Edmund Husserl's project of establishing phenomenology as philosophy of consciousness was very much aware of the dangers brought by its potential solipsism. Martin Heidegger and Maurice Merleau-Ponty made considerable efforts to set this objection aside: Heidegger, by formulating his concept of Da-sein as mode of being-in-the-world (Heidegger 1996: 213–40, 279–84, and particularly 317–20), Merleau-Ponty with his "elemental" notion of the flesh as intertwinement of world with self (Merleau-Ponty 1968: 130–55).

But it is Wittgenstein's propositions on solipsism that may help us consider how Nauman's and Dominguez's deployments of choreographic solipsism propose a way out of the idiotic being-toward-movement. Wittgenstein's brief reflections on solipsism in his *Tractatus Logico-Philosophicus* start with proposition 5.6: "The limits of my language mean the limits of my world," and end with proposition 5.621: "The world and life are one" (Wittgenstein 1961: 115). These two sentences already clarify both Nauman's relationship to his titles (and to his particular understanding of language in general which he explicitly attributed to his readings of Wittgenstein [Kraynak 2003: 5–10]) and Dominguez's self-closure behind a wall of text in *AGSAMA*. If the limits of "my language" means the limits of "my world," and if the constitution of the choreographic (as I proposed when discussing Arbeau's *Orchesographie*) means the coming into being of a body whose presence and kineticism is already informed, preformed, and performed thanks to its ontokinetic intertwining with writing, then to inhabit and to explore language profoundly, to come into being through language, and to push its logic to its limits, is also to throw oneself right into the midst of the world. But, in order to do so, it necessarily follows that one needs to refigure the common understanding of solipsism. One needs to transform it from a mode of subjectivization that privileges seclusion, the demise of the world, the demise of relationality, and the idiotic monadic, into a "methodological solipsism" (Natansom 1974: 242) where what matters is intensifying it for the creation of careful and systematic experimentation.

In proposition 5.62, Wittgenstein addresses "how much truth there is in solipsism," precisely in this sense of seeing in it a methodological possibility for a radical opening of thought and being:

> For what the solipsistic *means* is quite correct; only it cannot be *said*, but makes itself manifest. The world is *my* world: this is manifest in the fact that the limits of *language* (of that language which I alone understand) mean the limits of *my* world.
>
> (1961: 115, emphases in original)

Jaakko Hintikka argues that Wittgenstein's "peculiar interpretation of solipsism [. . .] can only be understood in the context of other doctrines of the *Tractatus*" and concludes, "If I can say that something is mine, it immediately follows that this something can possibly be yours too" (Hintikka 1958: 88, 89). This is the moment where the language that "I alone understand" conflates with "my world" – to affirm that this "I" and its language-world is all inclusive. In Wittgenstein, both the linguistic "I" and the world (onto)logically participate of the other. Thus, what solipsism *means* (without saying it, but certainly manifesting it) is that the continuum I–language–world *necessarily* contains, and is and contained by, the I–language–world of the other. O. H. Mounce associates Wittgenstein's notion of solipsism with Schopenhauer's, emphasizing that for the latter the solipsist's

> error is that he thinks he can [. . .] eliminate the world so that only he exists. He has failed to grasp that subject and object are correlative. Each needs the other. If he eliminates the world he eliminates himself.
>
> (Mounce 1997: 10)

Mounce states that Wittgenstein followed Schopenhauer to formulate in the *Tractatus* that "what is true in solipsism cannot be expressed without recognizing the truth in realism" (1997: 11). Given that the solipsistic "my world" *necessarily* includes and is included by the other, then "it can be seen that solipsism, when its implications are followed out strictly, coincides with pure realism. The self of solipsism shrinks to a point without extension, and there remains the reality co-ordinated with it" (Wittgenstein 1961: 117). Hintikka concludes,

> one can say that the reason why Wittgenstein claimed that solipsism is essentially correct is diametrically opposed to the reason usually given for solipsism. What is usually taken to be the claim of solipsism is the impossibility of getting "beyond the boundaries of myself." Wittgenstein's solipsism is based on the exactly opposite claim that all the ordinary boundaries of myself are completely contingent and hence irrelevant "for what is higher."
>
> (Hintikka 1958: 91)

We can start to understand now why Nauman and Dominguez must use choreographic solipsism. Choreographic solipsism is a way to dismantle modernity's subjectivization as a mode of idiotic, self-propelled, autonomous solitude from within. Solipsism becomes a critical and choreographic countermethodology, a mode to intensify critically and physically the hegemonic conditions of subjectivization and to explode them in improbable directions. In this sense, the solitary man transforms his chamber from cage into that *critical space* Phillip Zarrilli called "the metaphysical studio [. . .] a place of hypothesis, and therefore a place of possibility [. . .] where something can come out of nothing" (Zarrilli 2002: 160). This is why, by the end of *AGSAMA*, what started as an exhausting display of writing, solitude, masculinity, cadence, self-referentiality, slowly dissolves into an odd web of inclusions: narrative but also corporeal and experiential inclusions. Inclusions that show how the choreographic (precisely because it is a technology of subjectivization that morphs writing with movement with body with absence with presence) may also offer escape routes from its dubious project of senseless mobilization – and thus show how solipsism, when understood as a philosophical methodology that implicates the poetic force of language right at the core of the world, may become a means for transcending the self-contained, socially severed, self-propelled modern being-toward-movement.

It is at this point, which is the point where Wittgenstein, in the *Tractatus*, drops the notion of the subject, that an incredible solo by Xavier Le Roy, produced under the conditions of this expanded notion of methodological solipsism that disrupts notions of absolute seclusion, must be invoked. In *Self Unfinished* (1999), Le Roy also drops the notion of the subject – and consequently modes of arresting being within fixed categories: masculinity and femininity, human and animal, object and subject, passive and active, mechanical and organic, absence and presence, all the oppositions that psycho-philosophically have framed modern subjectivity within fixed binomial options. Le Roy replaces those categories with a series of pure becomings, in the strict sense Deleuze and Guattari gave to it:

> A becoming is not a correspondence between relations. But neither is it a resemblance, an imitation, or, at the limit, an identification. [B]ecoming produces nothing other than itself [. . .]. Becoming is a verb with a consistency all its own: it does not reduce to, or lead back to, "appearing," "being," "equaling," or "producing."
>
> (Deleuze and Guattari 1987: 238–9)

What does a becoming produce by producing itself? A power, a plane of consistency or composition of desire, a body without organs (Deleuze and Guattari 1987: 270). What a becoming produces is never a representation but a plane of immanence of desire, which, through the activation of those "experiments" proper to becoming, inaugurates a politics of microperceptions that occasions for whole sets of minoritarian positions and agencies: schizos, children, blacks, women, animals . . . (Deleuze and Guattari 1987: 247–51). This is precisely the bio-political force of any becoming: "all becoming is a becoming-minoritarian" (Deleuze and Guattari 1987: 291). Significantly, figments of each minoritarian position are constantly appearing and disappearing in *Self Unfinished*.

The key word is "experimentation" – as fundamental condition for reaching "other contemporaneous possibilities" that reveal the body as "organism, history, and subject of enunciation," while at the same time revealing those modes of hegemonic subjection that "steal the body from us in order to fabricate opposable organisms" (man or woman, boy or girl, human or animal, dancer or lawyer, priest or sculptor, choreographer or theorist) (Deleuze and Guattari 1987: 270). So, ongoing experimentation, ontologically unfinishable. Le Roy's solo never falls into those oppositions, thus restitutes to the body its power to constantly reinvent itself. In this example of methodological choreographic solipsism, we find the idiot leaving its plane of self-containment and becoming generatively and intelligently silly in his ongoing becoming machinic *and* organic, human *and* objectal, subjective *and* indeterminate, man *and* woman, animal *and* sculptural, black *and* white, active *and* passive, joyous *and* sad, solitary *and* multiple – by constantly disorganizing and reorganizing that fundamental question profoundly binding philosophy and dance: what can a body do?

As we enter the performance space, we find Le Roy at his desk, dressed in black pants and shirt, receiving his audience, acknowledging our entrance. For the following hour, he will engage in three series of acts: first, fully dressed with simple black pants and a shirt, he will move as a humorous rendition of a robotic being, voicing machinic sounds. Then, he will remove his shoes and pants and unfurl his shirt to reveal it as a long tube that stretches all the way down his legs as a dress. This becoming woman is quickly dissolved when he bends his body in an inverted V shape, and starts to move as a headless quadruped. On all fours, Le Roy goes to the back wall, stands on his hands for a while. Then, propped on his shoulders, facing the wall, he proceeds to take his clothes off. Naked now, and always propped on his shoulders, his arms are reorganized as flimsy organs of balance and spatial location – his body becomes a nonrecognizable figure (next to me at the Kitchen in New York in 2003, someone observed that this figure "looks like an uncooked processed chicken, sort of"). Le Roy spends a great amount of time like this: naked, on his shoulders, head hidden between his legs, buttocks up, moving pathetically inefficiently, becoming formless. Of all the works analyzed so far, this is the first time that representation totally, radically, and consistently subverts the hegemonic isomorphism between presence, masculinity, verticality, figure, proper name, frontality, faciality, and efficient motility.

Still, the ontohistorical choreographic emerges to haunt and to force its presence, even if now only in its most minimal elements: the choreographer-writer-philosopher's desk is still there with its inevitable chair; the white, empty, abstract space is there; just as a boom box is there on the floor, so that telecommunication with the voice of the absent other remains available. (By the end of the performance, Le Roy will exit the stage fully dressed again, leaving his audience with the boom box finally blasting Diana Ross singing "Upside down / now you're turning me / inside out / round and round . . .".) But the presence of hauntological inclusions in *Self Unfinished* is already their demise: halfway through the piece, naked, upside down, on his shoulders, head hidden, a formless mass of impossible description, already mutating at every passing moment, Le Roy slides under the desk and violently kicks it apart. And even though he presses the boom box "play" button many times throughout the piece, it never gets to work, thus delaying the delivery of the voice of the other. And the masculine body as privileged presence in the solitary space of choreography soon vanishes thanks to Le Roy's cross-gendered use of his clothes and the becoming animal suggested by the involutions and contortions of his naked body, whose face never faces us. Le Roy proposes an entirely different understanding of what a body is: not a stable,

Figure 2.4 Xavier Le Roy:
Self Unfinished (2000)

Photo: Katrin Schoof.
Courtesy Katrin Schoof
and Xavier Le Roy.

fleshy host for a subject, but a dynamic power, an ongoing experiment ready to achieve unforeseeable planes of immanence and consistency. In his radical use of choreographic solipsism Le Roy exhausts the being-toward-movement. For what matters in *Self Unfinished* is never the spectacle of kineticism, but the pack of affects and precepts unleashed by the many stillnesses, repetitions, reiterations, humorous images, and unnamable forms that Le Roy presents us with.

We are no longer before a notion of the self as proper home of the individuated subject, as presumed condition for a disciplined body to be inhabited by the choreographic. Le Roy's self is unfinished not because it has not been completed yet, but because it can never be completed. This incompletion does not derive from some tragic interruption of a teleological process, but from Le Roy's predication of ontology on radical incompleteness, on an ongoing process he calls "relation" (Le Roy 2002: 46). Explaining his idea of relation, Le Roy invokes Paul Schilder's notion of "body-image" (1964), and makes it work along Deleuze and Guattari's notions of becoming and of body without organs.[25] In a "Self-Interview" of November 2000, Le Roy writes:

> X5: I don't know. But very often I ask myself, why should our bodies end at the skin or include at best other beings, organisms or objects encapsulated by the skin?
>
> Y5: I don't know neither [*sic*] but you might talk about the fact that the body image is extremely fluid and dynamic. That its borders, edges, or contours are "osmotic" and that they have the remarkable power of incorporating and expelling outside and inside in an ongoing interchange?
>
> X6: Yes. As you say, body images are capable of accommodating and incorporating an extremely wide range of objects and discourses. Anything that comes into contact with surfaces of the body and remains there long enough will be incorporated into the body image [. . .]
>
> Y6: So in other words what you say is that the body image is as much a function of the subject's psychology and socio-historical context as of anatomy. And that there are all kinds of non-human influences woven into us.
>
> X7: Exactly. So it [*sic*] must exist another alternative to the body image than the anatomical one.
>
> X8: For example: I think about that the body could be perceived as space and time for trade, traffic and exchange . . .
>
> X9: . . . following that idea, would mean that each individual would be perceived as an infinity of extensive parts. In other terms, there would be only composed individuals. An individual would be a notion completely devoid of sense.
>
> (Le Roy 2002: 45–6)

Le Roy's *Self Unfinished* proposes an understanding of the body that challenges the confinement of the body brought by modernity. The individual body, the monadic body, has no longer a place. If, as Harvie Ferguson reminds us, "the distinctive feature of modern embodiment lies in the process of individuation, in the identification of the body with the person as unique individual and, therefore, as the bearer of values and legally enforceable rights" (Ferguson 2000: 38), we can see already the magnitude of Le Roy's gesture within the ontochoreographic enforcement of modernity's mode of self-reproduction. Le Roy's displacement of the notion of the individual is the ultimate exhaustion of modernity's mode of choreographing the dance of subjectivity. Without individuation, there is no possibility of assigning subjectivity within the economies of law, naming, and signification. Through the particular kind of intensely formless solipsism performed by Le Roy the dismantling of modernity's idiotic body and its replacement by a relational body renews choreography as practice for political potentiality.

3 Choreography's "slower ontology"

Jérôme Bel's critique of representation

This representation, whose structure is imprinted not only on the art, but on the entire culture of the West (its religions, philosophies, politics) therefore designates more than just a particular type of theatrical construction.

(Derrida 1978: 234)

In order to write on the work of French choreographer Jérôme Bel, it is important to contextualize it briefly within a particular movement in recent European dance. I am thinking here of the proposals made in the past decade by choreographers such as La Ribot, Jonathan Burrows, Boris Charmatz, Xavier Le Roy, Mårten Spångberg, Vera Mantero, Thomas Lehmen, Meg Stuart, Juan Dominguez, to mention just a few of the most recognizable names.[1] This movement has been gaining shape, visibility, and force since the mid-1990s but it is by no means an organized one, nor does it have a proper name.[2] Despite different modes of working, different dramaturgical approaches, and sometimes even open antagonisms between each choreographer's way of dealing with form, discourse, and content, it is possible to identify some quite remarkable convergences. One prevalent concern – particularly significant to the question I would like to tackle in this chapter, that is, the question of a dance that initiates a critique of representation by insisting on the still, on the slow, and on that particular form of repetition known in rhetoric as "paronomasia" – is the interrogation of choreography's political ontology. If such an interrogation has been carried out by many of the works of the choreographers mentioned above, no one has taken it to its limits more consistently and relentlessly than Jérôme Bel – since his first evening-length piece *Nom Donné par l'Auteur* (*Name Given by the Author*) (1994).

Bel's interrogation of dance's political ontology takes the form of a systematic critique of choreography's participation in the broader project of Western representation. The critique of representation is one of the main characteristics of early twentieth-century experimental performance, theatre, and dance – at least since Bertolt Brecht's "urgency to understand mimesis [. . .] as historically mediated" (Diamond 1997: viii), and Antonin Artaud's famous manifestos for a theatre of cruelty from the early 1930s which, as Derrida noted, not only announced the "limit of representation" but proposed a "system of critiques *shaking the entirety* of Occidental history" (Derrida 1978: 235, emphasis in the original).[3] Theoretically, the critique of representation announces "a fracture in the epistemological regime of modernity, a regime that rested on a faith in the reality effect" of representation as it secured the stability of discourse (Gordon 1997: 10). Critical theory (particularly after Horkheimer's and Adorno *Dialectics of Enlightenment* [1997]) and deconstruction (all of Derrida's work) have participated in and precipitated this epistemological fracture of the reality effect in representation in order to reveal how it reproduces discursive and performative forms of domination. In dance, the critique of representation was one of the distinguishing impulses behind North American postmodern dance of the 1960s, an impulse that made it particularly akin to the political project of performance art and to the esthetics of minimalism – as famously articulated by Yvonne Rainer in her famous "NO Manifesto": "NO to spectacle no to virtuosity no to transformations and magic and make believe" (in Banes 1987: 43).

Bel is fully aware of these esthetic, theoretical, and political experimentations. What distinguishes his particular mode of critiquing the representational is his insistence in uncovering how choreography specifically participates in, and is accomplice of, representation's "submission of subjectivity" under modern structures of power (Foucault 1997: 332).[4] Bel's work articulates the following proposition: in order to think the relation between choreography, representation, and subjectivity, one needs to understand representation not only as that which is specific to the mimetic (that is, to what is properly theatrical to theatre) but to consider it as an ontohistorical force, a power that in the West has entrapped subjectivity within a series of isomorphic equivalences. Particularly relevant for dance studies is Bel's disclosure "imprinted not only on the art, but on the entire culture of the West (its religions, philosophies, politics)" (Derrida 1978: 234) that representation establishes between visibility and presence, presence and unity of form, unity of form and identity. Bel's uses of stillness, slowness, and paronomastic reiteration show how choreography reinforces and reifies these series of equivalences in a spectacular display of the enclosure of subjectivity in the agitated kinetics of modernity's "being-toward-movement" (Sloterdijk 2000b: 36).[5]

Thinking about the political ontology of choreography in relationship to representation and subjectivity, Bel's work proposes the following questions: in which ways is Western choreography part of a general economy of mimesis[6] that frames subjectivity and encloses it? How can an exploration of choreography's conditions of possibility reveal its participation in the production of subjectivity in the space of representation? What mechanisms allow the dancer to become the choreographer's representative? What is that strange power at the core of the choreographic that subjects the dancer to rigorously follow predetermined steps even in the choreographer's absence? How does choreography's alliance to the imperative to move fuel, reproduce, and entrap subjectivity in the general economy of the representational?

Dramaturgically, compositionally, choreographically, Bel answers these questions by drastically distilling choreography to its most basic elements. Historically, these elements of choreography (I would like to insist on the particularities invoked by this word) have been: a closed room with a flat and smooth floor; at least one body, properly disciplined; a willingness of this body to subject to commands to move; a coming into visibility under the conditions of the theatrical (perspective, distance, illusion); and the belief in a stable unity between the visibility of the body, its presence, and its subjectivity. Throughout his work,

Bel addresses each of these elements by exposing them, exaggerating them, subverting them, destroying them, complicating them.

In his piece *The Last Performance* (1998), the question of presence, visibility, representation, and subjectivity are brought to the fore, and then examined, probed, exhausted. Throughout this hour-long work, four dancers (Antonio Carallo, Claire Haenni, Frédéric Seguette, Jérôme Bel) continuously exchange names, characters, subjectivities: a body that is not Jérôme Bel opens the piece by announcing to the audience, deadpan, alone center stage, by the standing microphone, "*Je suis Jérôme Bel*" (I am Jérôme Bel). After standing still for a minute (measured by his wristwatch), Frédéric Seguette-Jérôme Bel exits the stage and a body that is the legal carrier of the name Jérôme Bel, dressed in white tennis-player attire, enters to tell us deadpan, center stage, by the microphone, in English, "I am Andre Agassi." After hitting a few tennis balls against the back wall of the theatre, Bel-Agassi exits and dancer Antonio Carallo walks in, stands quietly by the microphone for a minute or so and tells us, deadpan, "I am Hamlet." His affirmation clarifies the question at stake in this piece, the question of ontology as it mingles with the history of (theatrical) representation. For, right after telling us who he represents, Carallo-Hamlet pronounces the famous lines of Act III, Scene 1. The words "to be," are uttered on stage, for the microphone; then he slowly walks off stage, shouts "or not to be," and calmly returns, to set forth the dramaturgical core of the piece: "that is the question." The question of Hamlet is, of course, the question of being, what Heidegger in *Introduction to Metaphysics* called "the fundamental question" (Heidegger 1987: 1–51). What Bel does in *The Last Performance* is to show how this question, when uttered under the sign of choreography on that particularly hyperbolic representational space that is the stage, has the potential to reveal a whole series of reified associations between presence and visibility, absence and invisibility.

I will return to *The Last Performance* later in this chapter. For now, let's just retain the piece's syntagmatic operation – in *The Last Performance* a restricted set of names are constantly being reassigned and exchanged, thus complicating any "proper" or stable assignment of subjectivity within the fundamental question of being (or not-being) in the expanded field of the representational. By exchanging names in a permutational game of ontologics, *The Last Performance* makes explicit that the fundamental question set forth by Heidegger and Hamlet – the question of ontology – is one that haunts any critical reflection on performance – as Richard Schechner indicated in his famous theorizations on the notions of twice-behaved behavior as predicated on a paradoxical ontology always oscillating between "not me – not not me" (Schechner 1985: 127), or as articulated by Peggy Phelan's proposition of the ontology of performance as being also an "ontology of subjectivity" (Phelan 1993: 146).[7]

The Last Performance displays very clearly how bodies and subjectivities are held captive within linguistic, cultural, but also within material and physical spaces of representation. All of Bel's works display how putative "outsides" of choreography (particularly language and the actual space of the theatre) are in fact accomplices to a collective subjection to representation. But his work also

Figure 3.1 Jérôme Bel. *The Last Performance* (1998).

Photo: Herman Sorgeloos. Courtesy Jérôme Bel.

displays how the end of representation remains both a project and an impossibility. Bel would agree with Derrida when he writes, "because it has always already begun, representation therefore has no end" (Derrida 1978: 250). Bel's play with names, with historical characters, with language, indicates that his work is informed by the fact that "presence, in order to be presence and self-presence, has always already begun to represent itself, has always already been penetrated [by representation]" (Derrida 1978: 249). His work displays the ambiguity of subjectivity that Deleuze and Guattari identify when they state, "we fall into a false alternative if we say that you either imitate or you are" (Deleuze and Guattari 1987: 238). But if representation's end remains an unfinishable political and esthetic project, the exploration of its *means* remains a necessity – given representation's entanglement with hegemonic forms of subjection. Bel insists on this exploration of representation's means by positing that the end of representation is the limit of its capacity to turn presence into a fixed, recognizable subjectivity. For this project to be carried out fully, a simultaneous interpellation of the historical, the ontological, and the spatial contexts where choreography appears is crucial. Thus, two constant elements in Bel's work: his use of isolated bodies (even in his group pieces, bodies appear as if wrapped in solipsism), and his interrogation of the architecture of the theatre itself as spatial representative of the isolated and isolating interiority of representation. Indeed, Bel's pieces constantly indicate that both performers and audiences are coextensively trapped in those particularly charged representational machines: language and the theatre.

In the piece *Jérôme Bel* (1995), four naked dancers walk onto the stage carrying only a lit light bulb and some white chalk.[8] That single light bulb will be the only light source for the hour-long piece (it's minimalist literality invoking Rainer's "no to illusion"). The bit of white chalk is used by dancers Claire Haenni and Frédéric Seguette to write their proper names on the back wall above their heads (indexing the overdetermination of presence performed by the legal force of the name), with their age, bank account balance, telephone numbers, weight, and height written vertically next to their bodies. They stand for a while under their names, next to their numerical information, as if their bodies subtitle the writing on the wall. The other two dancers write and stand under names that are not their own, names they represent, names that will be represented by what the dancers do. Thus, the old woman (Gisèle Tremey) holding the light bulb writes and stands under "Thomas Edison." The younger woman (Yseult Roch) who will sing the entire *The Rite of Spring* throughout almost all of *Jérôme Bel*, writes and stands under "Stravinsky, Igor." The former indexes the photology at the core of representation; the latter foregrounds the haunting force of dance trickling down across time. The localized light, the emptiness of the stage, the nakedness of the dancers, all the names overdetermining presence (including the choreographer's name, hovering throughout as the title of the piece), all show how representation operates as an isolating and centripetal force that constantly defines its space as one of pure interiority. Jérôme Bel's *Jérôme Bel* reminds us that, if representation allows for an experience of an outside, it is only in a subordinate relation to the inside that representation holds, preserves, and reproduces. And what representation endlessly reproduces is itself – representation reproduces its power for perpetually mirroring its self-embrace.[9]

Bel explores and destabilizes the self-enclosure of representation by messing up the reified isomorphism representation establishes between presence, visibility, character, name, body, subjectivity, and being – for representation, all functionally equivalent concepts sustaining the fantasy of the subject's unity. If a piece is titled *Jérôme Bel*, but the body represented by the name the title evokes seems not to make an appearance, seems not to be there, how can we identify presence with appearing, how can we assign full presence to a singular body?[10] Perhaps what Bel is proposing is a revision of our conceptions of presence, body, and being there.

In a short text published in 1999, Bel articulates his refusal to accept the notion of subject as a self-representational, closed entity, limited by its localizable and visible corporeal boundaries: "there is no such thing as a single subject or a central focus (a 'you' and a 'me')" (1999: 36). He continues the sentence by enumerating all the bodies that he *was* at the moment of his writing that text – thirty-three individual and collective names, from Gilles Deleuze to Myriam van Imschoot, from Samuel Beckett to "unknown individuals in the megalopolis where I live," from Peggy Phelan to "Claude Ramey (an invented name, maybe real)," from Hegel to Xavier Le Roy, to Madame Bovary, to Diana Ross, to Ballet Frankfurt, to "yourself" (Bel 1999: 36). And he reminds us how each of these names are also packs formed by other bodies, other collectivities. The subjectivity and the body Bel proposes are clearly not monads or self-mirroring singularities, but packs, open collectives, continuous processes of unfolding, multiplicities.[11] As Bel tells us, he is interested in subjectivities and bodies akin to the "body without organs" theorized by Gilles Deleuze and Félix Guattari – a rhizomatic body, an Artaudian project, an ongoing experiment.

Deleuze and Guattari proposed that "there is a mode of individuation very different from that of a person, subject, thing, or substance," what they called "the pack" (Deleuze and Guattari 1987: 261). This open subjectivity that will not be contained by the legal enclosure imposed by name, character, or the reification of the isomorphism between visible body and full-presence, resonates theoretically with Paul Schilder's concept of "body-image" – a concept contemporary to Artaud's second manifesto on the theatre of cruelty (1935), and that precedes by a decade Artaud's cry for a body without organs. For the Austrian psychoanalyst, one's body-image does not simply coincide with the visible presence of one's body. Rather, one's body-image extends itself to any place any particle of one's body has reached across space and across time. Wherever one has left a particle of one's body (feces, blood, menstruation, urine, sweat, tears, semen) there one finds the limits of one's body-image. Wherever one has left an imprint of one's body (including linguistic ones, affective ones, sensorial ones) there is a limit of one's body-image. Schilder's notion of the body as body-image is already rhizomatic, schizoid, in the sense that it posits a body that is always beyond its proper boundaries, beyond traditional metaphysical

notions of presence: a body that is always late to its arrival and a
its departure, a body that is never quite there in the context o
(Schilder 1964).

Jérôme Bel's opening up of the body and of subjectivity awa
enclosure proposes some methodological and epistemological
dance studies. If the dancing subject is no longer considered a sin
the visible body dancing on stage does not fully reveal its presence, how can
dance studies give an account of what it is disciplinarily supposed to be
accountable for: the moving presence of bodies in the confined space of the
stage? If the body is a pack, a rhizome, a body-image, if it is semantic as much
as it is somatic, if it extends across time and space, then in which ways can critical
writing assess choreographic work built upon this splayed-out model of the body
and of subjectivity? One answer for critical dance studies would be for it to
consider a radical questioning of the presumed stability (that has always been
secured by representation) between the appearance of a moving body on stage
(its presence), and the spectacle of its subjectivity (that representation always casts
as the spectacle of an identity).

But if one does engage in this critical operation, one will soon find out that it
is not only the status of the body of the dancer on stage that requires critical
revision. The assumed singularity of the author-choreographer must also be
revised.[12] Not surprisingly, the revision of the singularity of the author is one of
the elements Jérôme Bel is particularly interested in investigating in his critique
of choreography. No wonder that Bel's two first evening-length pieces (*Nom Donné
par l'Auteur*, 1994 and *Jérôme Bel*, 1995) explicitly address the question of
authorship, the figure of the author, and the economic and theological power of
the author as transcendental name-that-names – the power Foucault called "the
author-function" (Foucault 1977: 131).

> [T]he 'author-function' is tied to the legal and institutional systems that
> circumscribe, determine, and articulate the realm of discourses; it does not
> operate in a uniform manner in all discourses, at all times, and in any given
> culture; it is not defined by the spontaneous attribution of a text to its creator,
> but through a series of precise and complex procedures; it does not refer,
> purely and simply, to an actual individual insofar as it simultaneously gives
> rise to a variety of egos and to a series of subjective positions that individuals
> of any class may come to occupy.
>
> (Foucault 1977: 130–1)

In *Nom Donné par l'Auteur* (1994), it is precisely the mechanisms of the author-
function that are revealed, pulled apart, and recombined, by the means of a
series of precise and complex procedures. Throughout the whole piece, two male
performers (often, but not always Frédéric Seguette and Jérôme Bel)[13] quietly
explore the relationship between an object and its name. Surrounded by familiar
objects (a vacuum cleaner, a football, a rug, a carton of salt, a dictionary, a hair-
dryer, a stool, a torch light, a pair of ice skates, a money bill, all of which are Bel's

everyday personal belongings) the two performers silently place one object before another and place themselves in relation to the objects, in a series of arrangements and rearrangements of correspondences and permutations that create a very surprising, and very open, semic and syntagmatic visual game. Dance critic Helmut Ploebst quotes Bel on this piece: "[I was trying to] create meanings on stage, even if it was very difficult and boring for the audience – there was no dance, there was no music, there was no costume and no dancers" (in Ploebst 2001: 200). The question then is: without dance, music, and dancers, could there still be something of the choreographic in this piece?

To identify how *Nom Donné par l'Auteur* addresses choreography, one has to attend to its measured pacing of execution and to its performers' silence. In this piece, silence should not be defined negatively as a lack of sound, but positively as an activator, a force, a critical operation. Silence operates as an intensifier of attention; it gives density to the objects. Silence also places the performers at the level of the objects they manipulate, indexing the muting of the dancer's voice in Western choreography's ontohistorical process of becoming an autonomous art form. Lest we forget, Western dance achieved its representational autonomy (and therefore its claim for an ontology) by literally becoming dumb. Choreography's silencing of the body emphasizes its commitment to produce a pure being-toward-movement, a dazzling dumb-mobile.

Nom Donné par l'Auteur reminds us that a title is just a name given by the author to his or her work. By initiating his choreographic career with a piece that explicitly explores the question of naming in the space of muteness, Bel went to the bedrock of the choreographic to identify its paradoxical core. Choreography is not only an intriguing hypermimetic art form born out of early modernity. As I discussed in the previous chapter, choreography is the proper name given by a Jesuit priest judge to the technology of "writing down movements" lest one forgets them.[14] It should not be taken lightly that the birth of choreography – as name and as discipline – happened through the writings of a priest. This is where the history of choreography reveals its more than metaphoric entanglement with what Derrida, in his essay on Artaud, called representation's "theological stage." It is worthwhile quoting Derrida at some length in his description of such a stage.

> The stage is theological for as long as its structure, following the entirety of tradition, comports the following elements: an author-creator who, absent and from afar, is armed with a text and keeps watch over, assembles, regulates the time or the meaning of representation, letting this latter represent him as concerns what is called the content of his thoughts, his intentions, his ideas. He lets representation represent him through representatives, directors or actors, enslaved interpreters who represent characters who, primarily through what they say, more or less directly represent the thought of the "creator." Interpretive slaves who faithfully execute the providential designs of the "master."
>
> (Derrida 1978: 235)

Figure 3.2 Jérôme Bel. *Nôm Donné par l'Auteur* (1994).

Photo: Herman Sorgeloos. Courtesy Jérôme Bel.

On the theological stage, even if the actor speaks, it is on the condition of a necessary and previous muteness – for the actor's mouth must remain only an echo chamber for the master's voice. And if the theological stage hosts choreography, an art that had to mute the body in order to fully become autonomous,[15] then it is the dancer's body's expressivity that has to be muted, becoming nothing more than a faithful executer of the designs of the absent, remote, perhaps dead, yet haunting power of the master's will.[16]

By creating his first choreography in objectal muteness, Bel identifies the theological power of the author-choreographer at the foundation of choreography. As I have shown, this strategy is made explicit in *Jérôme Bel*, where the homonomy between the piece's title and the author's name underlines the controlling absence of the choreographer and indexes how on the theological stage the choreographer "lets representation represent him through representatives" (Derrida 1978: 235). (This is why Jérôme Bel must never perform in *Jérôme Bel*.)

In *Nom Donné par l'Auteur*, Bel's strategy for identifying the theological nature of the choreographic stage is slightly different, although still attached to the function of the name of the author. Here, Bel sets up the conditions for creating another kind of power relations in the viewing of his work. Derrida tells us that for the proper functioning of the theological stage one needs not only the passive subjectivity of the performer, but also a passive audience: "the theological stage comports a passive, seated public, a public of spectators, of consumers, of 'enjoyers' [. . .] attending a production that lacks true volume or depth, a production that is level, offered to their voyeuristic scrutiny" (Derrida 1978: 235). And it is at the level of activating the audience out of its consumeristic voyeurism that *Nom Donné par l'Auteur* displays its antirepresentational, antitheological force. For, even if the piece retains the spatial division between stage and audience, the persistent and quiet reiteration of forms and objects, their familiarity and their defamiliarization in improbable pairings, gradually start to dissolve the passivity of the audience. To just watch this piece is to certainly miss it. Rather, it is crucial to accept its invitation to engage in its playfulness, to move from a passive optical scrutiny to an active, multisensorial, polysemic receptivity. Then we find out that there is nothing silent, or quiet, in this piece's muteness. We discover that "silence as sonorous rest also marks the absolute state of movement" (Deleuze and Guattari 1987: 267). Indeed, there is nothing still in the objects' and performers' apparent stability and apparent nondancing. What *Nom Donné par l'Auteur* achieves is a playful joy in the muteness of objects and in the muteness of the dancers. The piece reveals not the silence of things, but the rustling of the signifier resonating on the crust of every object, the rustling of language running along the surface of every body, like salt poured on the pages of a French dictionary.

The rustle of objects, their nonlinguistic voicing, evokes a concept from one of Bel's acknowledged theoretical influences, Roland Barthes. Barthes writes that "the rustle is the very sound of plural delectation" implying "a community of bodies" but where "no voice is raised [. . .] no voice is constituted" (Barthes 1989: 77). *Nom Donné par l'Auteur*, because of its silence and of its calm pace, reveals the rustle of language operating in each of its objects – and, by extension, in each and every object. By activating the community of bodies (objects, performers, audience) rustling needs in order to operate its "plural delectation," the piece introduces another Barthian critical move: the destruction of the myth of the unitary figure of the master-author. Such destruction happens by a displacement and multiplication of the authorial voice: actively watching *Nom Donné par l'Auteur* turns each audience member into an author.

Bel opened up his choreographic career by cracking the question of authorial intent, and of authorial unity, within the field of representation: names are given by the author, the title tells us. But who is giving what to whom? Can we identify an author in its intentional singularity? The answer Bel gives us is clearly no: the author becomes an author-function, a multiplicity spreading across a broken fourth wall, thanks to the collective rustling of quiet naming.

Bel's insistence on the power of naming, on the pervasive rustle of language, on syntagmatic games, is particularly significant for dance studies, for his insistences propose for the dancing body an undeniable linguistic materiality – one that is as constitutive of its being as its kinetic, visceral, energetic, affective, or anatomical aspects. In *Shirtologie* (1997), body and language fuse one into the other to display modes of subjectivization. A male dancer stands still throughout most of its duration, as he peels off layers upon layers of T-shirts and sweatshirts with words, brand names, imprints.[17] In this solo, through metonymy, the dancer's body appears as a layered surface of inscription, in a way reminiscent of Foucault's description of the body as "the inscribed surface of events (traced by language and dissolved by ideas), the locus of a dissociated Self (adopting the illusion of a substantial unity), and a volume in perpetual disintegration" (Foucault 1977: 148). Bel shows us how the linguistic entangles the body within a representational layering that entraps subjectivity. The dancer in *Shirtologie* (usually Frédéric Seguette) stands still at the center of the stage, neutral, head down, almost removed.[18] He enters the stage three times throughout the piece. Each time, he wears dozens of shirts one on top of the other, layer upon layer, which he proceeds very simply, quietly, eyes cast down, to remove until he reaches the last. The dramaturgy is very clear from the start: with each new shirt displayed, there is either an indication of what that section is about (the piece's first section is simply a countdown following the numbers displayed on the shirts: from a shirt displaying "Lille 2004" all the way through "France 1998 World Cup," to "Euro-Disney 1992," to "Michigan Final Four," to "One T-Shirt for the Life") or the dancer enacts what the inscription, drawing, or logo on the shirt dictates: one T-shirt has a fragment of Mozart's *Eine kleine Nachtmusik*, which Seguette sings. The next shirt displays a woman in attitude, which Seguette emulates. In this sense, sections of *Shirtologie* disclose that peculiar alliance choreography has with the perlocutionary force of the performative speech act – that function of speech where "by saying it, I convinced him" (Austin 1980: 110). The first moment in this piece when the dancer steps out of his stillness and recognizably dances for a minute is when the T-shirt he uncovers shows a Keith Harring drawing with the words "Dance or Die." Following the persuasive statement, the dancer opts for life, dancing while he sings again the Mozart tune.

Since Jérôme Bel bought all the shirts for the piece in retail stores, *Shirtologie* displays the massive linguistic and image archive that constantly surrounds us, an archive we all wear and display as so many quasi-invisible commands ("Just Do It," "Dance or Die"), an archive that is part of our subjectivity and body-image in the society of the spectacle. *Shirtologie* reveals how the culture of representation, when allied to late-capitalist subjectivity, thrives in a ceaseless reproduction of a poetics of commodities, logos, and trademarks – all permeating our bodies, our language, our perception, forming subjectivities and informing identities. *Shirtologie* reveals how representation meets that other totalitarian mode of self-enclosure – capitalism. But, as Jérôme Bel stated, the piece also reveals how performance may allow liberation from capital's relentless branding of identities under the sign of the (trademarked) name. In 1997, Bel created a collective version of *Shirtologie* for a group of nontrained young people; with this version, a liberating humor was inserted into the dramaturgy. A young woman wearing a T-shirt with the face of pop singer Madonna will bring the song "Like a Prayer"; a young man wearing a T-shirt stating "No Time to Lose" quickly takes it off. Bel states that in this piece "we were using the energy of capitalism to express ourselves" (in Ploebst 2001: 204). Thus, there is the possibility of reenergizing language, reenergizing the forces of capital aligned with the representational and recode the speech act.

We saw how in *Nom Donné par l'Auteur* the poetics of silence opened up the possibility for listening to subtle and otherwise muted modulations of meaning, through a direct confrontation with objects. What happens when we are placed in direct confrontation with language? Are we all hopelessly submitted to its force, to its commanding, illocutionary and perlocutionary force, even to its violence? In the piece *Jérôme Bel*, we have a direct answer to this question. I described how language hovers in this piece, creating its conditions of visibility and overdetermining the presence of the dancers. But something extraordinary happens at the intersection between body and language in this beautiful piece, something fluid that suspends the house arrest of the body by language, by laws of signification and of signature. This fluidity appears through the action of what Georges Bataille called the "inassimilable excess" the body constantly produces. At a certain point in the piece, Frédéric Seguette and Claire Haenni urinate on the floor. Quietly, the visceral body acts, displaying an interiority that representation does not account for nor does it totally control. For many, this is a scandalous act, despite its tranquil rendition. It is certainly the cause for *Jérôme Bel*'s entanglement with obscenity laws in European courts.[19] But this act not only indexes the inner workings of the visceral body – this act also has a function. It will be used to indicate how the body is the primary agent for the transformation of language. When the two dancers are done, they scoop up their urine with their hands, and start erasing the letters and numbers on the wall. Names disappear, but some of the letters are left to form a sentence, to reveal a linguistic potential hidden in the previous writing: "*Eric chante Sting*" (Eric sings Sting). All performers leave the stage and a man, fully dressed, enters, stands in the darkness, and sings Sting's "An Englishman in New York." If language, name, history, property, titles can be erased, rearranged, played with, and if in this playing rewriting can invoke a new performance, a new body, a new performative, a new beginning, a new song, this happens thanks to an erasing and a rewriting activated by what the dancers' visceral body produces. Erasing, rewriting, renaming, recalling, all operations that happen after the force of names that structured the whole piece is undone by the inassimilable excess the body produces. This rewriting evokes Judith Butler's words, as she intriguingly recuperates Althusser's notion of subjectivization in relation to the Austinian speech act: "We do things with language, produce effects with language, but language is also the thing that we do. Language is the name for our doing" (Butler 1997b: 8). Bel proposes a very specific notion of language, one that is as malleable, as playful, and as dynamic as the body. He also proposes how the body, in its most visceral activation, is not only a surface of inscription, as Foucault noted, but an instrument of writing, an inassimilable agent that constantly rewrites history back.

So far, I have been discussing the basic elements of Jérôme Bel's critique of representation by emphasizing the importance of nonkinetic elements in his work: the critique of authorial power, the question of the indetermination of presence in the field of the name, the critique of the theological stage, the activation of the audience. Now, I would like to address why Bel's critique of choreography's participation in the subjecting machine of representation must involve a kinetic of the slow, the still – in other words, a particular deflation of movement.

Just as Bel deploys singularity to propose how subjectivity is always a multiplicity, I would argue that he deploys stillness and slowness to propose how movement is not only a question of kinetics, but also one of intensities, of generating an intensive field of microperceptions.[20] An understanding of movement as intensity allows for a critique of choreography's participation in the ontopolitical continuum of representation and subjectivity that takes us directly to the question of the still. Just as silence is not used by Bel as the negation of sound, so the still is not used as the negation of movement. Bel's critique of choreography's political ontology derives from the powerful epistemological and political activations contained in the still-act, which identifies for dance that which does not seem to be a proper part of its ontology.

Greek anthropologist Nadia Seremetakis proposed the concept of "still-act" to describe a politics of the senses that allows for "the perceptual capacity for elemental historical creation" (Seremetakis 1994: 13).[21] In Bel's critique of representation, the perceptual capacity that needs to be activated for "elemental historical creation" is one that discloses the political ontology of choreography as an essential technology of subjectivization. If, as I discussed in Chapter 1, we accept the premise laid out by Peter Sloterdijk that modernity's ontology is a pure "being-toward-movement," and if we recall the historical fact that power (theological power, regal power, stately power) is at the core of choreography's being through Arbeau and Capriol's pairing as the coupling of church and law, as well as through Louis XIV's founding of the first Academy of Dance in 1649 and dancing to manifest the pure totalitarian power of an autonomous moving body (Franko 2002: 36), then it must follow that what the intrusion of the still in choreography (the still-act) initiates is a direct ontopolitical critique of modernity's relentless *kinetic interpellation* of the subject.[22]

Sloterdijk noted that modernity creates its kinetic being based on a primary "accumulation of subjectivity" that must precede the primary accumulation of capital Marxist theory posits as essential for the unleashing of capitalist modernity. If we accept Sloterdijk's proposition that the mode of subjectivity in modernity is that of a pure "being-for-movement," that modernity interpellates its subjects to turn them into "auto-mobiles," then it follows that what subjectivity had to primarily accumulate in order to fully become a being-toward-movement was potential energy, that modernity unleashes as kinetic energy. Given that no living system is energetically autonomous, the very idea of an autonomously kinetic subjectivity, of a self-contained and self-mobilizing subjectivity, emerges as the manifestation of a deep ideological blindness. Teresa Brennan notes:

> The subject is palpably not the source of all agency if it's energetically connected to, and hence affected by, its context. The hubris of the modern subject finds this notion unpalatable; this subject clings to the notion that humans are energetically separate; that they are born this way, within a kind of shell that protects and separates them from this world. In fact they have acquired this shell, which is also called the ego.
>
> (Brennan 2000: 10)

Brennan's insight implies that modern subjectivity is predicated on a particularly exhausting and particularly predatory energetic project – one that demands, on one hand, a constant display of the ontological imperative to enter into a permanent agitation; and on the other hand, one that requires plundering whatever resources there might be available to sustain the spectacle of mobility. By constantly representing itself as a kinetic spectacle and disavowing its energetic lack of autonomy, modern subjectivity establishes its colonizing relation in regard to all sorts of energetic sources – whether those are natural, physiological resources, or affective ones: desires, affects, becomings.[23] The mode of performance that occasions the self-enclosure of subjectivity within representation as an entrapment in spectacular compulsive mobility is the one that early modernity invents and gives a proper name: choreography. Choreography is a necessary technology for an agitated subjectivity that can only find its ontological grounding as a perpetual being-toward-movement.[24]

Describing the main characteristics of the work of German choreographer Thomas Lehmen, dance theorist Gerald Siegmund indicates some traits that I believe could be extrapolated to characterize Jérôme Bel's own critique of dance's participation in this project of perpetual agitation. Siegmund notes that it is important "to avoid representing the body as a sign to be consumed by the audience as a representation of flexibility, mobility, youth, athleticism, strength and economic power" (Siegmund 2003: 84). It is no wonder, then, that dance must be slowed down – as a way of decelerating the blind and totalitarian impetus of the kinetic-representational machine.

Figure 3.3 Jérôme Bel.
Jérôme Bel (1995).

Photo: Herman
Sorgeloos. Courtesy
Jérôme Bel.

But Bel has a particular way of slowing dance down. At this point, I would like to return to *The Last Performance*, in order to propose a reading of its particular deployment of that intriguing rhetorical figure, paronomasia. For, in paronomasia, one can locate Bel's proposition for a slower political ontology for choreography.

I described earlier how *The Last Performance* unfolds by insisting on a constant destabilization of the proprietary relationships between body, self, identity, body-image, and name. I would like to return to that moment when, staring at the audience, dancer Antonio Carallo states: "I am Hamlet," and then, after a pause, he delivers "to be," walks offstage, into the wings, pauses briefly and shouts, "or not to be," walks back onto the stage, stands before the microphone dead center downstage and utters quietly "that is the question."

After a body claiming to be named Jérôme Bel and a body claiming to be named Andre Agassi, a Hamlet walks in. I would like to underline the indefinite article before the proper name; or rather, the couplet indefinite article–proper name. Deleuze proposed that the indefinite article is "the power [*puissance*] of an impersonal that is not a generality, but a singularity in the highest degree" (Deleuze 1997: 89); and, with Guattari, noted how "the proper name does not indicate a subject [. . .]. The proper name fundamentally designates something that is of the order of the event" (Deleuze and Guattari 1987: 264). Thus a Hamlet walking into *The Last Performance* means: a singular event in the highest degree is walking in. What is the power this singularity brings? What is the event this entrance announces? The power is that of the fundamental question, the power of the ontological. The event is that of prefacing the first eruption of choreographed dance in the entirety of Bel's work. After four years and three pieces, finally . . . dance!

Why is it that the event of choreographed dance in Bel's work has to be prefaced by a Hamlet's fundamental question? Francis Barker noted how Shakespeare's *Hamlet* first articulated, in a clear manner, a "system of presence" where "the deadly subjectivity of the modern is already beginning to emerge" (Barker 1995: 21). For Barker, Hamlet's conflicts are those informing the emergence of modern subjectivity as a system of presence subjugated to visibility, melancholia, and discipline. *Hamlet* announces the invention of the modern monadic subject, a subject centered on a self, contained by the limits of the body, isomorphic to that body perceived as private property, bearer of a biography, housing private secrets and unique ghosts, responsible before the state, strictly binomial in terms of gender, and tamed in the channeling of desire (Barker 1995: 10–37). It is important to note that this system of presence, because it entangles the spectacle of visibility right at the core of subjectivity, is also a system of representation: one that "designates more than just a particular type of theatrical construction," but the whole cultural logics of the West (to invoke Derrida's words that open this chapter).

Thus, the entrance of a Hamlet-event in *The Last Performance* starts to resonate ontohistorically and politically: a Hamlet enters so that the very advent of a choreographed dance may be possible. It is as if Jérôme Bel is proposing that without that monadic subject, without the melancholic question of being as a binomial decision between presence/visibility/inside *or* absence/invisibility/outside, that is to say, without a Hamlet, *there would have been no choreography.*[25] Thus, when Bel makes Hamlet-Carallo walk onto the stage in *The Last Performance*, his deliverance and his presence do not address only the history of theatre – they are extremely provocative statements aimed at the political ontology of Western theatrical dance.[26]

As soon as Hamlet-Carallo leaves the stage after posing the ontological question, dance walks in embodied by dancer Claire Haenni who will dance a fragment of Suzanne Linke's *Wandlung* (1978) to Franz Schubert's *Death and the Maiden.*[27] Haenni enters, white dress, blonde wig. Approaches the microphone and states, deadpan, "*Ich bin Suzanne Linke*" (I am Suzanne Linke). Then she moves upstage and starts to dance Linke's short piece. When I saw *The Last Performance* at Theatre am Hallescher Uffer, in Berlin, in August of 1999, there was huge release of tension at this point. The audience had been close to riotous.[28] But then there was motion at last! Finally, someone following music in the recognizable patterns of "dancing!" Flow, classical music, body, presence, woman, femininity, ongoing motion, pretty white dress – one could finally enter into the zone of recognition and relax with the kinetic familiar. But Linke's segment is short, no more than 4 minutes, starting with the dancer lying on the floor close and parallel to the back wall of the stage and continuing almost entirely on the floor. When the short dance ends, and Haenni-Linke leaves the stage, familiarity is soon slapped on the face. For, now Suzanne Linke reenters the stage in a body named Jérôme Bel. Bel-Linke tells us: "*Ich bin Suzanne Linke.*" The music starts again, and so does the dance, on the same spot previously occupied by Haenni-Linke, the same notes and the same steps performed with the same delicate precision. The dance ends, Bel-Linke leaves, and Carallo-Linke steps in, same white dress, announcing "*Ich bin Suzanne Linke.*" He dances, same sequence, and is followed by Seguette-Linke that starts the process once again. What is being claimed under the repetitious prefacing of each new dancing by the speech act uttered by each new dancer "*Ich bin Susanne Linke?*" What is at stake in this dance stuck in its continuous repetition, as if reconfiguring the linear teleological motions of time?

In a public lecture on *The Last Performance* that Bel has presented a few times in the past couple of years throughout Europe, he mentions how he conceived this dance scene around two main questions: the formal question of how to quote a dance piece, as a rapper samples a song from another musician, and the perceptual question of how repetition unleashes series of differences. Bel tells of being inspired by Deleuze's *Difference and Repetition* at the time of making the piece. In that book, Deleuze asks

> does not the paradox of repetition [lie] in the fact that one can speak of repetition only by virtue of the change or difference that it introduces in the mind which contemplates it? By virtue of a difference the mind *draws from* repetition?
>
> (Deleuze 1994: 70, emphasis in original)

Thus, each reiteration of steps, music, dress, and utterance of the name of the author inevitably discloses difference at the core of repetition.

Repetition creates a form of standing still that has nothing of the immobile. And the particular form of repetition used in this dance scene in *The Last Performance* is reminiscent of paronomasia, a composite word from the Greek *para*, both "alongside" and "beyond," and *onomos*, "name," that indicates slight variations on meaning proper to the pun. How does one perform this kind of paronomastic motion? Linguistically, by the careful reiteration of an idea through an ongoing stringing of different words that share the same "stem." This repetition with a difference performs a reiterative spacing of the idea, allowing for a specific kind of slow turning that "give 'intellectual objects' variation and hence shift their aspects or appearances. Thanks to paronomasia, language is capable of turning an object around and around" (Rapaport 1991: 108). But how does one dance the paronomastic movement? Dancing *Wandlung* over and over again, we see how the different bodies are less claiming to be Suzanne Linke, but experimenting on *what happens when one decides to move alongside a name* (to engage in a literal paronomasia). This particular form of moving repetition not only brings humor to the scene, but reveals how dancing alongside and beyond a name is also to stay with it, to reveal its undersides, to unfold it, to unleash its lines of force, to break open the illusion of fixity a name is supposed to bring to its referent.

What is being created in this intriguing moment where repetition confuses perception thanks to paronomasia? What is being proposed in the rigorous display of the choreographic machine? Didi-Huberman writes how any "*acte immobile*," because of its paradoxical nature, is a "discreet, but disturbing memory event" (Didi-Huberman 1998: 66, emphasis in original, my translation). In a similar way, paronomasia creates perceptual and critical conditions that reveal how choreography can escape the "system of presence" that in dance was reified and crystallized as a truism by those often quoted lines from W. B. Yeats's "Among School Children": "O body swayed to music, O brightening glance, / How can we know the dancer from the dance?"

Peggy Phelan rightly identified in Yeats's poem an intractable scopic desire attached to the spectacular entrapment of the dancing body in pure fleeting visibility:

> The fact that modern Western dance is *always* indexed back to the dancer is more than the logical proof of the *intractability* of Yeats's echoing question, and more a symptom of the desire to see the body of the other as a mirror *and* as a screen for one's own g/lancing body.
>
> (Phelan 1995: 206)

But every time *Wandlung* is danced once again in *The Last Performance*, every time paronomasia makes it appear differently in its sameness, every time a different body brings to the same piece of dance unconscious variations on emphasis and uncontrollable micromarks of individualities, we witness a moment in which that "intractable" identification of dancer and dance is fundamentally subverted.

Paronomasia reveals that dance is something independent of the dancer. It reveals choreography as a haunting machine, a body snatcher. It reveals the telepathic effect in the choreographic, a display of choreography's haunting and uncanny force. Under the paronomastic display of choreography, dance emerges as a disembodied power ready to be occupied by any body. By peeling off dance from the dancer, the dancer can be inhabited by other nonpreformed steps; and choreography reveals itself as always diluted by each body's tremors, involuntary acts, morphology, imbalances, and techniques. No longer subject to the "fleeting glance," but revealing choreography's nature as always participating of a paronomastic mode of being seen, the dancer can claim other ways to deal with the visible.

All repetition is a kind of falling; the falling into a trap called temporality. The falling into time that the still-act initiates is also the activation of a proposition for an ethics of being that is always an active entanglement with time. Sloterdijk explains how Heidegger purposefully chooses a word to characterize this falling into temporality that distances itself from any metaphysical or Christian notions of the Fall: *Verfallen*. In *Being and Time*, Heidegger writes: "Thus, neither must the entanglement (*Verfallen*) of Da-sein be interpreted as a 'fall' from a purer and higher 'primordial condition'" (1996:164). In her recent translation of Heidegger's *Being and Time*, Joan Stambaugh notes that "*Verfallen*, is, so to speak, a kind of 'movement' that does not get anywhere" (in Heidegger 1996: 403). This sort of mobility that stays put, this movement that does not get anywhere while going everywhere thanks to the still, is that of paronomasia. Herman Rapaport describes it as "a going beyond even as one stays in the same place" (1991: 14) and notes how paronomasia deeply informs the philosophy of Heidegger and Derrida. How does one literally go beyond while staying put? And what can be gained with such a step? I would claim that the paronomastic movement dissolves the temporal tyranny modernity's being-toward-movement imposes on subjectivity for it to be constantly *on* time. Paronomasia proposes to subjectivity alternative modalities of being *in* time. Paronomasia, through its insistence on reiterating what is forever not quite the same, through its slow yet uncertain, teetering pirouetting, triggers the possibility for the secretion of a temporality which allows the body to appear under a different regime of attention and stand on a different, less firm (ontological) ground. Here, movement belongs more to intensities and less to kinetics; and the appearing body must be seen less as solid form and rather as sliding along lines of intensities.

The paronomastic operation, which is a choreographic one, qualitatively transforms the ontological question of dance. It transforms it through a shift in velocities, through an attending that carefully uncovers otherwise unsuspected zones and flows of intensities. This temporal carving and expansion is performed through this most misunderstood act for dance: remaining still. This paronomastic intensification of the still not only demands a new regime of attention, a new caring regarding the mechanisms through which the dancing body makes itself apparent, but it challenges the very timing of ontology by opening up a radical temporality against dance's melancholic plaint: a temporality that exceeds the formal boundaries of presence, and that is not tied in to the presentation of presence. This is how I understand Gaston Bachelard's notion of a "slower ontology," which is an ontology of multiplications and intensifications, of energetic fluidities and micromovements, an ontology of vibrations and delays, an ontology in delay, which is to say: "one that is more certain than the ontology that reposes upon geometrical images" (1994: 215).

I would like to end by emphasizing that the choreographic inhabiting of paronomastic stillness necessitates a refiguring of the terms under which one can reflect theoretically, and act choreographically, on dance's political ontology. In the series of gestures, speech acts, characters, scenarios, and fantasies upon which Western theatrical dance has historically grounded itself up, dance was coopted by an exhausting program for subjectivity, an idiotic energetic economy, an impossible body, and a melancholic complaint regarding a very narrow understanding of time and temporality. Choreographic paronomasia as still-act offers a program for body, subjectivity, temporality, and politics that liquefies and slows down not only assumptions regarding dance's ontology, but the infelicities and idiocies embedded in dance's reproduction of modernity's kinetic project of endless acceleration and agitation. This ontological slowing down initiates a different energetic project, a new regime of attention, as it recasts the figure of the dancer and its subjectivity into new lines of potentiality for the political ontology of the choreographic at the moment of movement's ultimate exhaustion.

4 Toppling dance

The making of space in Trisha Brown and La Ribot

A prevalent feeling among many painters that lets them make a space in which anything can happen is a feeling dancers may have too.

(Cunningham 1997: 66)

Mid-March 2003. In two consecutive days, North American choreographer Trisha Brown performed at the Fabric Workshop and Museum (FWM) in Philadelphia an event titled *It's a Draw/Live Feed* – a collaboration with the Department of Modern and Contemporary Art of the Philadelphia Museum of Art. Brown's performance was an unusual one: alone in one of the museum's white gallery spaces she would create what FWM's press release called "monumental drawings in a public context." Brown's unqualifiable performance – a hybrid of improvised dance and automatic drawing – would be witnessed "live" by an audience placed in a separate space in the museum, where they could watch a live video feed of Brown drawing-dancing.

Mid-March 2003. In two consecutive days, Spanish choreographer Maria La Ribot performed at Tate Modern, London, an event titled *Panoramix* – a collaboration with Live Art Development Agency. La Ribot's performance was an unusual one: in one of the museum's white gallery spaces she would create what the press release called "a long duration performance," gathering her past ten years of work in a public context. As opposed to *It's a Draw/Live Feed,* La Ribot's *Panoramix* would be performed before an audience sharing the gallery space with the dancer.

These two temporally coincidental events – where dance happened in the space of, and in dialogue with, visual arts – were created by two women choreographers separated by nationality, style, geography, and generation. While extremely distinct, the two events were critically linked by their unique belaboring of dance's relationship to visual arts. In the case of Brown, her piece addressed dance's relation to drawing. In the case of La Ribot, to sculpture and installation art. Moreover, both pieces gestured explicitly towards a critical reassessment of dance and visual arts' complex relationship to horizontality. That is to say: both choreographers, in different manners, addressed with their work a plane with a particularly problematic relation to gender politics in twentieth-century visual art: the horizontal.

The use of horizontality in post-World War II twentieth-century visual art is usually traced back to Jackson Pollock's toppling of the canvas from the vertical plane to the horizontal in 1947. In her essay "Horizontality," Rosalind Krauss (Bois and Krauss 1997) writes that Pollock's lowering of the canvas from the vertical to the horizontal allowed not only the development of his dripping technique, but, more importantly, it opened the possibility for future subversions (never explored by Pollock himself) of the "phallic erectility" Henri Lefebvre says "bestows a special status to the perpendicular, proclaiming phallocracy as the orientation of space" (Lefebvre 1991: 287). Krauss draws her reading of horizontality from an early fragment by Walter Benjamin where the German philosopher proposes a distinction between the vertical and the horizontal planes based on each plane's relation to figuration and to writing. To Benjamin, the vertical plane is that of painting, of representation, of that which "contains objects," the horizontal is that of graphic marking, of writing – "it contains signs" (Benjamin 1996: 82).[1] Following this insight, Krauss argues that Pollock's toppling of the canvas subverts painting's privileging of verticality as plane of representation (Bois and Krauss 1997). I would like to add to Krauss's observation that toppling also allowed Pollock to literally transform the canvas into a ground, a terrain, empty territory where the artist could walk on at will and imprint traces of his or her meanderings. In this sense, Pollock's actions on the toppled canvas were equivalent to a territorialization, understood here as an act that seizes a milieu and turns it into property by the means of the mark (Deleuze and Guattari 1987: 314–16). Given the "founding father patrionics" (Schneider 2005: 26) that informs critical discourses on Pollock's action painting, his walking on the toppled blank canvas becomes infused with the mythical aura of claiming virgin territory, of colonizing the horizontal, as that "empty and wasted land where history has to be begun" (Bhabha 1994: 246).

Perhaps because his actions on the horizontal canvas were about marking virgin territory, Pollock was never able to commit to the border-crossing that his toppling of the representational plane suggested. He was never able to re-place painting outside the proper space of the canvas, to have painting follow the splatter of paint as it fell outside his territorialized domain. As Krauss points out, Pollock's toppling was just a transitory moment in the production of his paintings; not an end, but a means for the canvas to ascend back to the verticality privileged by representational imperatives in the visual economy of art consumption. But his actions on the toppled canvas, his walking on it, his spilling of paint on it, clearly suggested that there was a potential for trespassing that could be taken by whoever would be willing to venture out of the pictorial frame. In 1958, Allan Kaprow famously described how Pollock's actions on the toppled canvas inspired him to create his own actions and "happenings." Kaprow saw in Pollock's actions on the toppled canvas the potential for liberating not only painting itself, but art-making as a whole: the artist should step across the canvas's border and enter into the social sphere, or, as Kaprow put it, into "life" (Kaprow and Kelley 2003: 1–9).

Despite the liberating potential of Pollock's toppling identified and explored by Kaprow and other artists (particularly those gathered around Fluxus), it is also clear that Pollock's actions were informed by an extremely problematic gender politics.[2] Rosalind Krauss reminds us that Andy Warhol, already in the early 1960s, had clearly perceived in "the gesture that a standing man makes by spilling liquid onto a horizontal ground" the undeniable "machismo that surrounded action painting" (Bois and Krauss 1997: 99). A similar critique can be seen in some feminist performance art of the early 1960s as in Shigeko Kubota's *Vagina Painting* (1965) at the Perpetual Fluxfest in New York City when the Japanese artist squatted on a white paper and painted it with a brush extending from her vagina to create "a deliberately 'feminine' process of gestural painting, flowing from the creative core of the female body, in contrast to the 'ejaculation' of thrown, dripped and scattered paint" in Pollock (Reckitt 2001: 65).[3] Rebecca Schneider in her extraordinary essay "Solo Solo Solo" agrees with Warhol's and Kubota's diagnostic and also identifies an epistemological impasse brought about by Pollock's machismo – an impasse derived from what she perceives as an unabated deference in performance art history to Pollock's figure as patriarchical hero:

> Time and again we are told (in a reverberating echo from Allan Kaprow) that the American Action Painting Artist Jackson Pollock was responsible for the supremely masculine act of liberating art from the canvas and setting the entire performance-based art of the latter half of the twentieth-century into motion. All other possibilities become as if relegated to a footnote.
>
> (Schneider 2005: 36)

Being aware of Schneider's sharp comment, why do I invoke Pollock at the beginning of this chapter on Trisha Brown and La Ribot? Why bring up the figure of the dead father? Can't Brown and La Ribot be left alone, experimenting on their own? In her essay, Schneider provides an answer to these objections. Her critique of the modernist notion of the singularity and originality of the solo artist proposes a critical writing that stands against "the drive to 'single out' a unitary artist as against a consideration of the broader contexts of cross-national, cross-ethnic, cross-temporal pollination, dialogic collaboration and broadly diasporic influence" (2005: 35). Thus, I invoke Pollock precisely to indicate how the two distinct operations Trisha Brown and La Ribot execute on the horizontal plane – as their dances meet visual arts in the institutional context of the museum and in the discursive context of art historiography – are already in "cross-temporal" dialogue with, and already in a "cross-national" critique of, the art practices and master discourses that preceded them. Both women inevitably have to negotiate with the intrusion of Papa Pollock's specter, as well as with particularly powerful (performance) art history master narratives that privilege myths of patrilineal masculine origin and lineage. It is the legacy of the patriarchal lineages in art history, of art history's "machismo," the legacy of "historical originality" predicated on the heroic male genius discovering by and for himself the pleasures of temporarily walking on virgin territory (the blank horizontality of his canvas), that Brown and La Ribot are inevitably faced with in their performances and in the *reception* of their performances. It is also what they must escape at all costs in their distinct and particular uses of the horizontal – a plane whose immediate association with the Pollockian toppling erupts as a curse.

I would argue that Brown's *It's a Draw/Live Feed* and La Ribot's *Panoramix* propose modes of relating to the horizontal that allow for nonphallogocentric (to use Derrida's term) spatialities and noncolonialist territorializations. In that sense, as opposed to Pollock, these two performances indeed topple the plane of representation.[4] Belaboring dance's relationship to visual arts, Brown and La Ribot update and gender Merce Cunningham's observation in 1952 that dancers draw from painting not necessarily its formal aspects, but the utopian desire to make a space of pure potentiality. What does it mean for women choreographers to make for themselves a space of pure potentiality when working on horizontality in their dialogue with visual arts? I'd like to start answering this question by addressing first Trisha Brown's actions in *It's a Draw/Live Feed*.

Perspectiveless horizontality: dancing drawing falling

Trisha Brown has had a long relationship with drawing. French dance theorist Laurence Louppe writes in the catalogue of a recent touring exhibition on Trisha Brown's prolific career (*Art and Dialogue 1961–2001*) of the enduring, albeit somewhat secret (at least in the first decade of her work) "visual artist in Brown" (in Teicher 2002: 66). Some of Brown's dance pieces of the early 1970s seem to find direct counterparts in her sketches from the time (for instance, her drawing series *Quadrigrams* and her 1975 choreography *Locus*).[5] Throughout the 1980s and 1990s, Brown's drawings increasingly gained autonomous presence in the public display of her art. In the past few years, her drawings have been exhibited in galleries and museums across the world, including the Musée de Marseille (1998) and the Drawing Center and the New Museum in New York City (2004). The question then is of finding out what might justify the qualification of "unusual" that the FWM press release uses to describe *It's a Draw/Live Feed*. Certainly the drawings' "monumental" scale – although no novelty in painting – is unusual. Also, the fact that Brown draws in a public context subverts somehow drawing's more intimate nature – although, as noted above, the presence of the audience is deferred due to the live video feed (the only audience before Brown as she draws and dances is the video crew).[6] What I believe made this a very unusual event was none of the above elements, but rather how Brown choreographed a mode of appearing within the institutional and discursive space of visual arts by intimately fusing dancing and drawing and then inexorably linking both to horizontality through an approach to line exemplary of what Georges Bataille called "formless" (*informe*).

Yve-Alain Bois discusses the formless in Georges Bataille in terms of an antirepresentational operation: "Metaphor, figure, theme, morphology, meaning – everything that resembles something, everything that is gathered into the unity of a concept – that is what the *informe* operation crushes" (Bois and Krauss 1997: 79). In *It's a Draw/Live Feed*, it is precisely the dancing body's relation to figuration, theme, and meaning and to its mode of appearing within representational space that is put into question. Brown's uses of formless lines and moves in her drawing-dancing disrupt with meaning and its imperatives for clearly defined figures and themes. Her simultaneous dancing-drawing crushes all those concepts Bois describes as securing in place the smooth ideological reproduction of the economy of the representational. If the formless crushes meaning and figure, it also crushes the possibility of fixing representation within any grammatical or visual legibility. Let's see now how Brown formally accomplished these critical moves, and what she might have accomplished politically through them.

In *It's a Draw/Live Feed*, the audience sees Brown walking into an apparently empty white room: the abstract white cube of the modern museum. Lefebvre saw in "abstract space" a simultaneous material and ideological production of "an anaphorization [. . .] that transforms the body by transporting it outside itself and into the ideal-visual realm" (1991: 309). This transportation of the body into the ideal-visual realm is the necessary brutality at the core of the disembodiment that secures scopic and spatial hegemonies. In *It's a Draw/Live Feed*, we can say that the anaphoric transportation of the body into the ideal-visual realm is initiated by the force of the museum space itself, a force reiterated by the empty white room where Brown dances-draws and reinforced by the video camera's flattening of her image. The audience's point of view is predetermined by a fixed, unedited, and unmoving long shot rendered live by the camera feed to flat and vertical monitors.

If Brown's placing of herself directly into the abstract space of the museum is already a becoming ideal-visual, then the camera multiplies this becoming by placing Brown's image inside a highly perspectival composition. In the live-feed image, it's as if the many white surfaces and planes (floor, ceiling, walls, large sheet of paper on the floor) reflect and refract each other, creating a minimalist specularity; a visual tension that subsists throughout the whole performance between the orthogonality of multiple bidimensional surfaces (the sheet of paper, the television screens, the walls) and the obtuse effect of a body moving in tridimensional space.[7] In the Philadelphia version of *It's a Draw/Live Feed*, the camera remains still. The video image functions as a window, creating a perspectival illusion by placing the image's vanishing point somewhere close to the ideal viewpoint of a spectator facing the screen.[8]

Several layers of abstracted space then and Brown has not even started dancing-drawing. The first layer derives from the room's participation in the visual-ideological economy of the art museum. The second layer derives from Brown's performance being televised, thus further placing her dancing-drawing into the virtual. Third layer: the perspectival framing and its inevitable disembodiment of vision. Fourth layer, particularly relevant for dance studies, and brought by the specificity of the white space: the abstract space Brown walks in echoes historically with one particular foundational abstraction that initiated modern choreography. Brown's room for her dancing-drawing is conspicuously similar to the square French dance master Raoul-Auger Feuillet (the coiner of the neologism "choreography") proposed in 1700 as the ideal space for dance – an empty white square whose presence precedes that of the body and whose flat, smooth, blank surface is irrecoverably detached from the bumpy, mucky social terrain. Dance historian Susan Foster associated the abstracted space of dance created by Feuillet with the blank page: "Raoul-Auger Feuillet simulated the rectangular floor of the dancing area with the rectangular lay-out of the printed page" (Foster 1996: 24). A very similar overlapping of page and stage is proposed in *It's a Draw/Live Feed*. Such overlapping confuses the ground of drawing and the ground of dancing. The generative effects of this confusion at the level of perception, signification, and motility are the critical and esthetic impetus sustaining Brown's drawing-dancing in *It's a Draw/Live Feed*.

If the space where Brown draws and dances is reminiscent of Feuillet's room, then Brown's movements in that space profoundly disrupt the historical link. There is a deep difference between Brown's improvised moves and the historical apparatus of choreography as a set of predetermined steps. Moreover, Feuillet's system could only map the tracing of steps brushing the dance floor-page (his system was intensely critiqued by his contemporaries for not being able to account for arm, head, and hand movements).[9] In this sense, Feuillet's confusion between book page and dance floor reveals the graphic-signifying function Walter Benjamin attributed to the horizontal plane.

As opposed to both Feuillet's and Benjamin's assimilation of the page with the horizontal space of graphic signification, what Brown does at the moment she begins drawing-dancing on the "transversal cut" of the Benjaminian symbolic has very little to do with signing, or with writing. If she draws on the horizontal, she seems very unconcerned about enclosing in the transversal a symbolic, or a signifying marking. Additionally, she will often dance lying flat along the horizontal plane, refusing the association of figure and verticality that Benjamin identifies with the representational function of the vertical. By stepping out of the strict Benjaminian division of planes according to their semiotic functionality, Brown steps out of conventional axiomatics of signification and representation. Outside of writing, outside of the transversal cut of the symbolic, outside of longitudinal representational, what does she do then?

Brown enters the empty white room, about 6 by 6 meters, and walks around the historically resonant stage-page. In a concentrated and calm manner, almost hesitantly, she distributes charcoal and pastel sticks around the edges of the large sheet of paper (9 by10 feet). Holding the charcoal, Brown paces about, staying close to the periphery of the paper, not stepping into it right away. Moving closer to the drawing surface, she immediately suspends any possibility of associating her dancing-drawing with simply a tracing of steps or a recording of movement patterns. What Brown does as soon as she approaches the paper is first to ponder – to take her time pensively, concentrate, not to move – and then, to fall.

In a controlled manner, Brown falls outside the limits of the paper, defying its surface as boundary for her actions. From the start, a trespassing: she deterritorializes the horizontal, by performing a first move of her dancing-drawing outside the proper limits of the paper. She withdraws just enough tension from joints and muscle, so that her body may gently break away from the vertical alignment of the walking posture and surrender itself to gravity. Brown droops smoothly to the ground, with a slight rotation, in a controlled release sustained by her body's unique "undulation": that quality French dance scholar

Hubert Goddard has identified as Brown's specific "motility, a way of authorizing movement without restriction" (quoted by Louppe in Teicher 2002: 69). This controlled yet released falling, this temporary, willful withdrawal from the verticality of the figure is what unrestrictedly authorizes Brown's embrace of horizontality as a critique of the vertical-perspectival through the anti-representational and asymbolic game that is *It's a Draw/Live Feed*. There is already a politics in Brown's careful falling outside the limits of the page: a gesturing towards the fact that her dance will always exceed the imperative of imprinting as the sole mode for artists' relation to space. As opposed to Pollock's masculinist stand on the toppled canvas, as opposed to his refusal to step outside the proper borders of representation, Brown does not walk to dominate the flat surface, neither does she confine her moves to the limits of the paper. She will not be a standing figure on the blank, white page terrain. By giving up her verticality, she refuses the "phallic erectility" that organizes the hegemonic abstract "orientation of space" (Lefebvre 1991: 287). Rather, she will approach the horizontal by lying on it, by being with it, by rubbing and sliding against it. In other words: Brown's falling is more like a splattering: the formless splattering preventing figurability.

On the ground, Trisha Brown becomes not a grapheme, not a sign, not a symbol, not a figure, but as formless as paint hitting floor. Her falling is a becoming formless. Splattering, Brown's dancing-drawing escapes perspectival economies of the gaze and of symbolic signification. But, as opposed to paint, particularly as opposed to Pollock's drip paint, and adding yet another formless layer, another possibility to resist claiming possession over territory, Brown's splattering will not be pinned down, dried out, fixed. On the ground, she will keep moving, she will not stay put. And just as her fall and splatter is a becoming formless, so her doodling with charcoal will succumb neither to figuration, nor to signification, nor to representation. While lying on the transversal plane Benjamin associated with writing and graphic symbolism, Brown's dancing-drawing remains decidedly outside signification – nothing is being written, nothing is being symbolized. Her body, charcoal, and pastel move between the intentional and the accidental, between forethought and spontaneity, between marking and erasing, between almost drawing and almost writing but never quite. Both Brown's body and her drawings refer to nothing except themselves. This is the self-referentiality of the splatter, inexorably tied to the fallen. As she draws-dances, Brown creates nothing that proposes a theme, that foregrounds a full figure, that advances a well-rounded metaphor, that initiates meaning. The charcoal and pastel lines Brown traces while lying on the floor – lines traced with hands as well as with feet – vaporize in dust, twitch in hesitation, break under her attack, initiate flow, reflect precision, and fall into error. Occasionally, we see her tracing around a body part (arm, foot, knee). When viewing the drawings later, the most we get are possibilities for recognizing that a body might have been there on the canvas, that she might have opted to fully draw it – yet, the final result resists representing complete bodies or properly formed morphologies, just as they do not register steps that can be decoded, rehearsed, and danced again.

These dancing-drawings are definitely not representations. They are operations, performances.

And yet . . . something is inscribed on the paper. In order to understand the performativity of the inscriptions made by a woman choreographer falling, moving, rolling, skipping, rubbing, sliding hands, feet, legs, back, breasts, head, face, butt, and belly on an improbable, small paper stage (or, on an improbable, huge empty page left on the floor) it is important to account for the specificity of Brown's movements in relationship to their economy, that is, to their eventual destiny as traces. French dance theorist Laurence Louppe, when writing on the history of choreography's relationship to drawing, notes how "the paper in no way retains a record of the dance, it retains a trace which itself cannot be consigned anywhere else" (Louppe 1994: 22). This remainder that is not a recording of the dance is exactly what we witness in Brown's dancing-drawing. For what is fascinating in *It's a Draw / Live Feed* is not so much that a choreographer is drawing, nor that a choreographer is improvising dances while drawing, nor even that a choreographer is displaying so openly, so generously, her intimate moment of creation to an anonymous, absent present audience. What is fascinating is to see how Brown's dancing-drawing is not at all narrowly and exclusively aimed at producing a final work on paper. Rather, Brown generates an inordinate amount of movements, gestures, small steps, microdances that are not at all *aimed* at the paper, that will not at all imprint or leave their mark on the paper. In Brown's careful, quiet, attentively concentrated, and playful motility and gestures, there is a surplus of actions and steps and tracings that will not be arrested or bound to the horizontal, a plethora of actions that cannot leave a mark, that have nothing to do with marking, nothing to do with claiming possession over a territory, with territorializing. Some of Brown's dancing will result in inscriptions, as foot or hand rubs the sheet and leaves a mark. Others will remain unmarked as she dances with her focus away from the horizontal, as charcoal misses the page, or as pressure on the pastel is too weak to leave a mark.

Missing the mark: a traceless expenditure that is already a deterritorialization of art. Brown's particular mode of making space but not marking a territory brings with it some micropolitical implications. Gilles Deleuze and Félix Guattari associated what they called "the territorializing factor" with the becoming of art when they unequivocally posited "the territory a result of art" (1983: 316). They write: "The artist: first person to set out a boundary stone, or to make a mark" (1983: 316). It may well be so. At least, that seems to be the case with the masculinist mode of occupying the toppled canvas that Andy Warhol identified in Pollock's "machismo," where "the gesture that a standing man makes by spilling liquid onto a horizontal ground is simply decoded as urination" (Bois and Krauss 1997: 102). If the "urinary" character of action painting is in accordance with Deleuze and Guattari's notion of art as the marking of a territory, Brown's dance-drawing allows us to momentarily disagree with their proposition; or at least, allows us to consider other ways of making art, or of thinking about the relation between art and space that refuses the colonial implications of marking a territory with the artists' flag. Brown's dancing-drawing – where so much of

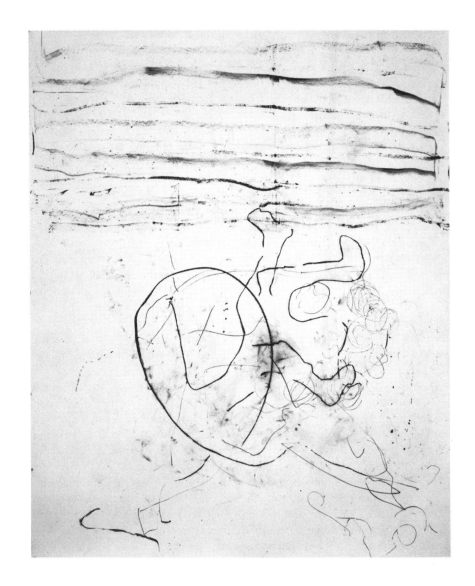

Figure 4.1 Trisha Brown. *It's a Draw* (2003).

Charcoal and pastel on paper.
Courtesy Trisha Brown.

dance and so much of drawing do not aim at leaving a mark – allows for a critique of Deleuze and Guattari's association between marking, territori- alization, the claiming of property, and the artistic act. In this sense, as drawings, Brown's are already talking back to the history of visual arts, to perform a profound critique of Pollock's use of the horizontal.

Let's return to the experience of watching *It's a Draw/Live Feed* on the flat, vertical screens. As Brown dances-draws, the audience's attention must go through a series of splits. Should it look at the paper to follow the making of the drawing? Or look at Brown's body, to follow the making of the dance? Should it look at lines, or at gestures? To keep track of both one has to look up and down and sideways simultaneously. In this dance of the gaze and of attention produced within an excessively parergonic space – frames within frames within frames: the still frame of the video screen, the still frame of the camera lens, the still frame of the gallery walls, the still frame of the paper on the floor – the audience must attend simultaneously to the vertical plane of representation of movement and to the horizontal plane of inscription of traces. Brown operates simultaneously in both, generating conglomerates of vanishing points in the bidimensional space feed live to the audience as hyperbolically perspectival. Thus, she creates a ceaseless dispersing where no act (dancing, drawing) or artistic genre (dancing, drawing) is privileged in relation to the other. Instead, there is a dizzying simultaneity of genres and acts. This dizziness is already a dismantling of the striated order of the perspectival.

Perspective is the effect created by a specific organization of lines on a representational surface (usually vertical) that secures a geometrically coherent figuration of spatial depth. Perspectival effect is predicated on a "central vanishing point" – the mathematical point where all orthogonals meet, "and which is determined by the perpendicular drawn from the eye to the picture plane" (Panofsky 1997: 28). Erwin Panofsky has shown that, although a correct perspectival representation may be obtained with more than one vanishing point on a single image, perspective's privileged relationship to hegemonic practices and ideologies of representation could only be secured once painting grounded its claim to truth on an image organized around one single vanishing point. The single vanishing point is essential to unify and harmonize the viewer's gaze with representational, theological, and discursive powers (Panofsky 1997: 141–2).

Panofsky reminds us: "'central perspective' makes two tacit but essential assumptions: first, that we see with a single and immobile eye, and second, that the planar cross section of the visual pyramid can pass for an adequate reproduction of our optical image" (1997: 29). Thus, perspective always operates by reduction. And what is reduced in perspective is not only the tridimensionality of space, but the embodied nature of perception as the corporeal grounding of sensation surrenders itself to algorithms of visibility. What is lost then is the embodiment of vision by the means of an operation that subtracts from perception our stereoscopic, decentered, constantly moving eyes and replaces them with an artificially monocular and monomaniacally fixed point of view.[10] This is why "perspectival construction is a systematic abstraction from the structure of psychophysiological space" (Panofsky 1997: 31). Of relevance for our discussion of Brown's creation of space in *It's a Draw/Live Feed* is that perspective's operation of abstraction, its perceptual reduction for the sake of monocular consistency, "is also true, of course, for the entirely analogous operation of the camera" (Panofsky 1997: 31).

But, in *It's a Draw/Live Feed*, the audience's eyes are never allowed to become immobile. Even if the piece is hyperbolically stilled by a multiple layering of frames (camera, monitor, walls, paper), Brown's movements and actions create a visual-kinetic troubling brought about by her constant creation, redistribution, and mobilization of multiplying vanishing points. What Brown accomplishes in her dancing-drawing is the transformation of the reductive operation of the camera as perspectival machine into a multiplying operation of vision. Distributing, creating, and destroying a multiplicity of vanishing points, Brown makes a space in a closed room that will not place her under the economy of the perspectival, that mode of gazing that historically consigned women to their house arrest.[11] Refusing to be placed under house arrest, Brown transforms space from a noun into a verb: her dancing-drawing, above all, adds to the vertical and the horizontal planes of inscription and representation an unsuspected dynamics, it transforms them from planar dimensions into zones of intensities, thanks to the formless, unfixable operations of a falling, bodied agency.

By the end of the *It's a Draw/Live Feed*, Brown will have created four different drawings. After the completion of each drawing, a process that takes somewhere between 10 and 12 minutes, Brown leaves the white room and two museum workers walk in pushing a scaffold. They carefully pick up the inscribed sheet of paper from the floor and hang it on one of the walls. As the assistants lift the marked sheet of paper, a clean one appears right below, ready to receive Brown's renewed moves and impressions. After completing their task of lifting up the drawing from its horizontal-choreographic plane of the floor and fixing it to its new vertical plane,[12] the two assistants leave the space, and soon the choreographer returns, starting the process all over again.

But it is in the final rising of the sheet of paper – a rising that all of a sudden reveals an unsuspected teleological impetus framing the whole event – from the horizontal into the vertical plane of representation and contemplation that we may find the limits of Brown's radical deterritorialization and the full activation of the territorializing force of the museum machine – a machine that must always erect something and fix it in the (vertical) plane of representation. After all the disruption of the gaze Brown performs by her yielding to gravity and to splattering, by the means of her undulating dancing, by the means of her ongoing dismantling and decentering and creation of so many vanishing points, by the means of her uses of formlessness in dancing and in drawing, something eventually *is erected* once Brown's dancing-drawing is completed. The entrance of the assistants marks the entrance of those visual-architectural-economic demands that characterize the museum as a territorializing machine. By fixing the paper back onto the vertical plane of display, the assistants as proxy of the museum machine transform deterritorialized spacing into a territory ruled by the imperative of displaying the (authorial) mark(ing). Thus the formless must be lifted from its horizontal plane of kinetic production for the sake of its relocation on the vertical as object for contemplation. This rising is a recoiling from the radical motions Brown had performed before us. It is reminiscent of the critique Rosalind Krauss makes of Pollock when she writes that Pollock embraced gravity and horizontality only to evacuate both at the moment the representational economy demanded the displaying of a final product, thus reinserting the toppled into the "proper" longitudinal plane of visual consumption (Bois and Krauss 1997: 93).

During the performance of *It's a Draw/Live Feed* the space of Brown's dancing-drawing explodes in a series of dizzying explorations between genres, between focal points, between confounding positions and certainties about spectatorship, authorship, artistic disciplines, documentation, original, copy, presence, liveness, dance, and art. But in the end, and because there must be an end (for museums have a hard time with incompleteness, the temporal aspect of *l'informe*), the entrance of the two museum assistants in black reminds us of the force of the vertical in the economy of representation, it reminds us of the lack of neutrality of any space whatsoever – no matter how abstract and empty that space appears to the viewer. No longer dancing-drawing: the end product must surrender itself to the destiny of art objects on the vertical-phallic space of representation.

The oblique: sculpting dancing wasting

Mid-March 2003. I am sitting next to a few dozen people on a cardboard floor in one of Tate Modern's large gallery spaces. Glued to the wall, as audiences of live art tend to be when not so sure about where the proscenium is, feeling the warmth of the cardboard, sensing its indefinable smell-color, we are all waiting for *Panoramix*, the durational performance where La Ribot presents, for just over 3 hours, all of her thirty-four *Piezas Distinguidas* (*Distinguished Pieces*, 1993–2003). This is the first time all of La Ribot's distinguished pieces will be performed in a single event. Thus the title *Panoramix* suggests a summation, a panoramic overview of ten years of its creation. However, as I settle into the large, white, gallery space, waiting for La Ribot's entrance, it becomes apparent that the set-up of the room undermines any possibility of framing *Panoramix* as an event participating in the overarching optical-historical drive that characterizes the representational function of the panorama.[13]

Piezas Distinguidas is the name of a series of short performances La Ribot started to create in 1993 and finished in 2003. The dramaturgical premises of this series were: each of its constitutive *piezas* had to take the form of a solo performed by La Ribot; each had to last somewhere between 30 seconds and 7 minutes; contents and duration of each *pieza* had to be negotiated with its "distinguished proprietor" – individuals or businesses who would acquire each distinguished piece from La Ribot. At first, these pieces were performed in theatrical spaces: small stages or black boxes. This was the case with *Piezas Distinguidas* (1993–4) and with *Mas Distinguidas* (1997). It was only with *Still*

Distinguished (2000) that La Ribot rethought the question of space and relocated all of the pieces outside of the theatre. This relocation brought obvious changes in terms of their presentation: light design would no longer be possible, thus radically changing the formal impact of the carefully constructed images that awed audiences of *Piezas Distinguidas*; frontal viewing would no longer be guaranteed, given the dismantling of the proscenium; sound sources would become localized and have less acoustic quality. Also, La Ribot appears in the gallery space naked. She only dresses up according to the requirements of each *pieza*. Once she finishes each *pieza*, she returns to nakedness, leaving her clothes scattered around, as detritus, or sculptural lumps on the horizontal. Thus, relocation did not only change the pieces esthetically, it changed them in *kind*. As La Ribot wrote,

> now the space belongs to the spectator and to me without hierarchies. My objects, their bags or coats; their commentaries and my sound; sometimes my stillness and their movement, other times my movement and their stillness. Everything and everyone is scattered around the floor, in an infinite surface, in which we are moving quietly, without any precise direction, without any definite order.
>
> (in Heathfield and Glendinning 2004: 30)

For La Ribot, relocation had a very important purpose: the dismantling of the hierarchical machine that is the theatre. The scattering of her audience and their stuff on the same floor that she and her objects perform, the leveling of "their commentaries and my sound," the sharing of an emphatic horizontality, reflect three important aspects of this change in kind in La Ribot's *Piezas Distinguidas*: a yielding to the gravitational pull, an intensification of the microperceptual, and a nonteleological presentation of small pieces. By privileging aimlessness, meandering, drifting (even as one stays put), by privileging the creation of indefinite points of view (no fixed place for the audience) and attention spans (the audience may come and go as they please), La Ribot deterritorializes the striated, orthogonal *space* of the institutional gallery and turns it into a *dimension* both indeterminate and precarious. Moreover, as her body and our body and her objects and our objects gather on the cardboard floor, there is an unavoidable emphasis on the pervasive effect produced on the art-works and on the audience alike by that unacknowledged transcendental force: the downward pull of gravity. *Panoramix* levels us all as already falling.

Yielding to gravity is the necessary consequence of La Ribot's moving away from the theatrical framing. Yielding to gravity also allows for reading in her desire to relocate her *piezas* a parallel desire to initiate a toppling, a debasing of whatever may be considered "well-built" – the well-organized, the directional, the teleological, the aimed, the representational, the perspectival, the architectural, and the choreographic. Rosalind Krauss, writing on sculptor Robert Morris's uses of gravity, horizontality, and weight in a 1961 performance where he toppled a 6-foot-tall column on a theatrical stage as a dance performance, observes: "A function of the well-built, form is thus vertical because it can resist gravity; what yields to gravity, then, is anti-form" (Bois and Krauss 1997: 97). Similarly in La Ribot's desire to debase the well-built choreographically, antiform is initiated by her moving away from the enframing performed by the proscenium and is immediately reinforced by a generalized yielding to gravity as equalizer of presence. La Ribot explained her move from a theatrical to a gallery context in these brief, yet telling words: "I would like to speak of presentation, rather than representation" (La Ribot in Heathfield and Glendinning 2004: 30).

La Ribot's move away from representation operates an inevitable change in kind regarding her body's presence. Now, her body deploys a positive relation to gravity that is ontologically crucial. There is a Heideggerian operation taking place here, as we saw in the previous chapter, one that understands presence as an ethical being-in-the-world associated to a particular kind of falling ("throwness," *Verfallen*). For Heidegger and for La Ribot, gravity appears as that given transcendental force (and law) to which we all submit without necessarily having to be submissive to it. Thus, one of the ethical tasks of Da-sein (the being who knows to be already in throwness and that must strive to master this condition) is of understanding how being-in-the-world is conditioned by that earthly imperative (Heidegger 1996: 319). Moreover, for Heidegger, the coming into being of the work of art is precisely the expression of this permanent tension between the earthly downward pull and the wordly antigravitational operations.[14] This is why La Ribot's withdrawal of her performances from the representational to the presentational must involve an attending to the earthly downward pull, an embracing of a transcendental falling, and thus her emphasis of the function of the horizontal plane as an active membrane, a tympan humming the tensile dialectics of world and earth as a dialectics overdetermined by the force of falling. As dance scholar Salazar-Condé once wrote, when we watch La Ribot performing in a gallery, "the only certainty is the weight of our bodies on the ground" (Salazar-Condé 2002: 62).

Even before La Ribot walks into the gallery space at Tate Modern, the invisible work of that persistent menace to the well-built called gravity already makes the space perform. The yellow-brown smooth surface of cardboard covering the horizontal plane is littered here and there with a couple of folded wooden chairs, one large piece of white cloth, some undistinguishable small stuff: matter and color and form lumping about just like our bodies squatting, our coats piling, our bags spilling out. On the four walls around us, hovering some 7 feet high, dozens of objects are held by brown tape. It seems as if any of our own stuff could be taped up there as well. The whole gallery becomes a sculpture; but a sculpture with all the instability and precariousness of the "badly built," all the aimless vibration brought about by the fact that the audience's "stillness and movement" are the foundational elements of that sculpture.

Visually, instability played itself out in *Panoramix* thanks to the tension between the soft yellow-brown cardboard floor where the audience squatted and the rigid orthogonality of the modernist esthetic imperative performed by the white walls

Figure 4.2 La Ribot. *Still Distinguished*. (Distinguished piece: *Candida Iluminaris*. Distinguished proprietor: Victor Ramos [Paris]).

Photo: Mario Del Curto. Courtesy La Ribot.

(Wigley 1995). This tension was reinforced by the colorful plethora of improbable objects cheaply taped on the white walls, objects that La Ribot would soon take down to manipulate or wear in the following 3 hours: scuba-diving goggles, translucent pair of pants, very large dark-blue paper wings, large yellow foam angel wings, glass of water, green dress, green dress with flowers, black dress with faces, pink dress, electric blue wig, boom box, "for sale" sign, white towel, red shoe, white enamel bedpan, microphone, rubber chicken, plastic bottle of water, brown coat, snorkel, pearl necklace, flashlight, red shoebox, bike helmet, black marker, and on and on. The objects hanging on the wall fixed with brown tape created two effects: a semantic confusion resulting from the incongruity of their display, object-nouns lining up as if they were jumbled words in a sentence yet to be organized into grammar; and a more physical effect resulting from the precariousness of their display, the cheap way they were fixed to Tate Modern's walls, emphasizing how these objects did not quite belong, how they were not quite art objects, not even (or no longer) ready-mades. The double nature of the objects' presence in space (as series of nouns, as series of forms) when associated into their precarious display indexed the constant menace of impending falling: their physical falling, and their linguistic one.

In *Panoramix*, the threat of this double falling generates one very specific result: La Ribot creates space that operates as an architectural disturbance. I am using architecture here in the sense Denis Hollier defines it in his reading of Georges Bataille – that is, architecture as a function of the "well-built," as a privileged accomplice to hegemonic economies of representational propriety (theoretical, theological, desiring): "Imperialism, philosophy, mathematics, architecture, etc., compose the system of petrification" of humanity (Hollier 1992: 50), a process where "the book and architecture are mutually supportive and foster such a monologic systematicity" (Hollier 1992: 42). This system of petrification as guarantor of the monological stability of form is predicated on an unwavering signification, the minimum requirement for representational success. That is why "architecture, before any other qualifications, is identical to the space of representation" (Hollier 1992: 31), and that is why, "when structure defines the general form of legibility, nothing becomes legible unless it is submitted to the architectural grid" (Hollier 1992: 33). In other words: architecture is an economy of legibility, a double structure of citationality and command legislated by the stability of the upright form. In *Panoramix*, the operation of architectural disturbance is achieved linguistically by the imminent threat of a falling into asignification of the object-nouns precariously fixed on the walls; it is achieved infralinguistically by the pervasive smell of the cardboard, by the pervasive yielding to the gravitational pull. The intrusion of asignifying objects, formless forces, and subtle sensations messes up the architectural as hardened orthogonality.

Thus, in *Panoramix*'s operation of architectural disturbance, a series of micromovements are set in motion right from the start, their quasi-invisibility attesting rather than undermining their force and impact. First micromovement: the subtle smell of the cardboard not only complicating the very constitution of the representational space of the gallery as purely visual, but relentlessly eroding the solidity of planar surfaces, undermining the gallery's trust on its planar orthogonality. Smell blurred straight lines and folded flat planes; it vaporized the rigid striation of the grid. Smell performed the distension of the horizontal and the vertical planes into so many obliques, folds, and curves, thus creating what Alain Borer (writing on the role of smell in the work of Joseph Beuys) called an *"impalpable dimension"* (Borer *et al.* 1996: 19). It is the production of such an impalpable and yet materially impacting oblique dimension (in contradistinction to the striated legibility of orthogonal space) that traverses *Panoramix*. Hence, the second micromovement: the replacement of spatiality by dimensionality. La Ribot makes for her pieces not a space but a *dimension*. Indeed, uses of dimensionality that stand against the spatial grid abound in La Ribot's work. Thus the centrality of scale in her pieces; the necessity of being out of scale in her pieces – actions out of proportion with their intention, or with the tone of voice, or gestures that are too grandiose for the dimensions of the room (dysfunctional scale); drawings that contain smaller versions of themselves within themselves (*Poema Infinito* [*Infinite Poem*] *Distinguished Piece* #21, 1997, property of Julia y Pedro Núñez, Madrid) or objects aligned according to a forced perspective (distorted scale). Both the distorted and the dysfunctional reveal the inadequacy of orthogonal spatiality before the impalpable dimensionality La Ribot creates for the presentation of her body. In *Candida Iluminaris* (*Distinguished Piece* #30, 2000, property of Victor Ramos, Paris), La Ribot switches on a pocket flashlight, places it on the floor aiming it at the farthest wall, and within the cone of light shed on the floor, proceeds to line up a series of objects, starting at the vertex with a minuscule piece of jewelry and going all the way up to one of the dismantled chairs on the floor, to finally end the sequence with her naked body lying on the floor, belly up, eyes closed, humming with mouth shut for some 2 or 3 minutes. Here, the forcing of perspective within a field of light leads from a sequence of odd objects to a vibrating, sonorous body, horizontally dancing its active stillness.

Third series of micromovements: La Ribot rigorously performing what I've called in previous chapters "still-acts" and their "slower ontology" – as if to emphasize the thickness of time contracting in the impalpable dimensionality of the nonrepresentational.[15] Thus, a still-act punctuates *Candida Iluminaris*, by also extending it into time; another one structures a whole *pieza* when, lying sideways, La Ribot dons a blonde wig and, covering her legs with white paper, lies on the floor to become a dying mermaid spasming quietly on dry cardboard, a sac of energy, an odd vision of femininity (*Muriéndose la Sirena* [*Death of the Mermaid*], *Pieza Distinguida* #1, 1993, in memory of Chinorris); another happens when, standing up, she drinks a liter and a half of water without catching her breath, then spreads herself on the floor, and does not piss (*Zurrutada, Pieza Distinguida* #32, 2000, distinguished proprietor Arteleku, San Sebastián); finally in *Another Bloody Mary* (*Pieza Distinguida* #27, distinguished proprietor Franko B. and Lois Keidan, London), she lies naked on the floor, a red patch of fake hair clamped to her pubic hair, legs spread out wide, red spilling out all around her (not paint, but red paper, red boxes, red dress), a revisiting of Duchamp's *Etant Donnés* (1946–66) or Courbet's *Origin of the World* (1866). Thus, a necessary condition for the third micromovement to be effective in *Panoramix* is La Ribot's nakedness. Many of her *piezas* are perfomed naked; when performing those that require a dress, or an angel wing, or a wig, she puts them on only for the *pieza's* duration, and disrobes as soon as it is over. And if her naked body operates sometimes as an image, this image is always subtly trembling, always revealing its physiological nature through its small tensions, its pulsations, hesitations, imbalances, shivers, contractions, expansions – the inexhaustible kinetic elements of La Ribot's small dances and still-acts.

La Ribot wrote about the function of the still at the time she moved her pieces from the theatre building to the gallery space. In her text, she mentions how stillness is a choreographic strategy, one that allows dance to step out of representation and into a different economy of presence. La Ribot explains how for her stillness also initiates an undermining of the rigid linear temporality of representation, replacing it with "the sense of being, or of feeling a corporeal presence and of contemplating inside a non-theatrical time, understanding 'theatrical' as something that starts and finishes" (in Heathfield and Glendinning 2004: 30).

With the "theatrical" defined by La Ribot as a teleological enterprise, one contained within a linear temporality marked by a clear beginning and aimed at closure, we arrive at the dramaturgical question *Panoramix* asks, imposes and provokes – a stupid question, a too literal question, but an absolutely necessary one. The question is this: where did all that cardboard covering the huge area of the gallery come from? First we laugh at the question, as laugh we must with several of La Ribot's incredibly humorous *piezas*. But, if after the laughter we stay with the literal question for one more second, we find out it is not at all an unreasonable one. Actually, *Panoramix* quickly seems to provide an answer – one weaving a nonteleological, nonchronometric time with the generative instability of badly built space.

Early on in the unfolding of the thirty-four *piezas*, La Ribot grabs from the wall a small square piece of cardboard (maybe 30 inches wide) and proceeds to walk back and forth across the gallery carrying it always parallel to the vertical plane of her body. This is *Pieza Distinguida #2* (*Fatelo Con Me* [*Do it With Me*], 1993, distinguished proprietor Daikin Air Conditioners, Madrid) performed to the sound of the homonymous Italian pop song by Anna Oxa. Right from the start of the *Piezas Distinguidas* series La Ribot takes as a privileged object a vertical plane of cardboard. While Oxa sings, emphatically asking to "do it with her," La Ribot walks naked back and forth with this cardboard square alongside her body, holding it always aligned with the vertical plane, as if to remind us precisely of the intrinsic alliance between the verticality of walls and the verticality of the body in representation. Could it be that this small cardboard square, which emerged apparently out of nowhere right at the very start of *Piezas Distinguidas*, ten years before *Panoramix* was conceived, is the origin of it all – a portable miniature, a perpendicular teasing, an anachronic announcement of the massive cardboard floor in *Panoramix*? If so, how come it traveled from verticality, from

Figure 4.3 La Ribot. *Still Distinguished*. (Distinguished piece: *Another Bloody Mary*.
Distinguished proprietor: Lois Keidan and Franko B. [London]).

Photo: Mario Del Curto. Courtesy La Ribot.

standing alongside La Ribot's upright naked body, to horizontality? How did it expand itself massively across the floor to the very limits of the gallery space?

Again, the question is that of architecture as structure of legibility. In the context of a proscenium theater, for which *Fatelo Con Me* was first conceived, the piece of cardboard had a specific visual-dramaturgical function: as La Ribot paced across the stage, she kept the cardboard always between her body and the audience, thus covering her breasts, buttocks, and sex. This choreography of humorous modesty was only possible due to the frontal position of the audience in relation to the perspectival proscenium. But, in the space of the gallery, such architectural legibility collapses: there is no front, no back, no proper placing of audience, no proper placing for the body to become image. Thus, at Tate Modern, just as in Trisha Brown's *It's a Draw/Live Feed* in Philadelphia, the organization of visibility is taken over by two museum workers. In the case of *It's a Draw/Live Feed*, we saw that two museum workers lifted Brown's drawings from the horizontal onto the vertical. During the rendition of *Fatelo Con Me* in *Panoramix*, two museum workers stood on opposite walls of the gallery and kept the audience behind an imaginary line running between them. The workers became living proxies of the proscenium arch, ensuring a proper point of view for the audience that could guarantee this particular *pieza*'s proper visual success. As stand-ins for an absent architectural construct, the museum workers prevented the audience from crossing over the boundary they defined. They were the embodiment of the architectural imperative of the representational.

This is an interesting moment; a moment where the choreographer's intention is sabotaged by a representational inertia embedded in the visual machines of the theatre and the museum. This is a moment that once again reveals the relationship between verticality, architecture, representation, and the gaze. As Jacques Lacan has shown, if there is something of the body that precedes its structuring while nevertheless determining its building, if there is something in perception that participates of the signifying-representational premises of the well built, that something is the gaze.[16] In this sense, the gaze can be considered the first antigravitational machine, the primary psycho-physiological technology allowing access to the visual only as vertically framed legibility. Paul Virilio discusses the parallels between gravity, representation, architecture, the vertical figure, legibility, and the weight of the gaze:

> Weight and gravity are key elements in the organization of perception. The notion of up and down linked to the earth's gravity is just one element of perspective. The Quattrocento perspective cannot be separated from the orientation effect of the field of vision caused by gravity, and also by the frontal dimension of the canvas which is never at a slant. Both painting and research on perspective have always been conducted on a frontal dimension.
> (Limon and Virilio 1995: 178)

It is interesting to see how, even after La Ribot abandons the frontal framing of the theatrical-perspectival, even after she embraces "presentation" through a yielding to gravity, to stillness, to horizontality, remnants of the well-built invade her work through the explicit marks of the institutional. And that is why the stupid question about the cardboard is so crucial. For, if a piece of cardboard appears to function for and with frontal viewing, the fact that years later it ends up extended on the floor of the gallery implies that the presentation La Ribot is so interested in must be one constantly oscillating between the (vertical plane of the) representational and the (horizontal plane of the) choreographic – the choreographic understood here as the inscription on a page of a symbolic of movement. This constant oscillation, these translational movements, imply the insertion of many obliques, of the slant Virilio sees as neglected in Western representation (and architecture). The slant refers not only to oblique angles, those mediating the vertical and the horizontal, but to the force of oblique looks, sliding glances with eyes at an angle. In the case of *Panoramix* this fundamental oscillation between vertical and horizontal that introduces the oblique – a plane on which everything is already sliding, falling, hard to hold – is performed via three antiarchitectural (the architectural being understood here as the well-building of form and signification) *operations*: the dilution of the orthogonal, the dilution of objecthood in the very objects used in *piezas*, and the dilution of a presence and a subjectivity subservient to the representational.

This is why, despite the vivid presence of visual arts in La Ribot's work, it is impossible to think *Panoramix* and the *Piezas Distinguidas* series outside of the ontohistorical grounding of Western theatrical dance. What this ontohistorical ground generates as its privileged model is a body that had to be able to simultaneously operate on the vertical plane of objectal and formal representation and the horizontal plane of writing and drawing. This is a body whose integration and congruence happens *by and in* the split between the two Benjaminian planes. This ontohistorically split body of the Western dancer, doubly inscribed simultaneously onto the vertical plane of representation (of the figure) and onto the horizontal plane of the symbolic (of writing), has created a specific mode of perceiving dance's coming into presence in the field of visibility. On the vertical plane, dance demands perception fall within the parameters of frontal representation and linear perspective (as already required by Georges Noverre in his famous *Letters on Dancing and Ballet*);[17] on the horizontal plane, dance demands perception to follow traces of steps, so as to guarantee the possibility of reading the choreographic design (as with Feuillet, for instance). In both cases, it is visibility as legibility that is privileged. It is the orthogonal fixity between the two planes that is required. La Ribot initiates a different relation, through her critique of the orthogonal, by requiring an attending to the oblique nature of the dancing body – one implying an impending falling off of visibility, legibility, verticality, the well-built, and teleology.

So far, I have discussed the generative spatial instability of *Panoramix* related to the slanted motions of the badly built. What of its temporality? Could there be a temporal slanting taking place? I mentioned how *Panoramix* is not about historical accumulation – a term whose connotative charge for dance history immediately evokes Trisha Brown's *Accumulation* pieces (1971–3, 1978, 1997). *Panoramix* produces a different temporality. Rather than accumulative, an operation predicated on repetition and sequentiality, *Panoramix* jumbles up the chronological sequence of production of its series. So, instead of repetition, it emphasizes a temporal effect that is contractile. In *Panoramix*, there is spatial obliqueness as much as there is temporal contraction, which is, as Deleuze and Guattari pointed out, already an introduction of oblique lines within temporality. Contraction implies an operation in temporality isomorphic to La Ribot's operation in spatiality. Contraction is a term drawn from the philosophy of Henri Bergson – it implies an understanding of the present as simultaneously and permanently splitting open towards the past in dilation and towards what-will-come in contraction.[18] For performance in general, and specifically for a performance that purposefully, explicitly, presents itself under the guise of the historical (the panorama-mix), the notion of contraction has profound implications for the understanding of the body's presence in relation to temporality, memory, and action. For contraction implies not only the body opening itself up towards what-will-come, but also to all the potencies of the temporally subjected body, in what Gilles Deleuze called contraction-subjectivity (Deleuze 1988: 53). Here, the past emerges as contemporaneous to the present that has been and extends itself as matter-memory. And what is that being that constantly performs this weaving of contemporaneity into pastness and back from the future if not *the body* – moving its presence not in a spatial grid, but in the multifolded dimensionality of its unstable, slanted, oblique throwness into time?

Panoramix acts in the present tense while pushing the past against the future of memory. This is the piece's operation of uniting the virtual with the material, absence with presence – contraction. But *Panoramix* proposes that contraction, which is a temporal operation through which matter and memory mingle ontologically, can happen only after the toppling of the archiframing of the vertical plane of representation and only after the angling of the horizontal plane of inscription. Disturbance of space, production of dimensions, contraction of all that has happened with all that is to come but still remains unannounced – all unfolding in those visual and kinetic exchanges between the orthogonal-representational grid holding up the gaze's weight and the oblique dimensionalities of folds, masses, and gravitational and antigravitational lines of vision. Like the image of La Ribot lying as dying mermaid on the cardboard, spasming next to our bodies huddled on the floor, receiving the weight of our gaze, expanding her presence across the glow-hum scent of the floor, becoming weight, becoming floor, pulsating on the floor, pulsating the floor, pulsing time, making space in the unstable obliqueness of the unconstructed.

5   Stumbling dance

William Pope.L's crawls

> Now the essent is no longer that which just happens to be present; it begins to waver and oscillate, regardless of whether or not we recognize the essent in all certainty, regardless of whether or not we apprehend it in its full scope.
>
> (Heidegger 1987: 28)

> 'Look, a negro!' [. . .] I stumbled.
>
> (Fanon 1967: 109)

Why frame a discussion on William Pope.L's crawls with epigraphs from Martin Heidegger and Frantz Fanon? As if the coupling of the two were not a risky endeavor, even a troubling one, due to what Pierre Bourdieu identified as the "ultra-revolutionary conservatism" embedded in Heidegger's writings – a conservatism that included Heidegger's "refusal to disavow the commitment to Nazism" (1991: viii)[1] – and to Fanon's radical leftist militancy in the critical-theoretical front, in the psychotherapeutic front, and in the armed anticolonialist front in Algeria.[2] A risky endeavor, a risky beginning, a risky coupling framing a very specific mode of moving by a black American artist whose trademark boasts: "The Friendliest Black Artist in America©."

A simple way of getting out of this risky spot would be to invoke a permission given by the friendliest artist himself. In the only essay authored by Pope.L published in the first comprehensive catalogue of his work, he writes:

> I am of African ancestry, but I do not speak to the gods. I speak to the MCI [telephone company] representative. I speak to my mother. I speak to Wittgenstein, Heidegger, Terry Eagleton, Bakhtin, and Frantz Fanon, but I do not speak to the gods.
>
> (Bessire 2002: 72)

Pope.L's confession of his ongoing conversations with philosophy and critical theory, and particularly with Heidegger and Fanon, should be enough for me to risk the framing. However, an artist's permission is still not quite enough to justify the critical necessity of such a pairing, particularly if such a pairing happens in a book whose aim is to rethink a politics of movement.

To side Heidegger's and Fanon's (necessarily very different) meditations on the fundamental question of being (Heidegger's aimed at the *destruktion* of old assumptions in Western metaphysics aligning being with a fully self-present visibility; Fanon's aimed at the dismantling of the psycho-political-philosophical alliance that sustained the project of Western colonialism and racism) is to agitate the ground of critical theory, it is to create a "seismology": that rippling critical and political effect that Roland Barthes saw in Brecht's theatre, an effect disturbing the proper functioning of closed semiotic systems (Barthes 1989: 254).[3] I am proposing in this chapter that the rippling effects of the critical seismic force generated by Fanon and by Heidegger's critiques of ontology animate the very ground on which Pope.L creates his art – and, more specifically, where he performs his crawls. While considering how Pope.L's work might critically inform a discussion of choreographic and political formations of bodies, subjectivities, and movements I will concentrate on the specific set of pieces that he has been performing in different configurations since 1978, known as "crawls." In them, Pope.L kinetically performs not only a profound critique of whiteness and blackness, of verticality and of horizontality, but also a general critique of ontology, a general critique of the kinetic dimension of our contemporaneity, and a general critique of abject processes of subjectivization and embodiment under the racist-colonialist machine – all by proposing a particular form of moving after the Fanonian stumble.

Thus, by siding Fanon, Heidegger and Pope.L we discover an ontopolitical ground that is not stable or flat, but ceaselessly quivering and grooving. Anyone that acknowledges to be moving on this ground already proposes a fundamental kinetic disturbance of ontology – a disturbance of ontology's alignment with the fantasy of temporal and geometrical stability of form and being. Under the seismological effect, being, body and figure all endure a radical blurring. I will propose that Pope.L's kinetic and critical identification and probing of this seismic ground and of its effects on processes of subjectification impacts on some deeply rooted assumptions regarding the political ontology of movement. This chapter aims at identifying some of those assumptions, particularly those that link movement, colonialism, and racism to the questions of presence, visibility, and the ground of dance.

It should not be taken lightly that in his extraordinary chapter in *Black Skin, White Masks* titled "The Fact of Blackness," Fanon raises the question of ontology even before the end of the first page, when he sharply states his critique of Hegel and Sartre: "every ontology is made unattainable in a colonized and civilized society" (Fanon 1967: 109). Let's note the specificity of Fanon's statement: Not that ontology is made impossible in a colonized and civilized society, but is made unattainable. Ontology's possibility, for Fanon, remains – but out of grasp. And what seems to make ontology out of grasp is the fact of colonization and its racisms. Facts that make Fanon state, further down, that "ontology [. . .] does not permit us to understand the being of the black man" (1967: 110). For Fanon, this happens not only because, for the colonized black man, being always happens in a (subordinate) relation to whiteness, but also, and as Homi Bhabha explains in his exegesis of "The Fact of Blackness," because of the particular "temporality of emergence" specific to the black man's coming into visibility on the colonized ground that defines modernity (Bhabha 1994: 237).[4] According to Bhabha, Fanon identifies how the black man is always in a belated relation to whiteness, when the latter is understood as emblem of modernity. It is this temporal lag, this not quite being there at the moment of emerging into presence, that "does not simply make the question of ontology inappropriate for black identity, but somehow *impossible* for the understanding of humanity in the [colonialist] world of modernity" (Bhabha 1994: 237, emphasis in the original).

Fanon's critical moves in most of his writings, but particularly in "The Fact of Blackness," reveal the unsustainability of general ontology while keeping its future possibility open. Since for Fanon, colonialism has no outside, since there is no society in a relation of exteriority to the process of colonization and the violence of racism, then ontology remains that open sore in philosophy's body. As Stuart Hall explained:

> the strategy of Fanon's text is to engage with certain positions which have been advanced as part of a general ontology, and then to show how this fails to operate or to explain the specific predicament of the black colonial subject.
>
> (Hall in Read 1996: 27)

Hall reminds us also that if we do not recognize that Fanon was a thinker who had "actually been in dialogue with themes of European philosophy" (1996: 26) we do a profound disservice to understanding his radical critical, clinical, political, and philosophical project. What was this project? That of bringing the question of racism and of colonialism to psychoanalysis's and to philosophy's understanding of how a subject's presence is formed, how being is always articulated within psychophilosophical formations of exclusion and violence. Fanon shows quite clearly how ontology's putatively transcendental mode of addressing the question of being is but the indispensable political strategy sustaining the colonialist-racist project: a project that reveals how politics and philosophy join forces by discursively framing all modes of appearing and of being present. After Fanon, in order for any ontology to be "attainable" again, it must first account for its (repressed) complicity with its colonialist-racist grounding.

What about Heidegger? His *destruktion* of Western metaphysics (articulated throughout his life since the publication of *Being and Time* in 1927) meant that in order for any ontology to be attainable (to use Fanon's expression) it had to first initiate a critique regarding its assumptions on direct relations between presence, stability, visibility, and unity.[5] With Heidegger, ontology could no longer be predicated on a being that "just happens to be present." As David Krell clarifies, Heidegger's critique of ontology proposes "a highly complex *Praesenz* [. . .], one that is ostensibly non-ecstatic and yet in some bewildering way includes *Absenz*" (Krell 1988: 115). Thus, one year after the publication of the first edition of *Black Skin, White Masks*, Heidegger is retelling us, when he finally publishes his 1935 lectures on metaphysics, that it is no longer enough for being to simply emerge in the field of presence, nor to just make itself appear in the field of light, nor to announce itself as that which fully occupies the present with its full presence. "What is" (that is, the "essent") can no longer be conceived as that which just happens to be there, presenting itself to our presencing at the moment of its appearing. Rather, for Heidegger what is, the essent, enters into the realm of being the moment it is infused with a minimum amount of movement. Heidegger is choreographically specific when describing the infusion of movement into ontology. The essent oscillates – between absence and presence, concealing and revealing, visibility and invisibility, unity and multiplicity. Only these particular movement-qualities guarantee the full emerging of being as presence: wavering, oscillation, vibration.

Oscillation already indexes a fundamental blurring of the essent's unity, a constitutional troubling of its being-for-vision. Oscillation is also Heidegger's way of revealing being's ambiguous nature in regard to its own presence. For being is always and simultaneously "half being, half not being" (Heidegger 1987: 28). It is both present and absent. Because being is both present and absent in and for itself, this is "also why we can belong entirely to no thing, not even to ourselves" (Heidegger 1987: 28). Let's retain these notions of ontologically never fully belonging not even to ourselves, of visually never quite being clearly there, of always being a least somewhat absent or delayed at the moment of being present. For these notions are essential for understanding how William Pope.L kinetically grounds the question of black masculinity's presence, visibility, and being in the field of racism by the means of his crawls.

Since the mid-1970s, William Pope.L has worked in many genres, from painting to sculpture, from installation art to performance art, from video art to poetry. His prolific work can be seen as an esthetic and a political statement about the impossibility for contemporary art to sustain the very notion of artistic genre. It is not even that his work is interdisciplinary or transdisciplinary. Rather, the question of discipline is dropped altogether from the equation, to be replaced by an emphasis on the ethics of the artist as laborer. A student of Allan Kaprow, Pope.L's *oeuvre* reveals influences of Fluxus (of which Kaprow was a member) in its use of cheap materials, found objects, and precarious substances, particularly processed food: mayonnaise (in *Broken Column*, 1995–8, he stacked broken mayonnaise-filled jars, packing tape, cardboard boxes, and leaning columns; or the performance *How Much is that Nigger in the Window*, 1990–1, he spread mayonnaise on his body); peanut butter (*The White Mountain* [*Wonder Bread Performance*] 1998); hot dogs (*Map of the World*, 2001: hot dogs, mustard, ketchup). Fluxus influences can be found also in Pope.L's acute use of humor to create what he calls "discomfort zones" for his audience. Importantly, the zones of discomfort Pope.L creates for and with his audience are zones neither of open confrontation, nor full-out antagonism. Pope.L is not at all interested in shocking, neither in *épater le bourgeois* – after all he *is* the friendliest black artist in America, as his trademark proclaims. Discomfort zones are carefully constructed by Pope.L always on foundations that allow for the possibility of their transformation into generative zones for dialoguing and relationality. In order to achieve this, he relies on dramaturgies that allow him to create, at least temporarily, a very real possibility of full-blown confrontation only to immediately dispel this threat through a disarming, often humorous, call for dialogue. As he once put it, he just wants to "bring fresh discomfort to an age-old problem" (Bessire 2002: 45).

Figure 5.1 William Pope.L. *Tompkins Square Crawl (a.k.a. How Much is that Nigger in the Window)*, New York City (1991).

Photo: James Pruznick. Courtesy William Pope.L.

In the manner of another African American performance artist-philosopher, Adrian Piper,[6] Pope.L's work is a relentless, sophisticated, and focused critique of that pervasive force so instrumental for the apparently endless regeneration of colonialism's contemporaneity – racism. Pope.L's pieces point out how discursive, esthetic, economic, philosophical, critical, and, yes, artistic mechanisms are constantly at risk of being coopted by one agenda: the reification and reproduction of racial exclusions. These exclusions, by the way, may happen in the friendliest of environments; for instance, in welcoming and enthusiastic critical appraisals of his work. In the text I already mentioned that Pope.L published in his recent catalogue, the artist writes about how two scholars described his work as "recollect[ing] African Vodun." Pope.L replies how, for him, this "is a very intriguing claim. I wish I could claim it for myself," and continues:

> I want Mr. Bessire and Ms. Crawford to find my work intriguing so I go along with the idea that there is, in fact, a link between my work and that of *bocio* [west African vodun artifacts] artist-activators. But in the same breath I also say to myself: Why is it not enough that I am a black American artist? Apparently, I need to get blacker. More authentic. I must become the black American artist with dark, mysterious, atavistic roots in some primitive Otherness. Who is speaking here? Who is telling me this?
>
> (in Bessire 2002: 71)

It is in this same text that Pope.L explains to his well-meaning admirers that he frequently speaks with philosophy and critical theory, with his mother, with costumer representatives, but not with "the gods." By naming with whom he has conversations with, Pope.L emphasizes how his contemporaneity is being denied to him by the two critics' desire to keep him in a belated "temporality of emergence" (Bhabha 1994: 237), one that keeps him captive of "atavistic roots in some primitive Otherness." Pope.L's artistic practices address precisely all those psychophilosophical and ontopolitical forces that create, reproduce, and keep in place the racist field and its discursive and physical blindnesses.

In his *White Drawings* (pen and marker on notebook paper, 2000–1), a series of forty-eight small framed drawings each containing a short phrase written in block letters in either red or yellow, Pope.L creates series of short sentences as so many minimal syntagmatic elements that both reveal and deploy a counternarrative to well-meaning systems of exclusion. We read: "WHITE PEOPLE ARE THE SKI, THE ROPE AND THE BONFIRE," "WHITE PEOPLE ARE THE COINS BENEATH THE CUSHIONS," "WHITE PEOPLE ARE THE CROOK OF MY ARM," "WHITE PEOPLE ARE THE SILENCE THEY CANNOT UNDERSTAND," "WHITE PEOPLE ARE THE CHEESE IN THE BURRITO," or – invoking that crucial Heideggerian concept – "WHITE PEOPLE ARE THE BLOOD AND THE HORIZON." In one of the drawings Pope.L proposes a devastating Lacanian reading of the constitution of racial desire within the claustrophobic space of white subjectivity: "WHITE PEOPLE ARE WHAT WHITE PEOPLE LACK."

The relation between lack and race in Pope.L's work is essential. It is also in this manner that we can start to understand his "giving up of verticality" and his embracing of the crawl as a choreopolitical statement. Pope.L's crawls propose a kinetic critique of verticality, of verticality's association with phallic erectility and its intimate association with the "brutality of political power, of the means of constraint: police, army, bureaucracy" (Lefebvre 1991: 287). Because they so clearly embrace horizontality, Pope.L's crawls reveal how the vertical "bestows a special status to the perpendicular, proclaiming phallocracy as the orientation of space" (Lefebvre 1991: 287). Pope.L's crawls initiate a deep and choreographic critique of ontology (and therefore of presence) akin to the critique Fanon articulates in "The Fact of Blackness." As I explained earlier, for Fanon, after the stumble in the racist terrain, there is no possibility for pure being. But Pope.L's crawls are also akin to Heidegger's relentless critique of "what is" as that stable unity which "just happens to be present" to view, fully immobile, and fully belonging to itself. Pope.L tackles the question of presence by positing as its condition of possibility the stumble of being and being never fully belonging to itself. He genders this question by emphasizing the specificity of black masculinity as it is "represented in Western culture as the central enigma of a humanity wrapped in the darkest and deepest subliminal fantasies of Europe and America's collective cultural id" (Louis Gates Jr. in Golden 1994: 13). It is in relation to these fantasies where both desire and violence intertwine and are then ambiguously aimed at the black male, that William Pope.L describes the black male body as constituted by a dialectics of having/not-having (the phallus):

> The black body is a lack worth having. The black male body (a.k.a. BAM), being male, attempts to preserve and promote its presence at the cost of its lack. Why? Because in our society, masculinity is measured in presence. However, no matter how much presence the BAM contrives, it will continue to be marked as lack. This is the dilemma for the BAM.
>
> (Pope.L in Bessire 2002: 62)

The black male's body dilemma is phrased by Pope.L in a way that allows us to think in psychoanalytic terms, particularly in relation to Lacan's understanding of castration as that indispensable wound that dominates a subject's entrance into the symbolic order "understood as the law on which this order is based [. . .], an agency that promulgates the law" as the law-of-the-Father (Laplanche 1973: 440). The wound-as-lack indexes an exclusion that patriarchy assigns to femininity but that can also be extended into patriarchy's ambivalent perception of the black male body's sexuality: simultaneously perceived as brutish and threatening while also "diffused by a process of fetishization that renders the black masculine 'menace' feminine through a process of patriarchal objectification," as bell hooks notes when writing on the body politics of black masculinity (in Golden 1994: 131). In his 1996 street performance *Member (a.k.a "Schlong Journey")*, Pope.L walks in the streets of Harlem with a six feet long plastic tube attached to his groin and propped on wheels. His long "schlong" creates a humorous scene on the streets. For his excessive phallic display is filled with ambivalences. If that black male body has a big member, it is made of white plastic; if it displays phallic ownership, it does not display the "phallic erectility" Lefebvre identified with the phallocratic orientation of space. Pope.L's "schlong" moves about – but exclusively on the horizontal plane, creating another mode of spatialization, one predicated on the toppling initiated by that lack worth having. At this point, it is useful to bring back Stuart Hall's reading of Fanon's critique of general ontology as one also predicated on a specific understanding of the operation of the lack in the construction of black masculine subjectivity in the field of racism.

In his essay "The After Life of Frantz Fanon," Hall writes that if for Lacan "the condition for the formation of subjectivity in the dialectics of desire 'from the place of the Other'" implies a "permanent 'lack' of fullness for the self" then the question for Fanon had to be of knowing whether this lack is "part of a general ontology or is historically specific to the colonial relation" (Hall in Read 1996: 27). Earlier, I stated that for Fanon this being-in-lack of the black body is a matter of historical circumstances. And, from the quote above, it seems that Pope.L agrees with Fanon. But I would like to note how Pope.L also complicates Fanon. According to art critic C. Carr, Pope.L has developed a "Hole Theory," which Pope.L explains as a theory of the specificity of inter-subjective relationality within the racist terrain: "Holes are connectors of lack [. . .]. If you have both female as 'less than' and black as 'less than', they're in relationship to patriarchy, all vying for acknowledgement through lack" (Bessire 2002: 52).

Pope.L complicates the Lacanian model by affirming that the lack black men are assigned to have by the symbolic is a thing worth having. But remember also that for Pope.L "White people is what white people lack." So, within the racist field, lack is a structuring force. BAM's lack is also what makes it whole. The performance of this empty-full w/hole is precisely what Fanon identifies in his description of the fantastical expansion that the black man's body in the colonialist-racist domain endures – an expansion that nevertheless keeps him in total invisibility: "In the train I was given not one but three places . . . I existed triply" (Fanon 1967: 112). It's as if the black body is perceived as incapable of properly belonging to a Cartesian system of coordinates, it is as if it is constantly swaying back and forth across space and time, its ontology accelerated into an unlocatable blur. The black body's being-there (its *Da-sein*) is always partially so, as if in excessive, wild Heideggerian oscillation. The empty seats next to the black man on the train are not fully empty, nor fully full. They show how the BAM's body is perceived as permanently taking too much space even when not being given the right to a proper place in the kinetic order of the visible.

Thinking about the function of the lack in black performance, or in the performance of blackness, Fred Moten writes about the operation of recuperating castration "as the condition of possibility of an engagement that calls castration radically and [. . .] irrevocably into an abounding or improvisational question" (Moten 2003: 177). This abounding questioning is a crucial function of the w/hole as a (black) disturbance not only of systems of interpretation (that is psychoanalysis), but of ontology itself, due to its involvement with the notion of abundance:

> The repression of the knowledge of the hole in the signifier is shadowed by another, not so easily sensed repression of the knowledge of the *whole* in the signifier. This is a repression of amplification, of sound and most specifically of abounding [. . .] where the whole expands beyond itself in the manner of an ensemble that pushes conventional ontological formulation over the edge. The hole speaks of lack, division, incompleteness; the whole speaks of an extremity, an incommensurability of excess, the going past the signifier . . .
>
> (Moten 2003: 173)

Going past the signifier by the means of the abundant lack – a movement that maps the complicated positionality of what Pope.L intriguingly calls BAM – a not so obvious acronym for Black Male Body. If the black male body signifies a raced masculinity that is paradoxically both affirmed and negated by the symbolic, then its odd acronym BAM aligns the question of being a black male body to an acoustics of conflict, to the ballistics of language in the field of racism: BAM! The black male body becomes an interruptive acoustic image, Saussure's classic definition of the signifier. As Fred Moten suggests, BAM as a w/hole that is both lack and incommensurable excess zooms right past this classic definition of the signifier. BAM zooms past the signifier only to reorient ontology by insisting in the fundamental paradoxicality affirming a black mode of being while standing on the ontohistorical ground of racism.

It was with a particularly powerful interruptive acoustic-image that Pope.L performed an intervention at Tate Modern in March of 2003. Invited to deliver a talk at the event *Live,* Pope.L arrived for his slotted time, walked to the podium and proceeded to read a 20-minute-long text of pure glossolalia. He then left the stage and disappeared from the event. According to some people I met who were part of the organization of the event, throughout his stay in London Pope.L apparently did not utter a single "proper" word. He communicated exclusively through the sonic power of pure, asignified, acoustic images.

With Heidegger, Fanon, and Pope.L, something fundamental at the level of ontology is being slanted, inclined, pushed over: the ground of being. Paul Virilio theorized the politics of the slant. Every time "one stands on an inclined plane, the instability of the position" affirms that "the individual will always be in a position of resistance" (Limon and Virilio 1995: 178). Virilio refers to physical resistance, but also to political resistance, to that explicit biopolitical momentum initiated by the instability offered by the slant. The operation Heidegger, Fanon, and Pope.L execute by slanting the ground of being also provokes an ontological instability, a kinetic uncertainty that disrupts the unity of presence, and the old association between presence, unity, being, and visibility. The Heideggerian oscillation and the Fanonian stumble – two very different modes of understanding the coming into presence of being – nevertheless reveal the necessity and impossibility of preserving and promoting one's presence at the cost of one's lack. Every time the stability of being is shaken, every time one initiates a critical seismology of presence (particularly when such a critical move is simultaneously philosophical and kinetic), general ontology and its dubious politics are threatened. Pope.L's "lack worth having" is yet another formulation shaking the ground of presence.

Thus, kinetic elements as well as the particular political, racial, gendered topographies of ontology impact on the definition of being. What Fanon's critique of ontology shows is that the oscillation of presence between being and nonbeing does not represent some vague and abstract theoretical reflection on the philosophical status of black subjectivity within colonialism, but that such an oscillation loops back to the corporeal and can be initiated by a nervous discharge, a muscular effort, by a strain, or a tremor. It may be provoked by the ground's sudden slant, by its unforeseen quakes, by its camouflaged grooves. Finally, the kinetic troubling of presence may also be initiated by the impact of language. Like the force rendered by a racial epithet making a black man stumble on the streets of Lyon, indicating how signifiers have their own powerful and precisely targeted ballistics.

Remember how Fanon felt exhilarated to be finally in the colonial metropole, a young doctor arriving from the colonized, colored, poor, far, and exotic elsewhere eager to offer his knowledge and skills to the scarred nation, eager to help France recover from the Nazi invasion? Remember how he thought of himself as a version of the Baudelairian *flâneur*, gliding smoothly on the planar surface of Europe, just another bourgeois man, a doctor no less, enjoying his freedom of movement, enjoying his ownership of civilized modernity's lure, promise, and reward – unbound movement, ownership of movement, or as Sloterdijk writes, "being-toward-movement" – by taking a careless stroll down a main artery in Lyon? And remember what happened then, during the stroll, when he stumbled for the first time against the fact of *his* blackness?[7] Not surprisingly, he stumbled thanks to the impact of the signifier.

"Look a Negro!" a boy yelled from across the street, pointing at Fanon, hailing him into a subject position: "Mama, a Negro. I am scared!" repeated the boy. And remember what happened then, when the ground shifted under his feet and Fanon tripped for the first time on the fact of *his* blackness? "I stumbled. [. . .] I burst apart" (Fanon 1967: 106). BAM. A not-so-obvious acronym, a piercing sound blasting a hole in the signifier of blackness, zooming through it. If BAM stands for the black male body, the acoustic imagery BAM produces is a powerful reminder of how within colonialism and racism the black male body becomes both ontology's bullet and its target. *Look a Negro!* BAM! *Mama, a Negro. I am scared!* BAM! BAM! Words pushing a black man to the ground, breaking up his body. After the stumble and the falling apart, Fanon describes the choreographic realignment required by this new mode of being, this new mode of presence forced by the ballistics of the racial epithet and by the shifting of the ground under his feet. Such choreographic realignment importantly points out the inadequacy of those bodily stances and temporal relations privileged by Western theatrical dance. For this realignment not only implies a paradoxical dancing, it reveals the impossibility of dance to remain unquestioned. If dance wants to attend to the dynamics and inertias traversing the racist terrain, if dance wants to find a way to address the politics of kinetics in the colonialist racist terrain, which is the ground of our contemporaneity, then dance must look at how Fanon describes his movements after suffering the full impact of the word-bullet in the stumbling ground of racism: "I progress by crawling. [. . .] I am *fixed*" (1967: 116).

What kind of dance was that, if any? This stumbling and falling, this scattering and loosening of one's own body, this forced crawling provoked by the ballistics of the speech act, this arduous movement which paradoxically fixates presence "in the sense in which a chemical solution is fixed by a dye" (Fanon 1967: 109)? And what exactly had happened to the ground under Fanon's feet? A private earthquake? The tectonics of racialization forces the question: how can one dance on such a treacherously racialized ground, where progress happens only by crawling, and where presence is put under arrest? Here, the speech act forces upon the racialized body both a posture and a kinesthesia and specifies the flow of temporality: "I move slowly in the world, accustomed now to seek no longer for upheaval" (Fanon 1967: 116). BAM. A black male body is down. BAM. He progresses by crawling. BAM. No longer seeking for upheaval. BAM. "Verticality is a ghetto" (Limon and Virilio 1995: 181).

Chris Thompson writes about Pope.L's "performance of horizontality" as "a commitment to the unpredictability of the encounters with others that produce social space" (Thompson 2004: 73). As Pope.L says,

> In Western society, we are given examples of the vertical: The rocket, the skyscraper, Reagan's and Bush's Star-Wars system . . . it's all about up. I want to contest and challenge that. In the crawl pieces, like *Great White Way*, I'm suggesting that just because a person is lying on the sidewalk doesn't mean they've given up their humanity. That verticality isn't what it's pumped up to be.
>
> (in Thompson 2004: 73)

Pope.L's first crawl, *Times Square Crawl*, took place in 1978. In this crawl, Pope.L, donning a brown suit, looking like any average middle-class citizen on the streets of the big city, surrendered his verticality and embraced the only possible mode of moving Fanon had identified as available to the black man after the stumble: slow crawling. The giving up of verticality, the slow progression along the sagittal plane,[8] is already a critique of the smooth kinetic functioning of the modern city, based on ideals of efficient flow of bodies and commodities. Crawling and its efforts, its clumsy temporality, reveal those many unmarked presumptions of citizenship in its relationship to velocities and proper stances of inclusion. Crawling cracks open all the kinetic assumptions related to ideological, racial, and gendered mechanisms of urban belonging, circulation, and abjection. If Walter Benjamin famously identified the consolidation of urban capitalist subjectivity with a particular mode of locomotion indexed by the distracted strolling of the *flâneur* (Benjamin 1999: 416–55),[9] Pope.L shows how, for some subjects, the motility and "intoxication" of the *flâneur* is unattainable, foreclosed. But why give up verticality? Is there a self-defeating gesture here? A reenactment of the traumatic encounter with racial interpellation? Or maybe something else might be under way?

"Have-not-ness permeates everything I do," states Pope.L (Bessire 2002: 49). Again, the emphasis on the lack fills up his art, his acts. But with the crawls, there is also the revelation of unsuspected relationships between lack and movement, between lack and the ground. Carr tells us that when Pope.L performed his *Time Square Crawl* in 1978 "he had a brother, an aunt, and a couple of uncles living on the street" and that, as of 2002, Pope.L's brother was still homeless (Carr 2002: 49). Pope.L's crawls inevitably challenge the presumption of free movement as a given of citizenry by revealing how certain subjects have a very different relationship to mobility, verticality, circulation, and ground, since they all stumbled and (as Fanon points out) were *fixed* by a speech act that "registers a certain force in language" (Butler 1997b: 9). Writing on how "language acts [...] upon its addressee in an injurious way" Judith Butler finds that the same force of language that injures also "both presages and inaugurates a subsequent force" (1997b: 9). This subsequent force, this counterforce, this force of moving against, can be identified in Pope.L's efforts to engage relentlessly in his slow progression on the sagittal plane after the Fanonian stumble.

Carr comments on Pope.L's state of mind in relation to the scattering of black bodies on city streets:

> When he [Pope.L] began the crawling, he was thinking about "the history of skills and knowledge," now dormant, in each inert body. "And I was wondering, how do I enter those images and build a tension between the stillness you see and the sense of recklessness that probably got them there. I wanted to show the struggle inherent in those bodies."
>
> (Carr 2002: 49)

As Frantz Fanon wrote after his stumble in Lyon, colonialism and racism demand that some subjects must only "slowly progress by crawling," while others participate of a different kinetics, an unbound mobility. Lest we forget, colonialism and racism are not buried in the past of explicit colonialist ruling. Before this simple geopolitical dynamic and ontological fact of contemporary modernity, what does Pope.L do? He "sometimes organizes group crawls, and others join him in 'giving up their verticality'" (2002: 49).

Summer of 2004. As curator of an artists' laboratorium at the festival *In Transit* in Berlin, I invited Pope.L to join us for a week at the Haus der Kulturen der Welt.[10] He graciously accepted my invitation and spent eight days with the laboratorium, developing a few projects in the city that did not involve crawls. On his last day with us at the lab, as a sort of farewell gift, Pope.L asked whether the group would be willing to give up its verticality and engage in a collective crawl. This collective crawl at Haus der Kulturen der Welt marked a critical moment in my relationship to Pope.L's performance. From the position of spectator – which, in the case of Pope.L's crawls, is a position that emphasizes the verticality of the spectators's stance – we all moved to an active horizontality, a difficult, Fanonian progression by crawling. On the ground, the first thing the group found out is that the terrain of cities and buildings has nothing to do with a planar surface. The moment one gives up one's verticality, the first thing one discovers is that even the smoothest ground is not flat. The ground is grooved, cracked, cool, painful, hot, smelly, dirty. The ground pricks, wounds, grabs, scratches. The ground, above all, weighs in. As we progress with difficulty, hurting, panting, looking silly, critical theorist Paul Carter's observation that "many layers come between us and the granular earth – an earth that in any case has already been displaced" resonates in all its political implications (Carter 1996: 2).

Carter advances his notion of a "politics of the ground" (Carter 1996: 302) in his extraordinary book *The Lie of the Land*, where he probes a troublesome question: what are the deep relations between "all that is comprehended by the Western arts of representation" (Carter 1996: 5) and the philosophical, political, kinetic and racial underpinnings of "the colonial experience" (Carter 1996: 13), particularly of colonialist racism? Carter ties the question of colonialism to the question of representation, to the question of ontology, and to the notion of the ground. For Carter, this ground should be understood not only as a metaphysical category but also as the very physical, material entity that it is. He asks for the ground to be theoretically grasped not as an abstract "surface but as manifold surfaces, their different amplitudes composing an environment [. . .] uniquely local, which could not be transposed" (Carter 1996: 16). The manifold consideration of the ground is for Carter fundamental to dispel "the modeling of movement as a sequence of ricochets calculated on a level, two dimensional ground [which] might be said to characterize the colonial experience more generally" (Carter 1996: 13). Carter's critique of the colonial experience is also a critique of the colonizing impetus of the tradition of Western metaphysics to create itself only on leveled ground:

> Western philosophy has in this respect operated little differently from the tunnellers, the earth-movers and the bulldozers: its first priority has always been to clear the ground of accidental impediments, to peg out its definitions and lemmata. Indeed, it is hard to imagine a philosophy, any more than a polis, founded on uneven ground, on ground that shifts or which already, by virtue of its natural obliquity, furnishes an infinity of positions, poses, points of rest to anyone prepared to traverse the ground in different directions.
>
> (Carter 1996: 3)

This is why Carter's politics of the ground finds in Heidegger's critique of Western metaphysics a generative partner, since Heidegger's critique of the traditional notion of being is a critique that "advances immediately toward a ground," "the ground for the oscillation of the essent," which for Heidegger is a ground-leap: "we call such a leap [. . .] the finding of one's own ground" (Heidegger 1987: 27, 28, 6). A ground-leap, a ground that allows for oscillation.

These antinomies are not to be read as arresting oxymorons. They are to be read as ontopolitical and choreopolitical challenges that can illuminate with particular force the conditions of mobility on the colonialist terrain, of how these conditions are bound to "the emotionally-catatonic and historically destructive opposition between mobility and stability" (Carter 1996: 5), for "if we were grounded, the cultural opposition between movement and stasis would disappear" (1996: 3). Carter proposes that what sustains colonialism is the creation of a subjectivity "without an attachment to the land" (Carter 1996: 294), a philosophical and topological flattening of the ground that is also a fleeing from it. This bulldozing of the ground, a colonialist gesture, is also a gesture that allows for representation to take place on an empty flatness, and that generates, sustains, and reproduces a subjectivity that perceives its own truth as a self-propelled "machine for free movement" (Carter 1996: 364) gliding along a flat and unmovable terrain.

For Carter, the first condition for the kind of free movement that colonialism requires must be the clearing of the ground, the creation of a planar surface, "and to do this, to render what is rough smooth, passive, passable, we linearize it, conceptualizing the ground, indeed the civilized world, as an ideally flat space, whose billiard-table surface can be skated over without hindrance" (Carter 1996: 2). Meanwhile, other bodies fall and inhabit unaccounted for grooves and folds. Meanwhile, the ground shifts and quakes, stirring up the fallen.

On the ground, crawling on the marbled and carpeted floors and stairs and elevators of the Haus der Kulturen der Welt, Pope.L teaches us the "military crawl." "The best way for you not to hurt yourself," he tells us. So, we find out that our crawl is not about self-inflicting pain. It is not a sacrificial act. It is certainly not a form of ordeal art. It is simply about understanding what happens once one gives up the privilege of the vertical and enters into a different relationship to effort and mobility. This is the crawl's performative biopolitics. It is also about identifying who detains knowledge of the ground – whether for the sake of survival or for imperial conquest. Here we are in Berlin, at the same time that Afghanistan and Iraq are violent stages of colonialism's new guise, and we find ourselves doing the military crawl as taught by Pope.L. What does this tell us about Pope.L's creation of a critique of racism as the authorized mode of socialization in the not quite postcolonial, certainly neoimperial moment of late capitalism? This is where Paul Carter's observation that a politics of the ground, if it wants to initiate a truly postcolonial and anticolonialist poetics, must do so by first generating discursive and kinetic practices that highlight the body in motion as always already an extension of the terrain that sustains it. Therefore, any politics of the ground is not only a political topography, but it is also a political kinesis.

Since *Times Square Crawl* in 1978, Pope.L has crawled in Budapest, Berlin, Prague, Madrid (all in 1999) and Tokyo (*Shopping Crawl*, 2001). He also returned to Manhattan to perform *Tompkins Square Crawl* (July 18, 1991) and, in 2002, to initiate his longest crawl. Titled *The Great White Way*, this 22-mile-long crawl is to be performed in yearly installments until its completion scheduled for 2007. For *The Great White Way* Pope.L started to crawl from the Statue of Liberty and plans to move up Broadway, until his final destination in the Bronx, close to his mother's home. In this crawl, Pope.L has included visual and kinetic elements that were absent from his other crawls in Manhattan. Instead of the business suit, he wears a Superman suit, but without the cape, which was replaced by a skateboard strapped to his back. The skateboard has an important function: it allows him to negotiate a particularly difficult or dangerous portion of terrain by turning on his back and rolling. As he once told me, the skateboard is especially handy when he needs to cross a street without interrupting traffic or endangering himself.

In the winter of 2003 I was able to see an installment of this 5-year crawl in downtown Manhattan, between Ground Zero and City Hall. As I recall Pope.L's body advancing on the frozen ground, in freezing temperature, his effort to progress as he painstakingly negotiated the cold, dirty, inhospitable terrain, the few people standing around him, also shivering, I cannot help but think of a passage from "The Fact of Blackness" where the racist encounter is depicted as a frosty one:

> look a nigger, it's cold, the nigger is shivering, the nigger is shivering because he is cold, the little boy is shivering because he is afraid of the nigger, the nigger is shivering with cold, that cold that goes through your bones, the handsome little boy is quivering because he thinks the nigger is quivering with rage.
>
> (Fanon 1967: 113–14)

On that particular winter day, the conversations Pope.L has with Fanon become transparent. Pope.L's exertion, his visible pain, his slow progressing are vividly supplemented by the unavoidable quivering provoked by the chilling temperature and by the cold ground, half frozen, laced with ice and snow. BAM. William Pope.L on the ground and shivering. BAM. We stand tall next to him shivering. BAM. Next to us, the hole where the Twin Towers once stood, compressing in its inordinate topography the whole history of colonialism's violence. This unbearably frosty environment, this mode of presencing on the racist ground, this uncontrollable shivering made out of misread signs and bodies, this cold that Fanon describes becomes all of a sudden not only the climate of racist encounters but the critical temperature in which a melting away of the fixed distinctions between inside and outside may occur. Cold and shivering are the physical and kinetic evidence of the racialized space where rage, fear, words, performances and bodies all stumble upon each other in a not-at-all-innocent quivering of being.

Within the colonial field of racism, the question of movement becomes a question of targeting, of tactical ballistics, of what is made to fall and of what must remain upright. Buildings, bodies, monuments, oil towers, meaning. If it is a fact that *The Great White Way* had been conceived before the attacks on the Twin Towers of September 11, 2001, and its first installment (*Training Crawl [For the Great White Way]*, Lewiston, ME, 2001) had also happened before that date, it is also true that – as Chris Thompson reminds us – "Pope.L's crawl has become bound inextricably to them" (Thompson 2004: 67). Thus, *The Great White Way* inevitably undergoes dramaturgical and political changes as its path intersects historical unfolding. For this unfolding literally changes the ground where we stand and the performance that we witness. Pope.L started *The Great White Way* in a particular historical and geopolitical context. But as Pope.L keeps following the original trajectory, it becomes clear that any linear progression is as much a choreographic myth as the myth of a linear and predictable unfolding of history. As the geopolitics of neoimperialism and the legacy of colonization and racism gain new modes of visibility and unleash unsuspected actions, the whole relationship between movement and intention is radically shaken up. Distending itself across the time of the event and through the space of historical rubble, Pope.L's military-crawling black Superman already fallen on the frozen ground of downtown Manhattan becomes a boiling performance of untold colonialist narratives and barely hidden racial legacies which still inform modes of being, modes of moving, and modes of tacking bodies down.

In this sense, Pope.L's crawling body constantly rewrites history. This is the power that long durational performance brings about: the unfolding of events is never fully under the spell of the performer's intention. All the performer can do is to make sure he or she remains alert to historical forces as they traverse their bodies and the bodies of his or her audience. The performer's body becomes more a conduit for historicity than for teleological intentionality. Paul Carter explains how Richard Dennet's critique of the notion of intentionality (of the author) departs from the observation that the word "intent" comes to us "by metaphor" from the Latin "*intendere arcum in,* which means to aim a bow and arrow at something" (Dennet in Carter 1996: 329). Following Dennet, Carter proposes that the whole system of Western metaphysics and of historiography, which allows for the phallogocentric invasiveness and bulldozing of the colonized ground, is based on "this technologically-reinforced tradition of thinking in straight lines [which has] contributed to a deficiency in Western poetics," and also of Western notions of historiography. As Pope.L's crawls progress and history unfolds, as the ground shakes and rumbles, cracks and opens, in unforeseen ways, the initial line of intention of the crawl gets diverted. His motions indicate crooked historical lines, opened by the unpredictability of the event, lines crawling up Pope.L's body and those bodies his crawls interpellate.

Thompson narrates how an angry crowd gathered around Pope.L as he passed by Ground Zero, with some screaming at him, accusing his performance of being some sort of desacralization, a mockery of the dead. Eventually, a policeman interrupted Pope.L, demanding that he get up, telling him he needed a permit if he wanted to continue. As Thompson narrates, Pope.L calmly kept repeating, "I just want to crawl. I want to crawl. I did not know I need a permit to crawl" (Thompson 2004: 78). Because of his calm demeanor and persistence, the policeman eventually gave up. Pope.L resumed his crawling, and, at that moment, the crowd (even the angrier among them) cheered Pope.L. As Thompson writes in the same essay:

Thus, in waves, as it were, it became apparent to its viewers that the crawl – however irreverent the Superman costume might have made it appear at the outset, however much it might have appeared to be a making-light of the loss of life caused by the September 11 terrorist attacks – was or had permitted itself to become a decidedly serious, and indeed compassionate, response to these violences and their legacies.

(2004: 78–9)

I agree with Thompson on this particular reading. But I do think that within the kinetic parameters set up by the Fanonian stumble, the question of violence as indexed by the shattering of the body through the force of the signifier as described by Fanon and as performed by Pope.L's use of the military crawl needs further probing. What needs to be probed is the relationship between the embracing of horizontality, the "progessing by crawling," and the kinetics of how to more efficiently negotiate the body's relationship to the ground.

Pope.L's crawlings allow for a performative rethinking of Fanon's stumbling of ontology's presumptive temporality and vertical stance in the racist field. Giving up verticality is to be already fallen. Pope.L's coming into presence after the stumble through crawling invents a choreographic program, a slow dance, which retells Fanon's relation to movement and verticality after stumbling in the racist field: "I move slowly in the world, accustomed now to seek no longer for upheaval" (Fanon 1967: 116). This giving-up of verticality has nothing of the formal neutrality some choreography may search for and encounter when it entertains the horizontal line. This becoming ground, this fallen presence, this embracing of painful horizontality, this understanding of the grooves and temperatures of the physical and historical ground where one inevitably negotiates one's own presence is acknowledgement that the "discomfort zone" is the place where we all live and move about. In this zone, Pope.L's body becomes ground, rather than form, and in this field he creates "a real dialectics between the body and the world" (Bessire 2002: 49). This real dialectics includes directly addressing the pervasiveness of violence in everyday life. To directly address the brutality of violence as a major organizational agent within supposedly enlightened modern democracies is to create a zone of discomfort in much political and critical theory. Allen Feldman argues quite poignantly that "conceptualizing political violence as routinized element of everyday life" remains one the biggest obstacles in current sociological and anthropological theorization of violence, since most scholarship is still caught up in Norbert Elias's famous proposition that "modernization entails the progressive withdrawal of violence from everyday life in tandem with its increasing monopolization by the state," a proposition Feldman sees as revealing "the evolutionary drive of Norbert Elias' notion of civilizational process" (1994: 87, 88). Feldman argues that most political theory still conceptualizes violence as only occupying "the verges of civilizational process and European modernity" as well as Western modernity at large (1994: 88). Thus, to identify violence as one of the main organizing political principles in contemporary democracies, to point out

Figure 5.2
William Pope.L.
*Tompkins Square
Crawl (a.k.a. How
Much is that Nigger
in the Window),*
New York City
(1991).

Photo: James
Pruznick.
Courtesy William
Pope.L.

violence's pervasiveness, its deep relation to the constitution of political power, and to those rhythms, habits, and performances of everyday life, is an important act not only to understand Pope.L's desire to create "zones of discomfort" but to understand also how he continues his dialogues with Fanon beyond questions of ontology and right into questions of political performances. The military crawl is just one more element in the indexing of kinetic techniques of violence, associated with the imperial power of Superman, of White America, all revealed and activated by an extremely nice black man crawling on *The Great White Way*, alongside the mass graves the legacy of colonialist and imperial policies keep opening around us daily. BAM. In Pope.L's dialectics between body and the world, in the discomfort zone he creates, the Fanonian stumble asserts a different eloquence.

How can we define being after the stumble of general ontology? What kind of moves might this being perform now that we have charted with Fanon, Heidegger, and Pope.L the problematics of presence on the racialized ground? Perhaps every moving body on the racist ground is always already a stumbling one. The landing of presence and performance onto the stumbling foot allows for the creation of what Alain Badiou called "an ethics of the situation" (Badiou and Hallward 2001). It allows for the possibility of creating a critical response to the violence of racism that is also a choreopolitical one. Such a particular mode of mobilization informed by the stumble, the quiver, the oscillation of being, proposes different ways of mediating dance and politics. This is the point where we radically jump from Heidegger's general notion of the quivering of being into Fanon's contextually specific description of stumbling and of quivering in the racist-colonialist terrain. A terrain informed both by a shifting and shifty ground as well as by blunt wordings, a charged terrain where the body sustains radical reconfigurations before the illocutionary and perlocutionary force of the performative speech-act but where the body also stumbles into its own capacity to abound in the lack, to move within its fixity, to negotiate an otherwise inhospitable terrain. This is the impact of the crawl, not as an act of submission, but as the choreopolitical effort that transcends the condemnation of the symbolic order by resolutely moving into the quivering ground of being.

6 The melancholic dance of the postcolonial spectral

Vera Mantero summoning Josephine Baker

An intolerance
A non-vision
An inability
A desire
An emptiness
An emptiness
An emptiness
An emptiness
A tenderness
A fall
An abyss
A joy.

Vera Mantero, 1996

Indeed, racial melancholia [. . .] has always existed for raced subjects both as a sign of rejection and as a psychic strategy in response to that rejection.

(Cheng 2001: 20)

Where does history rest, if at all? And how is history reawakened and put into motion? How is it that it finds its grounding, its pacing, its anatomy? These questions are the starting points for a consideration of the critical, artistic, and political effects brought about by a recent historical invocation – the choreographic resurfacing of a particularly haunting, a particularly iconic image that once filled the European imagination regarding African Americans, dance, and black femininity. Indeed, from the early1920s to the mid-1930s, the dancing image of a certain African American woman vividly illustrated and troubled the complicated dynamics of what Brett Berliner has called twentieth-century colonialist melancholia. That ambivalent sentiment in the colonizer to both sensually own and to methodically brutalize the colonial and racial other (Berliner 2002: 200). As indicated in the title of this chapter, the iconic, troubling, ghostly image in question, the figure and the voice that I am casting as denouncers of European colonialist and postcolonialist melancholia are those of Josephine Baker.

To summon the ghostly in Josephine Baker is to reclaim Baker as a contemporary critical voice, one that remains posthumously active and resistant. It is to acknowledge that Baker's force still moves; that to invoke her presence is to perform a specific political calling. To accept the possibility of Baker's agency today is to acknowledge her participation in the cohort of what [...] identified as "improperly buried bodies" of history: bodies ab[...] death, denied ground, place and peace by history's hegemonic [...] forces (Gordon 1997: 16). For Gordon, those improperly burie[...] racialized, congregate in so many shadowy communities, condemn[...] invisibility under the authority of meticulously enforced violence: [...] of the spectral, and the invisibility at the heart of racialization. Writing on the links between scopic racial regimes and the affective regimes of racialization, Anne Anlin Cheng suggests that "the racial moment" happens precisely within a social field of "mutual invisibility" (2001: 16) between white and colored subjects. But, as Cheng also points out while analyzing Ellison's novel *Invisible Man*, racial invisibility does not mean lack of materiality. It is precisely this paradoxical condition of being a material body that nevertheless remains to be seen that initiates the history of violent collisions, clashes, and missed encounters between racialized subjects.

Gordon follows the signs, scars, and markings grafted by history's collisions onto the bodies of those subjects inhabiting the racial field of invisibility to suggest that forces of racial exclusion do leave material traces on those they enforce their violence upon. In a move reminiscent of Michel Foucault, Gordon proposes that history's inscription onto marginalized bodies as the marking of "the violence of the force that made them" (Gordon 1997: 22) generates counteractions of resistance. For Gordon, those acts of resistance constitute precisely the spectral's force across time – performances as well as "stories concerning exclusions and invisibilities" where the ghost emerges as a "crucible for political mediation and historical memory" (1997: 17,18).

In this chapter, I analyze a contemporary choreographic reflection by Portuguese choreographer Vera Mantero on current European racism and European forgetting of its quite recent colonialist history. This reflection happens precisely through Mantero's staging of a linguistic and scopic field of invisibility while choreographing the effects of this field on a hyperbolically racialized body. Moreover, Mantero's choreographic reflection came into being and was performed with the help of the haunting figure of Josephine Baker. I will read Mantero's 1996 piece *uma misteriosa Coisa disse e.e. cummings* (*a mysterious Thing said e.e. cummings*), based on the figure of the African American performer, as informed by, and as proposing a powerful political counterperformance against racism and colonialism. Mantero achieves this by the means of a strategic use of melancholia against racial and colonialist abjection. I will situate Mantero's solo piece as a choreopoetic proposal for a political meditation on European historical amnesias regarding its colonialist brutality and will show how it is through Mantero's uncanny evocation of Josephine Baker's ghostly force that such a political proposal can be successfully made. This means that in Mantero's piece, as well as throughout this chapter, Baker's figure emerges as the teetering bridge between European melancholia (as a mode of subjectivity structured around oscillating feelings of loss and anger, as suggested by Cheng and Judith Butler [1997a]) and the historical cohort of living and dead colored, colonized peoples, condemned to a subjectivity in which deep grief must always be transformed into a moving spectacle for the colonizer by colonialism's melancholic imbalance.

Movement takes an important place in my reflections on the spectral, the melancholic, and the postcolonialist subject. Indeed, if recent critical theory and political thought, after Jacques Derrida's *Specters of Marx*, has legitimated the spectral as critical concept, the term has recently emerged as instrumental for race studies as well – particularly through the works of Gordon and Cheng. Critical considerations of the spectral, the invisible, the absent-present, the disappeared have also allowed for important developments in critical, political, and philosophical readings of performances – most notably by Peggy Phelan (1993), Diana Taylor (1997), and José Muñoz (1999). However, the spectral's other face in the constitution of its uncanny appearing, movement, still has to find its place as fundamental critical fact and tool in race, performance, and critical studies.

Randy Martin's *Critical Moves* offered a sophisticated and engaged Marxist reading of both theatrical and vernacular North American dance (Martin 1998).[1] Through the notion of "mobilization," Martin clearly articulated the added value to performance and social theory of considering movement critically, epistemologically, and politically. What I am attempting here is to take Martin's proposal on the political centrality of movement seriously, but consider it under a different scale. I am attending to a movement less concerned with mass social mobilization than with the creation of micro-countermemories and small counteractions happening at the threshold of the significantly apparent – that is, precisely within the haunted territories of Europe's racist and colonialist melancholia and disavowal. This attending to small perceptions responds not only to the challenges of a micropolitics and a choreography of small gestures embedded in Mantero's piece, but also to the phenomenological capacity for "melancholia [to be] kept from view; it is an absorption by something that cannot be accommodated by vision, that resists being brought into the open, neither seen nor declared" (Butler 1997a: 186).

Finally, and to conclude this introduction on method, I would like to add that to invoke haunting theoretically means paying particular attention to the role of the uncanny in the construction of colonialist and countercolonialist narratives and performances.

Freud, in his 1919 essay "The Uncanny," addressed the spectral and its esthetic impact as one of the two major characteristics of any uncanny experience. But it is the other major, defining element in the Freudian uncanny that becomes of particular relevance for my argument: unexpected, uncontrolled, unruly forms of motion. Indeed, to attend to actions and words taking place within haunted territories is to pursue the theoretical implications for dance, performance, and race studies of what Freud deemed to be one of the uncanny's most explicit signatures: motion happening where it should not happen, motion occupying a body that should be still, motion occurring at an improper time, with an improper tempo, and in skewed intensities. Indeed, it is striking how Freud's essay is filled with examples of the uncanny as motion misbehaving, motion improperly disturbing the homely sense of a body's "normal" stance or normative behavior.[2] This means that the uncanny would be but motion unexpectedly defying the laws of the home, whose source and agency cannot be accounted for visually or scientifically. The motions of the uncanny resist documentation, certification, and economy. What is uncanny in movement then, what turns any moment uncanny, is its apparent lack of purpose, efficiency, and function. Instead, in the uncanny, movement always happens for the sake of movement.

Here, we turn to the ontological problem of Western dancing as fantastically conceived, at least since the beginning of the nineteenth century, by Heinrich von Kleist, but already in the sixteenth century by Thoinot Arbeau, as that mysterious animation of a body otherwise defunct, or apathetic. In this European fantasy equating dance to life, or dance to soul, we see the eruption of a familiar theme in critical race studies: that of the animation of whiteness's melancholic nature (whiteness's gloom, as painstakingly diagnosed since Robert Burton's famous 1658 treaty *The Anatomy of Melancholy* [2001], and as theorized more recently by Giorgio Agamben [1993] and Harvie Ferguson [2000] as the mark of European modern subjectivity) by energizing, contagious, black "soul power." The animation of whiteness by black soul and black motions participates entirely and symmetrically of narratives that equate dance with the uncanny infusion of life in the corpse. This "soul power," this surge of motion in the apathetic European body that infects and suspends the endemic melancholia of whiteness every time it witnesses the spectacle of uncanny motions, whether marveling in the colonial plantation at slave dances, or seeking some groove in the postcolonial dance halls. This contagious movement bringing whiteness back to life reintroduces in the esthetic domain the primal fantasy underlying the mode of colonialist exploitation.[3]

Treating the uncanny epistemologically means to first project and then find meaning where there should be but the careless motions of chance.[4] In other words, it means to theoretically foreground the coincidental. To treat coincidences epistemologically is to set the ground for a thicker historical analysis, one that allows for improbable readings, particularly for readings colonialist narratives have foreclosed, prohibited, censored. It is to treat the geographical distribution and temporal-coincidental collisions of facts, names, and events as designing improbable yet thoroughly historically significant choreographies of encounters and missed encounters. If the history of the colonialist European project has always been one of discursive as well as of adventurous fantasies, of producing teleologically exculpatory narratives for the occupation of lands always depicted as empty (despite the presence of "natives") and of generating stories for justifying the erasure of others, to invoke improbable histories is to dismantle such a colonialist narrative-machine. It is to identify alternative patterns informing alternative through-lines, a movement Paul Carter sees as the ethical precondition for any project of historicizing, performing, and creating in a colonial (or postcolonial) context.[5] Carter's essays on colonialism are influential at yet another level. Following Jacques Derrida (Patton and Derrida 2001), Carter sees no distinction between a postcolonial and a colonial moment, except as a linguistic detour, a flimsy camouflage for the perpetuation of atrocious racist subjection and geopolitical exploitation essentially in place since the colonial period, despite official independence of former colonies. I abide to Carter's and Derrida's position, which is the reason why throughout this chapter, while I use "colonial" and "postcolonial" to chronologically demarcate Portugal before and after the independence of its colonies, I believe both terms must synonymically conflate once they are used to describe contemporary Western hegemonic political and cultural attitudes in regard to the developing world. This is also why I have modified the terms "colonial" and "postcolonial" to the harsher "colonialist" and "postcolonialist" so that the record remains straight about the purpose and the nature of the ongoing colonial endeavor.

What are the uncanny historical coincidences surrounding Josephine Baker and the fate of Europe's colonialist projects and fantasies? One could start with the haphazard parallel between Baker's ascendancy on the European stage and the beginning of the decline of European colonialist control in Africa. Indeed, the African American singer, dancer, and performer saw the peak of her notoriety in France and in Europe coincide with the beginning of the end of Europe's explicit political self-definition as a colonialist continent, right before the beginning of World War II – a decline that would only accelerate after the end of the war. One could add that Baker's death in 1975 at the Hôpital de la Salpêtrière in Paris, coincided with the independence of the last five European colonies in the African continent: Angola, Cape-Verde, Guinea-Bissau, St. Thomas and Prince and Mozambique. These were all former Portuguese colonies whose independence was preceded by a military coup in Portugal in 1974 (against the fascist régime in place since 1928), and by thirteen years of bloody colonial wars (in Angola, Mozambique, and Guinea-Bissau, between 1961 and 1974). Perhaps these are not too impressive coincidences; perhaps I am indeed pushing the uncanny unfolding of parallels too hard here. But perhaps the haphazard parallel between Baker's death and the European colonial collapse may become historically and theoretically thicker once I foreground how they delineate an uncanny design allowing for the possibility of an unsuspected mobilization in critical race and dance studies.

Motion happening where there should be stillness announces the spectral creeping in with the force of an uncontainable agency, exercising its call upon the fields of visibility, movement, and historical awareness. This is the moment when we must consider the fact that it was indeed in Lisbon, in 1996, twenty-one years after Josephine Baker's death and twenty-one years after the débâcle of the Portuguese colonial empire, that Baker's figure was posthumously summoned back to stage in order to dance once more for a fascinated, cosmopolitan, mostly white European audience. Baker was back to Lisbon (where she had performed in the 1950s during the fascist régime), answering to a call placed by a state-owned bank of the last colonialist capital of that not-too-distant colonialist European continent.

Such an eccentric resurfacing of Baker's dancing body resulted from an invitation/invocation made by António Pinto Ribeiro, then curator and director of programming for the cultural services of Portugal's largest state-owned bank, Caixa Geral de Depósitos. Ribeiro asked three choreographers to create each a 20-minute solo "inspired" by Josephine Baker. The three choreographers were the North American (but based in Paris) Mark Tompkins, the African American Blondell Cummins, and the Portuguese Vera Mantero. Although all three solos presented by these important contemporary choreographers were extraordinary, I will exclusively address Mantero's *uma misteriosa Coisa, disse e.e. cummings*. I am interested in the ways Mantero's piece provides indications for an understanding of how an African American woman's dancing presence – moreover, her spectral dancing presence – disturbs and subverts current European historical narratives and silences regarding its quite recent, quite brutal, colonialist past. I am also interested in how Mantero's piece may point at Europe's political self-denial regarding its current racist present.

Mantero's task as a performer and as a choreographer was not an easy one. She had to overcome a series of ethical obstacles to create her dance: how does a white European woman, coming from a country that until 1974 saw as its essence and its mission that "of colonizing peoples and lands," portray, invoke, reclaim, and dance in the name, and in the body, of an African American dead dancer?[6]

I am arguing that the way Mantero's European, female, white body chose to address (the ghost of) Josephine Baker as precisely a haunting subjectivity and a haunted body thickens the streams of European colonialist histories and memories, of current European racial fantasies and current colonialist amnesia, by offering an uncanny presentation of a challenging, improbable image of a woman, of a dancer, and of a subjectivity. I will also argue that, from a European audience's perspective, the presencing of Baker's resurfacing through Mantero's body proposes an even more complicated affective-mnemonic dynamic – what can be called (expanding Berliner's concept) postcolonialist melancholia. In this particular case, where melancholia mixes itself up with processes of racialization and brutalized exploitation, what informs the dynamic of postcolonialist fantasies is not only the ambivalent desire for absolute sensual possession of the other along with the other's absolute, violent abjection, but also ambivalence's particular psychic mechanism – the mechanism Judith Butler has depicted as leaving the melancholic subject always lingering in between loss and rage (1997a: 167–98). Relevant in Butler's analysis is her emphasis (following Walter Benjamin) not only on a psychology of melancholia, but on the centrality of what she calls the "topography of melancholia" (1997a: 174). Such a psychic topography is important in addressing European postcolonialist fantasies regarding the "proper" place of and for African Americans within the racial mapping of European subjectivity. It is also crucial for identifying where and when "improper," unruly movements of colored bodies find their place and timing for (re)action.

The topographic clarifies yet another important element in what I am calling postcolonialist melancholia. Freud notes that one may mourn not only "the loss of a loved person" but significantly also "the loss of some abstraction which has taken the place of [a loved person], such as fatherland, liberty, an ideal, and so on" (Freud 1991a: 164). Such mourning of an ideal, or of a lost land, may very well develop into the "morbid pathological condition" of melancholia (Freud 1991: 164). This is a point I would like to keep in mind throughout this chapter. That the feeling of "loss" of Europe's "beloved colonies" creates a morbid melancholic subjectivity that gets energized as rage in contemporary European racism. Melancholia – that incapacity for the subject to let go of the lost object and to accept loss – establishes an odd and perverse symmetry in postcolonialist European affection and racism. In this skewed symmetry, the plaint of the colonized is misheard as voicing the colonizer's own loss. The European's incapacity to overcome colonial loss creates as psychic topography that turns Europe into a space where specific kinds of (non)encountering take place. The lament of the colonized singing, dancing, or performing the loss of her homeland finds an odd, affective, unexpected reverberation in the colonizer's own (antithetical, racist, angry) sense of loss. This explains the type of European fascination with Josephine Baker's body and voice, as I will discuss in a moment. It also clarifies Mantero's use of her own voice while choreographing Baker's invocation.

Why is Vera Mantero's piece, which first took place in a peripheric European country, and whose spectatorship will always be limited to the few attending European international dance festivals, relevant for a discussion of how Europe blackens itself up in its twentieth-century minstrel fascination with African Americans? And how can we start reconsidering contemporary European fantasies regarding movement, the animation of bodies, and black femininity alongside Europe's old fascination with black North Americans dancing in its colonial metropoles? This point is relevant historically and ontologically. Historically, Berliner documents in his book on European desire toward the black other from the 1910s to the 1930s how African American dance and music started to circulate in France as "civilized" alternatives to images and sonorities produced by colonized black Africans, who were perceived by the European audience as being more "savage," and therefore unredeemable inferiors, than their North American brothers. Berliner distinguishes between the ways *sauvage* and *primitif* were used in French vernacular as well as in ethnographic texts from the first few decades of the twentieth century.

> While *sauvage* was reserved mostly for black Africans and for their descendents in the French colonies, the term *primitif* [. . .] referred to someone who lacked civilization – but who possessed some morality and capacity for civilization. The primitive, more so than the savage, was often exalted in the 1920s and was the object of many exotic fantasies and quests.
>
> (Berliner 2002: 7)

Those exotic (and erotic) fantasies fomented by "the primitive," whose main symbol was the African American performer (dancer, singer, musician), produced in the European an incontrollable kinesthetic response: an impetus to wander, to

move about, to get lost, to get off. Movement as quest, as voy
of the self is but movement for the sake of movement,
modernism's new understanding of movement, as famously a
Martin, when in 1933 he writes about how modern dance 1
break with the entire Western dance tradition by finally disco
essence is indeed movement (Martin 1972: 6).[7] Modernis
movement for movement's sake is contemporary to the v
made by the average European dancing in "Negro" clubs, a place where white
bodies are inflamed to move by the sheer contaminating presence of African
American "primitive" sounds and dances. I would like to press this point, this
fibrillating alliance of erotic/exotic fantasies, African American dances and
sounds, and the instigation in the white European of the desire to start moving
for the adventurous sake of movement. For this alliance cuts across ontological
(and historical) master narratives of Western theatrical dance – narratives that
refuse to see in Western dance's very foundation projects of embodiment and
discipline not only profoundly racialized, but also profoundly invested in a
colonialist "exotic fantasy and quest." It is this movement at the core of Western
dance towards a complicated desire that necessitates a reinvention of the white
body's ability to move before the mirror of racial colonial alterity that I am
addressing as European dance's melancholic and colonialist ground.

How did Mantero inhabit this troubled, troubling ground when she was asked
to invoke the ghost of Josephine Baker in the main theatre of the national bank,
twenty-one years after the Portuguese colonial empire collapsed with a whisper
so significant in its historical, political, and moral disavowal that it lead
Portuguese philosopher Eduardo Lourenço to wonder how it was possible that

> an event as spectacular as the downfall of a five-hundred-year old "empire"
> – whose possession seemed so essential for holding our own historical reality
> and, even more, for holding our own corporeal, ethical, and metaphysical
> image as Portuguese – ends without drama?
>
> (Lourenço 1991: 43, translation mine)

This is how Mantero laid the ground for her choreographic reflection on the
haunting presence of African Americans in the midst of Portuguese (and
European) colonialist amnesia. The stage is dark as the audience enters the
theatre. Lights go down, and darkness becomes complete. Time passes and we
hear some hesitant knocking sounds on the wood floor. The knocking is
uncertain, and it moves around the stage. It soon stops close to us, center stage.
Slowly, a faint trace of light, a very narrowly focused spot, reveals a wide, very
white woman's face, with very red lipstick on her lips, and very long eyelashes and
sparkling blue shadow on her eyelids. This is a hyperbolically staged face, a mask
of a white woman performing a clichéd image of certain vaudevillian seduction.
The face, however, does not smile or seduce. It is calm, alert. Under the faint
spotlight, the face seems to hover, bodiless. After a moment, the very red mouth
opens, and endlessly, calmly, quietly, starts to recite, with some accelerations and

rruptions, a litany. She begins, in Portuguese: *"uma tristeza, um abismo, uma não-vontade, uma cegueira . . . atrozes. atrozes* [A sadness, an abyss, a nonwillingness, a blindness . . . atrocious. atrocious]." As time passes, the spotlight gradually widens its field of action and Mantero's body becomes increasingly more visible. As the very white face gains a body, we realize that hers is a racialized body, the naked body of a white woman who decided to cover most of herself with brown make-up in order to recreate the illusion of blackness. It is a self-conscious illusion not only because Mantero's face remains white (as if marking that whiteness already participates in a theatre of race, race's masquerade), but her hands also remain uncovered by the brown powder. Both hands and neck become separated from the rest of the body by straight lines of paint. Thus, the brown make-up works not as a minstrelsy device, in the sense that minstrelsy "caricatured blacks for sport and profit" (Lott 1993: 3), but rather as a gestic marker of a hyperbolically, artificially constructed racialized body: part brown, part white, both parts emphatically made up.

Dance historian Susan Manning has recently proposed the concept of "metaphorical minstrelsy" to refer to a "convention whereby white dancers' bodies made reference to nonwhite subjects" on the American theatrical dance stage of the 1930s. Manning argues that, "in contrast to blackface performers, modern dancers did not engage in impersonation. Rather their bodies became the vehicles for the tenors of nonwhite subjects" (Manning 2004: 10). I argue that Mantero is doing something altogether different than "metaphorical minstrelsy." For, her body is not a "vehicle" for Baker's body, it does not intend to represent it. If something is being voiced, if something is being referenced, it is not the body of the other, or the voice of the other, but the lament of the shared violence and profound sadness produced on the racialized field.

What we have with Mantero's use of makeup in her blackening of her body is precisely the marking of both whiteness and blackness as forces of tension for the mutual construction of women's identities across the color line – and particularly the construction of a white woman's sexuality as already in dialogue with blackness. Once we add the third element in Mantero's "costuming" of her body in *uma misteriosa Coisa disse e.e. cummings*, we have an even more complex figure disturbing the binary opposition of whiteness and blackness. This third element appears first in the piece aurally, with the knocking sounds about the stage; it is then visually indexed and supplemented by Mantero's constant lack of balance (while the light is still too dim to disclose her body fully), and, once her body is finally fully revealed, it becomes the visual punch line of the dance: Mantero is standing, precariously, strenuously, on goat's hooves. The doubly racialized woman uncovers yet another trap of colonialist, patriarchal, and choreographic subjectivities – her body is also bestial. The beast is the lurking danger of woman's genitalia, it is the "savage" animalization of the body in the racist view of blackness, and it is the savage image Mantero uses as her explicit body in performance. The image of the animal she chooses to prosthetically incorporate into her nakedness has a very specific connotation in Portuguese – a connotation that ultimately makes this solo bend over itself in its stream of signification as it gets layered on Mantero's composite figure and this figure's imbrications with Portuguese colonial history, and with Portuguese current efforts of forgetting that history as the country moves after a desirable "Europeanness." The she-goat is, in Portuguese, *cabra*, the coarse synonym for whore.[8] Here, signifiers loop around the feminine force field on the ideological terrain of modernity as a project always already, engendering, racializing, colonizing.

By replacing the ballerina's pointe shoes with animalesque hooves, Mantero stages two powerful visual statements. Choreographically, she proposes for Josephine Baker a dance of unbalance and pain (she has to stand for over 25 minutes on *demi-pointe*, thus foregrounding dance as strenuous labor). Semantically, she brings us back to the figure of the whore. A third element must be added to the composition of this particular plaint – Mantero's litany, almost repeating itself endlessly, calmly, matter-of-factly, insistently, hovering between factual statement, minimal poetry, and blunt accusation. She starts her recitation:

a sorrow
an impossibility
atrocious, atrocious
an impossibility
a sorrow
atrocious, atrocious
a sorrow
a sadness
an impossibility
atrocious, atrocious
a bad-will
an impossibility
a sorrow
atrocious, atrocious

. . .

a fall
an impossibility
an absence
atrocious, atrocious
a fall
an impossibility
a sorrow
a sadness
atrocious, atrocious
a fall
an absence
a sadness
an impossibility
atrocious, atrocious

. . .

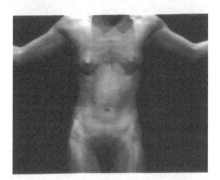

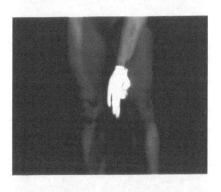

Figure 6.1 VM/JB Videostill composition by Luciana Fina (1999). Vera Mantero in *uma misteriosa Coisa, disse e.e. cummings* (1995).

Photo: Luciana Fina. Courtesy Luciana Fina.

This solo is no happy "tribute" to Josephine Baker. Mantero, while never loosening her focus from the figure of the African American dancer, does not attempt to represent Baker. Rather, she carefully constructs a figure in which she animates not a historical Baker, but Baker's resonating absence as central to the collusion of dance, colonialism, race, and melancholia in the body of woman. Mantero cannot just embody the semblance of Baker, not with the history of minstrelsy, of the appropriation of the black woman's body by white women, not with the recent Portuguese colonial past. Mantero takes pains to undo the mimetic machine of racism and minstrelsy, but she does so by indicating precisely the mechanism by which mimicry does bodies.

Homi Bhabha has shown how mimicry plays a central role in the construction of colonial discourses and policies, "as one of the most elusive and effective strategies of colonial power and knowledge" (Bhabha 2002: 114). Such a strategy, for Bhabha, operates at the level of a methodical destruction of "body and book," the anatomical and the verbal, running across colonialism's project (2002: 121). What is striking in Bhabha's understanding of colonial mimicry and what I find particularly relevant for an understanding of Mantero's piece as both spectral and melancholic is that Bhabha sees colonial mimicry as fundamentally ambivalent. Mimicry must remain an incomplete project so that the other remains familiar "but not quite," and menacing but not quite (2002: 114–15): "the ambivalence of colonial authority repeatedly turns from mimicry – a difference that is almost nothing but not quite – to menace – a difference that is almost total but not quite" (2002: 121). This ambivalence towards the discursive creation of a disturbingly unfamiliar familiarity immediately positions the question of colonial mimicry within the operational field of the Freudian uncanny. Moreover, as discussed above, the ambivalence of colonial mimicry has striking similarities to the one Berliner identified in colonial melancholia, and to Butler's understanding of melancholia's operation at the level of subject formation. Here, it is not surprising to find that, according to Bhabha, colonialism's ambivalent grounding generates the colonized, racialized other as a spectral, uncanny subjectivity. Indeed, Bhabha offers, "the ambivalence of colonial mimicry [. . .] fixes the colonial subject as partial presence [. . .] both 'incomplete' and 'virtual'" (2002: 115). It is at this juncture of a colonialist fixation of the racialized other as an incomplete, not quite present, menacingly almost familiar presence that we can paradoxically start to witness the resistant surfacing of the spectral and racial uncanny as unruly motions in the almost familiar – that is, as the colonized's strategically melancholic performance of plaint. How is it that the other can generate and sustain counteridentities and countermovements of resistance once they have been condemned to move and to exist as a half-presence within the field of racial invisibility? This is precisely the choreographic question (how to appear in a body moving the necessary steps) recent race theory has probed through the psychoanalytic concept of melancholia; this is where Mantero's fantastical body and poetic plaint occupies and resubverts once again colonialist and postcolonialist representational strategies.

José Muñoz, in his book *Disidentifications*, mobilizes a critical rethinking of both staged and vernacular performance practices that directly address what he calls resistant "disidentificatory acts" within hegemonic regimes of identity formation. Not surprisingly, Muñoz's notion of disidentification also engages the psychoanalytic concept of melancholia. Muñoz promotes practices of performance and theoretical practices that lead to fruitful, social, and critical mobilization. Thus, he sees an ethical imperative in reframing melancholia from "a pathology or [. . .] self-absorbed mood that inhibits activism," to consider it instead as "a mechanism that helps us (re)construct identity" (Muñoz 1999: 74). More recently, David L. Eng and Shinhee Han have taken Muñoz's argument further to investigate how "melancholia might be thought of as underpinning our everyday conflicts and struggles with experiences of immigration, assimilation, and racialization" (Eng and Han 2003: 344). What is critical in Muñoz's project is that his reframing of melancholia as mechanism of disidentification can only happen through the invocation and mobilization of the spectral within the fields of political critique, social mobilization, and subject formation. As Muñoz puts it, under this new light, melancholia allows us to "take our dead with us to the various battles we must wage in their names – and in our names" (Muñoz 1999: 74).

Dancing in the name of Josephine Baker in the former capital of the last European colonial empire, a hyperbolically (not) naked woman performs a series of half-presences before us. Sweating, made up, she proposes an image that refuses to ground itself within a set of fixed identities within representation. She is, as Bhabha described, fully inhabiting those partial presences colonialism has to offer its racialized others. Within the blind field of mutual racial invisibility, her body anatomically reveals the signs and marks of unsuspected collisions. She is partly whore, partly enchantress, partly accuser; she might be in pain, she may be a monster, she is perhaps beautiful, but she definitely and defiantly teeters at the threshold of what may perhaps still be dance. She attempts to stand, but that is the most excruciating physical task. She methodically and insistently tells us of an atrociously pervasive field of blindness while staring directly into our eyes. We can no longer rest neutrally in our places. Her pain and her repetitive recitation summon us into the timing of the piece she carefully weaves. This timing, her time, the time of the specter, of the plaint, secretes a space that becomes metonymic to her body. This is the moment where voice and body, motion and skins generate a topography of (racialized) melancholia. Mantero's wobbling feet, her unbalance, metonymically reveal otherwise invisible cracks in the terrain, denouncing the stage as hollow ground, as a gathering place for those bodies atrociously improperly buried by the hands of colonialism. Importantly, this ground (Mantero's, Baker's, the mysterious Thing's) is contiguous to where the audience stands.

So, gradually, the invisible field of racism starts to fill up with presences, voices, and lands. And we cannot avert our eyes from that body under strain, trapped within itself, trapped under its many layers of skin, each skin as historically overdetermined as the other. In her simultaneous exacerbation and deferral of full presence Mantero's partial stillness functions as a sort of visual reiteration of the poetic repetition of the word "atrocious" throughout her speech. Atrocious blindness, atrocious pain, atrocious silence, atrocious lack of will, atrocious impossibilities, atrocious sadness – at least for the duration of Mantero's summoning of Baker, of her plaint of the beast, of her appearing in the half-presence, half-shadows of a racialized, mysterious Thing, the audience cannot escape the position of being utterly contemporary to that lamenting body. Cheng notes:

> When we turn to the long history of grief and the equally protracted history of physically and emotionally managing that grief on the part of the marginalized, racialized people, we see that there has always been an interaction between melancholy in the vernacular sense of affect, as "sadness" or the "blues," and melancholia in the sense of a structural, identificatory formation predicated on – while being an active negotiation of – the loss of self as legitimacy.
>
> (Cheng 2001: 20)

Pain happens due to Mantero's insistence in trying to stand on her improbable goat feet, and by her choreographic decision to stay put in one place, that is, by her decision to not move as one expects dancers to move. As Mantero tries to find balance in her grotesque, bestial hooves, thus expanding and exploding with definitions and expectations of what is "dance," she deactivates yet another register in the field of colonial mimicry and representation. As she strains, as she recites, as she stays put under the spotlight, streams of sweat quietly streak down her body. If aurally she provokes with her sad recitation, visually she disturbs the field of dance by making sweat and tremor into explicit agents of meaning. Sweat signifies Mantero's labor when apparently there is none (she seems not to be giving her audience its money's worth). As her physical strain increases, sweat also subtly removes the dark paint from her skin, opening white scars in her body, showing it is all fiction, an image, an image of women-whores condemned to dance to tunes whistled by someone else's lips.

Indeed, through Baker's haunting, the naked body of a contemporary Portuguese female dancer becomes neither excuse nor proxy for voyeuristic jubilation of European fetishism toward African Americans. Nor does it become a vehicle for the reiteration of racial harmonies, but rather it functions as the powerful trigger of an uncanny nausea drawn by the sudden revelation: in its unveiled presence, that woman-whore-beast body is crying out a history of blindness and misencountering, a history of untold violence and labor, a history of meticulous destruction of bodies that remain to be properly seen and buried.

This is when Mantero's composite body reshuffles the ground upon which spectatorship and dance stand. We are not seeing Josephine, despite her being there. We are not seeing Vera, despite her exposure. Mantero's naked body transpires opaqueness, literally, as her dark coloration becomes sweat, streaming down her skin and revealing a white body under the overdetermined body of the dancer-whore. Ultimately presence is deferred. The spotlight that first illuminated only her face and then, in a 20-minute fade-in, gradually reveals the rest of her body, creates a reverse effect of illumination. For the more light is shed onto Mantero's body, the less we are able to see her, the less we see Josephine Baker, the less we see the she-goat. Instead, what fills our sensory is sweat, tremor, and mostly her voice. What is left of Mantero's dance is an acoustic image. It is as if the field of light defined on the stage also defines the field of racial blindness, of mutual racial blindness, a field only the aural could break – as in the uncanny tappings of ghosts on furniture, as in the knocking sounds on the stage preceding the piece. In Lisbon, when I saw the piece in 1996, Mantero's recitation provoked an increased and quite raucous amount of discomfort in the audience. Her words became sources for agitation and unrest. The plural form of "atrocious," the word that modifies every other one in the piece, is in Portuguese, *atrozes*. As Mantero stood on the spot trying to balance, telling us of the abyss, the blindness, the bad faith, one member of the audience, a middle-aged white woman, talked back to Mantero, loudly, disapprovingly: "*Artrose! Artrose!* [Arthritis! Arthritis!]."

In the verbal interpellation of Mantero performed by the anonymous Portuguese woman in that odd choreographic séance in postcolonial Portugal, we see how the field of racial invisibility and deafness unfolds across the stage. As one plaints, tells a history of hurt, the other mocks, accusing the suffering body of being diseased – accusing it of not being able to perform what it should, a dance. This is where European fantasies of dance once again match the colonial project: the body of the dancer, just like that of the slave, is only relevant, productive, meaningful, and valuable as long as it produces properly contained and efficient movement. The slave's biggest crime is to have a body in pain and to voice that pain in direct, noncamouflaged, nonspectacular, uncanny ways. However, despite the slave's condemnation to a half-presence, despite the field of invisibility covering the bodies of colored peoples, despite the current disavowal of the European colonialist past and current endemic racism, the ghostly knockings and plaints are always heard by white colonists within the walls of properly guarded homes. The spectral lament always hits its mark, thus initiating white melancholia, that ambivalent subjectivity hovering between loss and rage.

One question remains to be answered. Why Josephine Baker? Why was her call heard by the Portuguese postcolonialist cultural programmer, and why was the programmer's call for Mantero to perform Baker answered at all? If we consider that Baker is one of the few African American women that stood out significantly within the field of visibility, representation, and recognition in twentieth-century European imaginary, then we apparently arrive at a paradox. How can we talk of Baker's force in terms of a colonized half-presence if she seems so inescapable? Or how can we discuss her performances in terms of a practice of complicity with counteracts of resistance performed by less visible bodies of colonized Africans? How can we talk about Baker's use of uncannily resistant movements of the melancholic spectral, if she had been so successful, so present, so forcibly all over? These questions are further complicated once one takes into account that Baker's characters in three of her four French films *La Sirène des Tropiques* (1927), *Zou Zou* (1934), and *Princess Tam Tam* (1935) appear as proxies for otherwise unseen, unrepresentable, less noble, indeed (for the European colonizer) "savage," colonized African bodies. In these three films, Baker does not play an African American. She plays a Martinican, a black French (from the Antilles), or an "African." Baker's African American body stands in for those other colored bodies that seem to cause so much discomfort to the European proper, neat, regulated, colonialist home. As a proxy for the colonized African and Martinican, Baker emerges as a complicated half-presence in the general field of racial invisibility, because as an African American she could be cast as a colonized African.

But a paradox does not necessarily mean an impasse, neither a giving in. Baker's uncanny agency relies precisely on her quiet understanding of what was at stake in her success in Europe. This awareness can be read everywhere in her autobiography. And it can be seen best in the ways that Baker, throughout her career, voiced and channeled a plaint that markedly situated her right along with the plaint of the colonized – directly within the influence of the colonized's melancholic counteracts of resistance. In all her movies, Baker's characters always appear hovering between wild spontaneity and deep melancholia. This ambivalence in her character's behavior was certainly a part given to her by her French directors, script-writers, and collaborators. But if it was given to her, she took it – and it is no less certain that she fully embodied those parts with a reciprocal ambivalence and wisdom. What is truly stunning in Baker's film performances is that despite the proximity of the camera, despite the filmic structure of command, despite editing and the rudimentary special effects, her dancing remains to be captured – and therefore to be both properly placed and properly seen. A case can be made that Baker's dances for film perform a refusal to enter into the field of the visible. It is almost as if the camera could find neither its proper place nor Baker's placement in space. It is as if Baker's movements could not be properly pinned down, captured, entrapped by the machinic gaze. What we witness mostly while watching Princess Tam Tam's final, "wild" dancing in a Parisian cabaret, or Zou Zou's skits in the vaudeville stage, is the prevalence of a blurred absence made of quick cuts, strange edits, and odd camera moves. And what glides across this ongoing visual disruption, what moves along Baker's filmic half-presence, is a partly disembodied voice, longing for Martinique, Africa, or freedom. The French loved that noble display of grief by an African American portraying what they thought would represent proper African and Caribbean nostalgia. But the problem she poses to this enchanted European audience, or the uncanny shadow her movements cast in all her movies, is the fact that neither the colonized African nor Baker were ever quite there. Baker knew quite well what she was doing in the moving field of colonial mimicry, half-presences, colonialism, and spectral melancholia. She choreographed and danced not for the eye to capture, but for other senses – those activated in the improper field of melancholic subjectivity. Senses attuned to all that "cannot be accommodated by vision, that resists being brought to the open, neither seen nor declared," to repeat Butler's formulation on the particular phenomenology of melancholy (Butler 1997a: 186).

Michael Taussig describes Josephine Baker's dance as "disorganizing the mimesis of mimesis" (Taussig 1993: 68). For Taussig, Baker fully understands what is at stake for the colonizer in colonial mimicry – the colonizer's integrity as both body and subject whose very being is predicated upon the blunt appropriation and absolute erasure of any independent, autonomous voice, and full presence of the colonized, racialized body. Baker's way to escape the colonialist drive informing her European admirers is precisely by eluding the possibility of Europeans replicating, repeating, and reproducing her movements. When Baker attended a soirée at Count Harry Kessler's in Berlin in 1926, the white guests "implored" her to dance. As the Count remembers the episode, his guests soon started imitating Baker's movements, "Now and again, Luli Meiern also improvised a few movements, very delightful and harmonious; but one twist of the arm by Josephine Baker and their grace was extinguished, dissolved into thin air like mountain mist" (in Taussig 1993: 69).

This understanding of dance as an improper practice, a practice that presents itself as essentially antirepertoire, a practice impossible for a certain subjectivity and body to grasp, to retain; this understanding of dance's potential for the uncanny; this claiming of a movement that is not for the eye to behold; this strategic choreography of the colonized plaint as partly never present; this enactment of the dancer's half-presence within the field of invisibilities that racialization and colonialism inaugurate; this understanding of race and of dance an ontological and epistemological invocations of ghosts, all coalesce in Baker's project of direct destruction of dance's own colonialist premises. This destruction is what turns Mantero and Baker into accomplices and partners in each other's struggles – each an uncanny, unruly half-presence of the other in the melancholic field of the European postcolonial.

7   Conclusion

Exhausting dance – to be done with the vanishing point

> We have great difficulty in understanding a survival of the past in itself because we believe that the past is no longer, that it has ceased to be. We have thus confused Being with being-present.
>
> (Deleuze 1988: 55)

In Chapter 2, I discussed how Arbeau's *Orchesographie* first alloyed a neologism that fused dance with writing. I noted how this alloying had implications not only at the level of signification but also at the level of subjectification. I argued that the moment Arbeau chose for *Orchesograpie*'s epigraph a line from Ecclesiastes, "A time to mourn, & a time to dance," the centrality of the spectral in that dance manual profoundly transformed the function of that conjunctive "&" in the biblical quote. Rather than separating the time of dancing *from* the time of mourning, that "&" ontologically connected both dancing time *and* mourning time as emblematic of the temporality of the new technology of telepresence, choreography. Arbeau's alloying of dance *and* writing into one word corresponded to the fusing of the "time to dance" *and* the "time to mourn" into a single temporality – thus creating a new mode of understanding the coming into presence of the dancing subject. Such semantic and affective operations at the core of choreography reaffirm how Western theatrical dance's coming into being was profoundly tied to a very modern affect: the mournful perception of the temporality of the present as an ongoing, ceaseless passing away of the "now."

Theorizing the consequences of such investment on the now for dance studies, Randy Martin reminds us how Nietzsche's critique of history attempts

> to articulate the experience of modernity as an awareness of the interminable loss of the present that is possible only when what is felt as "just now" (modernus) becomes a central cultural referent. It is the culture of an incessantly passing "now" that allows the past to figure as compensation for the imminent death of what is.
>
> (Martin 1998: 40)

In this sense, dance's complaint in regards to the perception of its being as constitutionally ephemeral became its modernity – and soon this complaint developed *melancholic* characteristics. Giorgio Agamben rightly indicates in his reading of Freud's 1917 essay "Mourning and Melancholia" (Freud 1991a) that,

> in melancholia the object is neither appropriated nor lost, but both *possessed and lost at the same time* [. . .] so the object of the melancholic project is at once real and unreal, incorporated and lost, affirmed and denied.
>
> (Agamben 1993: 21, emphasis added)

Note in melancholia the intromission of the ambiguous status of the reality of the lost object as both present and absent. But note also Agamben's characterization of melancholia as a *project*. A project of subjectification establishing modernity's relationship to the ways it negotiates presence and absence. Harvie Ferguson notes how modern subjectivity "having established itself as melancholy [. . .] infected every form of sensuousness with a certain morbidity" (Ferguson 2000: 134).

Choreography comes into being as a technology particularly able to answer and foster *modernity's melancholic project*. Its drive is to fixate absence in presence, to occasion the dancer's "joining again" those already departed.[1] The advent of choreography is tied to the perception of the moving body's relationship to temporality as always already under a melancholic spell – once the kinetic becomes modernity's emblem, nothing guarantees the permanence of being.[2] This perception suggests for critical dance studies that Western theatrical dance – as it confined itself in increasingly more abstracted rooms (the court, the salon, the theatre, the studio) in its drive toward artistic autonomy – must be theoretically approached not just as a kinetic project but as an affective one. An affective project profoundly marked by the infusion of the kinetic at the core of subjectivity generating continuous complaints of dance always going away, irremediably bound to its own loss, of never quite being there at the fleeting moment when it visibly moves.

Arbeau, 1589: "As regards ancient dances all I can tell you is that the passage of time, the indolence of man or the difficulty of describing them has robbed us of any knowledge thereof" (Arbeau 1966: 15). Jean-Georges Noverre, 1760: "Why are the names of *maîtres de ballets* unknown to us? It is because works of this kind endure only for a moment, and are forgotten as soon as the impressions they had produced" (Noverre 1968: 1). Dance's modernity is grounded on this unbearable perception of the dancing body's relation to temporality. But note a subtlety in dance's lament, and in its lamentable condition of being doomed to forgetfulness as soon as it is performed. Note how in the melancholic complaint it is not only dance's present that is always being lost. As both Arbeau's and Noverre's quotes show, the loss of dance's present implies also the *loss of dance's past*. The former complains of how we do not know how to dance ancient dances; the latter of how we forget the names of old masters. Nothing seems to remain in the archives of dance. Dance loses all. Mostly it loses itself. This is dance's curse in the temporality of modernity – it forgets too much, it retains nothing. Dance silently moves towards its future only to reveal it as a vast amnesiac past. Within the melancholic perceptual and affective field of modernity, dance offers nothing but fleeting vanishing visions of its momentary brilliance in a series of irretrievable nows.

Choreography emerges precisely to counter this ontological condition. Choreography activates writing in the realm of dancing to guarantee that dance's present is given a past, and therefore, a future. Note that, in this operation, choreography does not dispel the melancholic; it actually reinforces it, by constantly being in a state of dissatisfaction before its own project.

If the birth of choreography is ontohistorically associated with melancholic complaints about dance's inability to stick around, could this condition still be operating today? In contemporary dance studies, one of the most famous and explicit reiterations of dance's full participation in the melancholic project of modernity can be found in Marcia Siegel's opening paragraph in her book *At the Vanishing Point.* She writes:

> Dancing exists at a perpetual vanishing point. At the moment of its creation it is gone. All of a dancer's years of training in the studio, all the choreographer's planning, the rehearsals, the coordination of designers, composers, and technicians, the raising of money and the gathering together of an audience, all these are only a preparation for an event that disappears in the very act of materializing. No other art is so hard to catch, so impossible to hold.
>
> (Siegel 1972: 1)

Note how in Siegel's account it is not only the performance of dancing that is depicted as ephemeral. All the labor and all the preparation that allow dance to come into being are described almost as funereal rites – "*a preparation for an event that disappears in the very act of materializing.*" If such a description is applied to the work of "designers, composers, and technicians," imagine the implications for the work of the dancer. Under Siegel's framework, the dancer's years of training, of conditioning body and mind for the fleeting moment of dancing, are but the embracing of a sacrificial subjectivity, the creation of a particular mode of being-in-the-world that would amount to nothing more than a lifetime of rehearsing and performing endless successions of living-burials. It is as if existing at the vanishing point transforms years of training, learning, creating, and dancing into years of continuous anticipated mourning and reiterated retrospective melancholia. Under these conditions, the dancer is always already an absent presence in the field of the gaze, somewhere between body and ghost, a flash suspended between past and future.

Siegel proposes that dance's inability to be held, the inability for it to acquire an endurable temporality and a density, is what clogs its inclusion in economy: "precisely because it does not lend itself to any form of reproduction, dance was the only one of the arts that had not been cut up into handy packages and distributed to a mass market" (1972: 5). She concludes: dance is not "ready for recycling" (Siegel 1972: 5). But I would argue that not lending oneself to reproduction does not extricate one from hegemonic forces and ontological violences proper of the representational, of the economy of representation, what Derrida called "economimesis" (Derrida 1981). For it is precisely dance's self-depiction as a lamentably ephemeral art form, the melancholic drive at its core, that generates systems and performances of high reproducibility: strict techniques named after dead masters applied to carefully selected bodies, continuous modeling of bodies through endless repetition of exercises, dieting, surgeries, the perpetuation of systems of racial exclusion for the sake of "proper" visibility, an endemic eruption of archival fevers, the international and transcultural spreading of national ballets performing nineteenth-century steps for the sake and glory of dancing their status as modern nations (particularly in "developing" nations, those former formal colonies of the West, where the national company becomes a staple of the state's ability to escape the "belatedness" of their emergence as nations), the merchandising of brands and names, the franchising, the fetishes. A whole economy of dance and its supplements energized by the melancholic plaint of the lawyer Capriol allows precisely for dance and dances to constantly be recycled, reproduced, packaged, distributed, institutionalized, sold. Siegel's depiction of dance's existence at the vanishing point ironically places it right back at the core of the psycho-philosophical system that allows the reproducibility of representation at the (ontotheological) core of the visible. For, as I discussed in Chapter 4, it is this particularly modern optical invention, the vanishing point, that sustains perspectival representation and its politics of figuration, presence, and visibility. To exist at the vanishing point means never to be *figured* within perspectival representation, it is to exist at the abstract, mathematical point of a virtual singularity. But if the vanishing point is in itself an invisibility, it is one that secures the relationship between scopic representation and modernity's ideologies of subjectification and visibility.[3] To exist at the vanishing point is to exist right at the core of that which guarantees the very possibility of representation, it is to exist at the core of the power in representation. In that sense, the locus attributed by melancholic modernity to dance's being becomes a transcendental articulator for the possibility of representational visibility always tied to the figuration of ontothological and ontopolitical stabilities as demonstrated by Erwin Panofsky (1997) and Allen Weiss (1995).

Siegel's observations in the early 1970s on dance's ontological relationship to ephemerality and on dance's complicated relationship to economy anticipate an influential proposal for the ontology of performance made two decades later. There are some striking similarities between Siegel's description of dance's existence at the vanishing point and the description of performance's ontology as articulated by Peggy Phelan in her celebrated essay "The Ontology of Performance: Representation without Reproduction" (Phelan 1993). I would like to explore those similarities, not to establish putative lines of direct influence, which may or may not be there, but to focus on why Phelan's ontology of performance (consciously or unconsciously) dialogues so strongly with the ontohistoric formation of choreography as the kinetic emblem of the modern project of melancholia.

The opening lines of Phelan's essay are well known: "Performance's only life is in the present." Phelan concludes the opening paragraph of her essay by remarking: "Performance's being, *like the ontology of subjectivity proposed here*, becomes itself through disappearance" (Phelan 1993: 146, emphasis mine). In a way reminiscent of Siegel's, Phelan notes that such an ontology predicated on disappearance defies economy: "without a copy, live performance plunges into visibility – in a maniacally charged present – and disappears into memory, into the realm of invisibility and the unconscious where it eludes regulation and control" (1993: 148), thus clogging "the smooth machinery of reproductive representation necessary to the circulation of capital" (148).

Phelan's theoretical framework is informed by psychoanalysis, and her scholarship proposes a unique and important feminist reading of Freud and Lacan. When Phelan states that performance disappears into memory, it is to indicate that it enters into the atemporal, deregulated realm of the unconscious. But it is at this moment of performance's "plunge" that one needs to identify the precise topography of that place where performance "disappears into." Here, some problems arise in terms of the political project of such disappearing – particularly given its proximity to, and reification of, the melancholic project of modern and choreographic subjectification. Depending where one positions oneself theoretically in relation to the development of Freud's work, the unconscious does not at all escape regulation. It is precisely Lacan who reminds us that in order for psychoanalysis to critically assess the structuring of the symbolic order around the name of the Father understood as the Father's "no," Freud had to develop his second "topography" of the unconscious, the one articulated in 1920 in *The Ego and the Id*. In this book, Freud sophisticates his notion of the unconscious. The unconscious is no longer just a place for the repressed, but it now encompasses more clearly the operations of the ego and of the superego – particularly those related to "parenting prohibitions" (Laplanche and Pontalis 1973: 453). In Freud's second topography the unconscious carries with it highly regulatory functions. Thus, any plunge into the unconscious may not necessarily mean an escape from regulation.

Moreover, if performance's only life is in the present, it should be noted that the Freudian unconscious (in both topographies, pre- and post-1920) is informed by its radical atemporality – the unconscious fully belongs not to "the present," but to *its* own present. If the unconscious is structured as a language, to use Lacan's famous formulation, then it would be a language without verbal inflexion. Freud: "The processes of the system Ucs [unconscious] are timeless; i.e., they are not ordered temporally, are not altered by the passage of time, in fact bear no relation to time at all" (Freud 1991b: 135). The intrusion of this particular timelessness of the unconscious gives a double meaning to Phelan's opening sentence in her essay. If performance's only life happens in the present, its plunge into the unconscious is what guarantees its persistent (yet atemporal) presentness, for the unconscious reveals only the atemporal present tense of memory. This is one of the reasons why the melancholic must always reminisce: remembering as total surrender to memory is a very effective way to elude the passing of time.

To disappear into memory is the first step to remain in the present. The melancholic understands that, and plunges him or herself into memory in order to preserve the lost object within the presentness of memory (even if this preservation endures the operations of the unconscious – displacement, repression, condensation, and sublimation). It is in this sense that Phelan's ontology of performance shares with dance's ontology an overarching *melancholic affect* in relationship to the dance-event. This affect remains untheorized in dance history, despite the fact that Phelan's "Ontology of Performance" allows for the possibility of such theorization (Phelan 1993). I would like to propose as one of the implications of such theorization the following: to be done with choreography's modernity, to be done with the affective project binding the choreographic with the melancholic, would be to be done with the temporality at the core of vanishing point – the temporality that assimilates the present with the instantaneous "now."

As we saw in the previous chapter, to be done with melancholia, to be done with existing at the vanishing point, poses some ethical difficulties. As my discussion of Vera Mantero's summoning of Josephine Baker proposed, if melancholia is a condition of modernity, if it is one of modernity's main projects of subjectification, it is important to have in mind that recent critical race theory reminds us that it is through melancholia that in modernity one *exchanges affects in the racialized and racist field*. This exchange indicates a generative potential in embracing melancholia as subjectivity and as political project. For, if melancholia keeps in place particularly morbid subjectivities and their constitutive relational blindness – it is also the affect allowing for an ethics of remembering and for the exchange of affects after colonialism. Moreover, queer theory and critical race studies have recently posited how there is a privileging and a violence embedded in certain modes of forgetting. José Muñoz in particular writes poignantly on the need for not forgetting those who are no longer living, those who have succumbed to overwhelming violence, to hateful ignorance, to injurious neglect (Muñoz 1999). In this sense, the melancholic position, or to emphasize again Agamben's term, the melancholic *project*, is inextricably bound to resistant subjectivities, to what Julia Kristeva called "the metaphysical lucidity of depression" (Kristeva 1989: 4).

Perhaps, then, the question for a political ontology of choreography and for a temporality of dance that refuses to live bound to the vanishing point should *not* be articulated as a choice between taking sides with forgetting or with remembering. The question perhaps should be posed in terms of knowing how to detach not forgetting from the morbid implications melancholy always carries with it. This question fuses the affective with the theoretical, the political with the choreographic. All must work in tandem for the production of other possibilities of experiencing and thinking the temporality of dance that does not cast it as always doomed to disappearing. This would mean to follow Deleuze's advice in the epigraph to this chapter and not to confound Being with being-present, disappearance with invisibility, the past with memory.

Here, notions of temporality brought by nonpsychoanalytic models could be of use. For instance, the particular temporality of memory and perception that Henri Bergson advances in *Matter and Memory*. Bergson's notions allow for refiguring what constitutes the past and what constitutes remembering. In simple terms, for

Bergson "the past is *that which acts no longer*" (Bergson 1991: 68, emphasis in the original). In order for this statement to make sense, it demands detaching the "act" from the understanding that frames it as the immediate visibility of an action at the moment of its performance. For Bergson, any act, as long as it continues generating an effect and an affect, remains in the present. As long as there is act, there is becoming; for Bergson, all that is present is becoming, only the past *is*. In other words, "the past is pure ontology" (Deleuze 1988: 56). In Chapter 3, I discussed how Paul Schilder replaced the singular notion of the body, the body as stable unit bound by the surface of its skin, the body as spatially and temporally belonging only to the place-instant of its appearing, with the centrifugal notion of a body-image as unfolding multiplicity spreading in time and space. With Bergson, we are before an analogous operation in terms of memory and time: whatever action remains active in its effects (no matter when that action first took place) there we encounter and walk along a line of our present. If the past's pure passivity is its encounter with ontology, then whatever stirs and makes us stir (a force, an affect, a memory, an image) no matter whether visible or invisible, at hand or at a distance, physical or metaphysical, linguistic or visceral, constitutes a present understood as a becoming. Direct consequence: an unprecedented opening-up of the restricted understanding of the "present" that had been assigned to it to by the melancholic casting of time as an irrecoverable passing away of irreversible unique instants performed by a series of "nows."[4] Because, as Deleuze explains Bergson's understanding of time, "a succession of instants does not constitute time any more than it causes it to disappear," because "time is constituted only in the originary synthesis which operates in the repetition of instants," and because "this synthesis contracts the successive independent instants into one another, thereby constituting the lived, or living, present," the present opens away from its investment in the now (Deleuze 1994: 70).

Dance's melancholic framing of its temporality (of temporality in general) as aligned with the irrecoverable passing away of the "now" left dance barely with a present, certainly without a past (no memory), and also without a future (no activation of memory for the futurity of dance). What Bergson's notions of temporality, matter, and memory propose are modes of being in the present that can escape the melancholia of the fleeting "now." With Bergson, the present is no longer equivalent to the now. The present spreads out in activity, affects and effects, outside the moment of the now. As Deleuze explains,

> the past and the future do not designate instants distinct from a supposed present instant, but rather the dimensions of the present itself in so far as it is a contraction of instants. The present does not have to go outside itself in order to pass from past to future.
>
> (Deleuze 1994: 71)

Expansion of the present then – but also its multiplication thanks to its living. Deleuze identifies in Bergson the demise of the definite article to qualify "present," thanks to the living. The living implies and reveals no longer *the* present, but presents: "two successive presents may be contemporaneous with a third present" (Deleuze 1994: 77). This other present, these other contemporaneous presents may be more or less "extended by virtue of the number of instants" each present contracts (Deleuze 1994: 77).

A matter of contraction then, but also a matter of identifying every body, every mode of subjectification as modes of contracting temporality, of creating and multiplying synthesis, that is to say, of creating, multiplying, and identifying living as fundamentally constituted by a multiplicity of presents, extending towards past and future in different modes, according to different vectors, intensities, affects. It is not by chance that such a temporality has an antikinetic component in it; or at least, an immanent critique of the being-toward-movement that has been the central conceptual character of this book, in its relation to the choreographic-melancholic project of modernity. For, in order to fundamentally access and accept the multiplication of presents in any mode of being-in-the-world, a certain stillness is needed:

> the duration of an organism's present, or of its various presents, will vary according to the natural contractile range of its contemplative souls. In other words, fatigue is a real component of contemplation. It is correctly said that those who do nothing tire themselves most.
>
> (Deleuze 1994: 77)

What happens with Bergson's and Deleuze's expanded notions of the present when applied to the temporality of dancing at the vanishing point, understood as one bound to the notion of the present disappearing as soon as it is performed? It is the very notion of present as series of forever lost "nows" that can no longer be sustained. For *the present is to be found in whatever still-acts*. The activation of all that is not properly supposed to be there at the moment of its assigned temporality, the expansion of presents towards the past and the future, their coexistence, indexes the possibility for an ethical remembering necessary for a politics of the dead, for accessing the endless motility of absent presents. It points at the possibility for an accounting of the ghostly that could dispel the morbid forces of melancholia, and propose a joy at the edge of the temporal abyss (such as the one Mantero dances when she summons Josephine Baker). The expanded and always multiplying presents in dances, in performances, acting away across time and space, accessed and revealed thanks to fatigues and contemplations, would activate sensations, perceptions, and memories as so many stirring affects bound not to what had once happened and then disappeared into a "lost time" – but to an intimacy to whatever insists to keep happening.

Intimacy is the generative theoretical and phenomenological affect of a temporality that escapes dancing at the vanishing point, and yet could still account for an ethics of remembering. To this affect of temporality Bergson gave the name of "duration," which is "defined less by succession than by coexistence" (Delenge 1988: 60). Bound to situated temporalities, this coexistence would allow for the production of "a theory of the contingency of chronotopic, or space-time, environments," that would allow "dance studies [to track] how units of temporality circulate within a given performance" (Martin 1998: 209). To track the coexistence of multiple temporalities within the temporality of dance, to identify multiple presents in the dancing performance, to expand the notion of the present from its melancholic fate, from its entrapment in the microscopy of the now, to the extension of the present along lines of whatever still-acts, to reveal the intimacy of duration, are all theoretical and political moves producing and proposing alternative affects through which dance studies could extract itself from its melancholic entrapment at the vanishing point.

Figure 7.1 Jérôme Bel. *The Last Performance* (1998).

Photo: Herman Sorgeloos. Courtesy Jérôme Bel.

Notes

1 Introduction: the political ontology of movement

1 I discuss Jérôme Bel's work in detail in Chapter 3.
2 One of the other reasons for the superiority of the puppet is its lack of inner psychological life, which prevents it to displace the "natural centers of gravity" to other parts of the body, thus guaranteeing full expression of graceful moves. Kleist's text is the subject of numerous readings and critical analysis. The most influential is undoubtedly Paul de Man's in *The Rhetoric of Romanticism* (1984). Briefly, de Man understands Kleist's text as a parable on the act of reading, where reading is cast as an unfinishable test to a reader who will always miss the marks of writing. Without precluding such a reading, I would argue that "On the Puppet Theatre" demands an expansion of its interpretation as being only a commentary on reading due to the three ontokinetic-theological arguments it proposes between human movement, animal movement, and puppet movement in their relations to expressivity, truth, God, and being. It should also be mentioned that Kleist's evocation of "elves" in the passage quoted is historically telling, and that his description of dancing puppets resisting gravity could very well fit the performances staged by Charles Didelot's "flying techniques" – theatrical machines that could create, at the end of the eighteenth century, the illusion of flight on stage.
3 For Derrida, the entire history of Western metaphysics (which he identified with the "history of the West") revolved around a fixed center: that of "Being as presence in all senses of the word" (Derrida 1978: 279). For Derrida, it is only with Nietzsche, Freud, and Heidegger that presence as Truth, presence as Subject, and presence as Being, respectively, are fundamentally decentered (1978: 279).
4 Derrida remains a philosopher of the body in the sense he radically reframes the question of language as the question of a grammatology, as he carefully attends to the practice of writing and to the haunting effects of writing. The fact that the body, for Derrida, is already linguistic, already within a writing machine, in the sense Kafka understands the body, does not mean it is less corporeal. See also Derrida's concern with actual performances and with the centrality of performatives in some of his most cherished themes: the force of law, giving, ethics, dying, listening to the other, theology.
5 Thoinot Arbeau coins "*orchesographie*" – a writing ("*graphie*") of the dance ("*orchesis*") in 1589. The synonym currently used, "choreography," was introduced in 1700 by Raoul-Auger Feuillet in his eponymous classic treatise. Interestingly, in 1706 John Weaver published *An Exact and Just Translation from the French of Monsieur Feuillet* where he translates Feuillet's original title *Choréographie* as "orchesography" thus indicating the currency of the older version in the eighteenth century. In either configuration of the word, the fusing of dance with writing names a practice whose programmatic, technical, discursive, economic, ideological, and symbolic forces remain active today.

6 "The distinctive feature of modern embodiment lies in the process of individuation, in the identification of the body with the person as a unique individual and, therefore, as the bearer of values and legally enforceable rights" (Ferguson 2000: 38).

7 Jameson pushes his argument a bit when he identifies in Deleuze "a quintessential modernist" (2002: 4).

8

> It is a fantasy which accords certain attributes to the subject, and dispossesses the other of them as and by the process that makes the other into an object, a surrounds (as Heidegger might say), an absent background against which it is present. It is a fantasy that relies on a divorce between mental design and bodily action to sustain its omnipotent denial. In this fantasy, the subject must also deny its history, in so far as that history reveals its dependence on a maternal origin.
>
> (Brennan 2000: 36)

9 "Much contemporary dance criticism and scholarship is still inflected with the assumptions [. . .] that looking at dance politically might somehow interfere with its efficacy" (Martin 1998: 14).

10 "The philosophers have only *interpreted* the world, in various ways; the point is to *change* it" (Marx and Engels 1969: 15).

11 Throughout this book, all quotes from Sloterdijk's different works are my translations from the French editions.

12 See Banes 1989, Manning 1988. See also Siegel 1992.

13 I discuss Bachelard's "slower ontology" in Chapter 3.

14 The man in question is French critic and programmer Jean-Marc Adolphe.

2 Masculinity, solipsism, choreography: Bruce Nauman, Juan Dominguez, Xavier Le Roy

1 Film, 16 mm, black and white, silent, 400 feet, approximately 10 minutes.

2 Film, 16 mm, black and white, sound, 400 feet, approximately 10 minutes.

3 Videotape, black and white, silent, 8 minutes.

4 I thank Ramsay Burt for directing me to this interview.

5 Members of the Judson Dance Theater and artists that were close to Judson and who took Halprin's workshop in San Francisco included Yvonne Rainer, Ruth Emerson, Simone Forti, Robert Morris, Trisha Brown, and La Monte Young. Later, Meredith Monk also took classes with Halprin (see Banes 1993: 141–2; Banes 1995: *passim*). Janice Ross writes: "For Halprin it was modern dance establishments and all its rules of representation, theatricality, and illusion" that she wanted to escape (in Banes and Baryshnikov 2003: 29). Halprin's refusal of theatricality and stifling rules of representation anticipates Rainer's later alignment with minimalism and explicit refusal of illusion and representation as famously stated in her "NO Manifesto."

6 My thanks to Jenn Joy for her diligent research on this matter.

7 In 1969, Nauman performed a trio version of his studio film *Bouncing in the Corner, No. 1* (1968) with Meredith Monk and with his wife at the time, Judy Nauman, at the *Anti-Illusions: Procedures/Materials* (1969) exhibition at the Whitney Museum of American Art, New York.

8 The dating of Nauman's films and tapes is sometimes contradictory and varies somewhat depending on the sources consulted. I am following Nauman's "Videography" listed in Robert C. Morgan's *Bruce Nauman* (Morgan 2002).

9 For a critique of the notion of movement as "language" in dance see José Gil's notion of "infra-language" in *Metamorphoses of the Body* (Gil 1998).

10 Mark Franko notes that although as early as the sixteenth century "the dance is often called a language, the effects of steps and movements in the communication of a

message is not treated, nor is their possible sign value taken up" (Franko 1986: 8). The distinction between language and writing that I am proposing at this point will be of particular significance when I discuss the spectral effect of writing within the choreographic.

11 On the commanding function of titles in Nauman's sculptures and drawings see Paul Schimmel's essay "Pay Attention" (in Simon 1994).

12 The author's real name was Jehan Tabourot (1519–93). From 1542 until his death, Tabourot served at the Cathedral of Langres, where he held the office of treasurer and also ecclesiastic judge and vicar-general. The political and historical ties between choreography, the theological, and the juridical are thus much more than just narrative flourishes performed by Tabourot's alter-ego Arbeau.

13 I discuss Sloterdjik's concept in the introduction.

14 I refer to a desire that is expressed as primary in the production of "choreography" as neologism and technology of writing movement – a production resulting from a pedagogical encounter between two men. This does not mean that many dances in Arbeau's book do not include women. Indeed, one of the major social purposes of Renaissance dance is to occasion heterosexual socialization and mating. However, except as partners for dances, women do not take any role whatever in the textual duet between the dancing priest and the dancing lawyer. The birth of that powerful new word for modernity – orchesography – is the result of a homosocial encounter and desire to hold on to the loved object: the master.

15 A citationality that, moreover, Butler links to the question of law:

> The forming, crafting, bearing, circulation, signification of that sexed body will not be a set of actions performed in compliance with the law; on the contrary, they will be a set of actions mobilized by the law, the citational accumulation and dissimulation of the law that produces material effects, the lived necessity of those effects as well as the lived contestation of that necessity.
>
> (Butler 1993: 12)

16 "A writing that was not structurally legible – iterable – beyond the death of the addressee would not be writing" (Derrida 1986: 315).

17 For an outline of a sociology and an epistemology of haunting, see Gordon (1997).

18 For a history of the grave as private space in the West see Philippe Ariès (1974, 1977, 1982) and Alain Corbin (1986).

19 I discuss Feuillet's square in Chapter 4.

20 I write "often" because some of Nauman's studio films show the artist pacing around in less choreographed manners. This is particularly the case with *Playing a Note on the Violin While I Walk Around the Studio* (1967–8), and *Violin Tuned D E A D* (1969). However, I find significant that in those two films the perlocutionary force of the title aims not at movement itself, but at the execution of a different task (playing the violin). The only other studio film that is significantly achoreographic (explicitly dealing with chance, accidents and the improbability of movement) is *Bouncing Two Balls between the Floor and the Ceiling with Changing Rhythms* (1967–8). But this exception has a powerful connotation, which I explore more in detail further on.

21 Film, 16 mm, black and white, sound, approximately 10 minutes.

22 Film, 16 mm, black and white, silent, 9 minutes.

23 I saw *AGSAMA* in Berlin, during its world premiere at the festival *Tanz in August* in 2003. The piece was performed neither in a black box nor in an auditorium, but in a large, white, rectangular room, with tall windows along one of its walls. On the opposite wall two regular doors allowed audience and performer to enter and exit the room. The fact that the audience was seated in bleachers did not diminish the visual and spatial impact of the fact that we were all in a *room*, not in a theatre.

24 Title of Dominguez's previous piece, premiered in 2000.

25 I discuss Schilder's notion of "body-image" in the next chapter.

3 Choreography's "slower ontology": Jérôme Bel's critique of representation

1 For a discussion of La Ribot's work, see Chapter 4; for a discussion of Juan Dominguez's work, see Chapter 2; for a discussion of Vera Mantero's work see Chapter 6. For more on this recent European dance movement, see Lepecki 2000, 2004; Ploebst 2001; Burt 2004; Siegmund 2004.

2 Dance critics tend to refer to this movement as "conceptual dance." Many of the choreographers involved do not accept this name, see for instance Xavier Le Roy's statement "I don't consider myself as a conceptual artist and I don't know of one choreographer who works in dance without a concept" (Le Roy *et al.* 2004: 10). In 2001, a group composed of many of the choreographers and critics (including La Ribot, Xavier Le Roy and Christophe Wavelet) aligned with this experimental scene met in Vienna to draft a document to be submitted to the European Union as suggestions for guidelines for a European dance and performance policy. In this document there was a purposeful resistance to naming current choreographic practices under a single word:

> Our practices can be called: "performance art," "live art," "happenings," "events," "body art," "contemporary dance/theatre," "experimental dance," "new dance," "multimedia performance," "site specific," "body installation," "physical theatre," "laboratory," "conceptual dance," "independence," "postcolonial dance/performance," "street dance," "urban dance," "dance theatre," "dance performance" – to name but a few . . .
>
> (Manifesto for a European Performance Policy 2001)

I do think, however, that "conceptual dance" at least allows for historically locating this movement within a genealogy of twentieth-century performance and visual arts, by referring to the conceptual art movement of the late 1960s and early 1970s that shared its critique of representation, its insistence on politics, its fusion of the visual with the linguistic, its drive for a dissolution of genres, its critique of authorship, its dispersion of the art-work, its privileging of the event, its critique of institutions, and its esthetic emphasis on minimalism – all traits that are recurrent in many recent works in Europe of which Jérôme Bel is one of the initiators. "Conceptual dance" at least prevents claiming absolute historical originality to this movement, something I believe its participants would agree with, given their open dialogue with the history of performance art and postmodern dance.

3 For an account of a whole tradition of representational critique in contemporary performance deriving from Bertolt Brecht's epic theatre see Elin Diamond's *Unmaking Mimesis* (1997). For an account of performance art's critique of representation see Amelia Jones's *Body Art/Performing the Subject* (1998).

4 Foucault writes retrospectively in 1982, "it is not power, but the subject, that is the general theme of my work" (Foucault 1997: 327). He clarifies:

> There are two meanings to the word 'subject': subject to someone else by control and dependence, and tied to his own identity by a conscience or self-knowledge. Both meanings suggest a form of power that subjugates and makes subject to.
>
> (Foucault 1997: 331)

Thus, as Deleuze explains, Foucault is not reinserting a transcendental notion of "the subject" back into his theory, but understanding the "subject" as a function of power: "It's idiotic to say Foucault discovers or reintroduces a hidden subject after having rejected it. There's no subject, but a production of subjectivity: subjectivity has to be produced, when its time arrives, precisely because there is no subject" (Deleuze 1995: 113–14).

5 For a detailed discussion of this concept, see introduction and Chapter 2.

6 Derrida called the fusion of general *and* restricted economy with the logic of the mimetic (of representation) "economimesis" – a term that emphasizes how the law (*nomos*) of representation is the house (*oikos*) where Western metaphysics and esthetics dwell (Derrida 1981).

7 See also Phelan (1993: 27, 148). Phelan more explicitly expands her ontological research on performance as an ontological research on subjectivity in *Mourning Sex* (1997).

8 The performers usually are: Claire Haenni, Éric Lamoureux, Yseult Roch, Frédéric Seguette, Gisèle Tremey. Occasionally, Patrick Harlay replaces Yseulth Roch.

9 This is how Jean-Luc Nancy describes representation's functioning in his short essay "The Birth to Presence." For Nancy, "representation is what determines itself by its own limit" (Nancy 1993: 1). Thus, the temporal and geographical expansion of the West corresponds to an endless, centripetal reiteration of the West's confinement within its own "closure . . . named representation" (1993: 1).

10 The splitting of the notion of presence from the perception of a fully appearing being was proposed by some early twentieth-century philosophy. Departing from and complicating Husserl's phenomenology, Martin Heidegger was one of those who performed what John Sallis called a "decisive [. . .] displacement of presence." Sallis explained how for Heidegger "there is no pure presence; for in whatever presents itself there is already in play the operation of signification" (Sallis 1984: 598). For a further discussion of Heidegger's displacement of presence and its implications for perfomance and dance studies see Chapter 4. Another important contribution for this displacement, but coming from a different tradition in philosophy, and aiming at different set of concerns, is that of Henri Bergson, whose theory of memory (particularly as articulated in *Matter and Memory*) led him to show how Western metaphysics had always "confused Being with being-present" (Deleuze 1988: 55). I discuss Bergson's theory of memory and temporality in the conclusion.

11 "A multiplicity is defined not by the elements that compose it in extension, not by the characteristics that compose it in comprehension, but by the lines and dimensions it encompasses in 'intension.'" The author's "intension" (rather than "intention") is the activation of his or her affect across "lines and dimensions" that "constitute the pack at a given moment" (Deleuze and Guattari 1987: 245).

12 The critique of the singularity of the author gains momentum at the end of the 1960s, particularly with Barthes's 1968 essay "The Death of the Author," Derrida's 1968 essay "La différance," and Foucault's 1969 essay "What is an Author?" For a recent consideration of this critique's impact in performance theory see Schneider (2005).

13 Sometimes dancer Claire Haenni replaces Jérôme Bel and dancer Jean Torrent replaces Frédéric Seguette. In an email exchange with Jérôme Bel during the writing of this chapter, he told me that, although Claire Haenni had replaced him a few times, this is not something Bel prefers – for it creates the possibility of flattening the reading of the piece as being a piece about heterosexual "couple relations," a possibility he finds "not interesting at all." So Claire Haenni is asked to perform *Nom Donné par l'Auteur* only when Jérôme Bel is, for some reason, unavailable.

14 It was Jesuit priest and dance master Thoinot Arbeau (a pen name for Jehan Tabourot), who alloyed for the first time in one name the kinetic with the linguistic, creating in 1589 the first signifier for modernity's being-toward-movement, "*orchesographie*" (the *graphie*, writing, of the *orchesis*, dance). For a more detailed discussion see Chapters 1 and 2.

15 It is not by chance that one of the great liberators of the dancer's voice, Pina Bausch, had to break with the tradition of choreographic composition and subjectivity. Bausch famously stated that what matters for her was not how people move but *what* moves people. Her Tanztheater comes out of a deep dialogue with other

antirepresentational forces in early 1970s visual arts and performance (Joseph Beuys' ssocial sculpture, Fluxus). Not surprisingly, Bausch's method for breaking the dancer's mute subjectivity was that of bombarding him or her with questions. To answer the question was both a way to fill the dancer's mouth with his or her own voice and also to reshape the dancer's body, to give him or her a new corporeality. Even today, Bausch's method even encounters resistance with many dancers and choreographers. For an excellent "inside" narrative of this process, see Hoghe (1987). See also Fernandes (2002).

16 Here, Heinrich von Kleist's famous parable of "The Puppet Theatre," written in 1810, clearly outlines what kind of subjectivity the ideal dancer must have on the theological stage. The ideal dancer is a puppet, devoid of affectation and inner psychological life, mute, with a supple body, loose joints, and infinite receptivity for the master's movements, which are directly and mysteriously transmitted from the master's center of gravity to the puppet's center of gravity. That this parable is one that invokes "the book of Moses" and the biblical fall as the main reason for why humans are less perfect dancers than puppets should not be taken as mere coincidence. Kleist (ironically) identifies the theological stage operating full blast in theatrical dance. For a deeper discussion of choreography's relation to an absent yet commanding power, see Chapter 2.

17 A first version of *Shirtologie* was created in 1997 for Portuguese dancer Miguel Pereira, a commission from Centro Cultural de Belém, Lisbon. In 1998, Bel recreated and adapted the piece for dancer Frédéric Seguette, who performs it now most of the times. On one occasion, I had the chance to see it performed by Jérôme Bel himself.

18 In a personal exchange, Bel told me that he appreciates the capacity Seguette has of "being still" and almost "disappearing" from his own presence on stage while performing this piece.

19 For a discussion of the obscenity lawsuit brought against the International Dance Festival in Ireland for programming *Jérôme Bel* in 2002, see Chapter 1.

20 For a phenomenology of the microperceptual of the still in twentieth-century dance see my essay "Still: On the Vibratile Microscopy of Dance" (Brandstetter *et al.* 2000).

21 For a discussion of Seremetakis's notions of "still-act" see Chapter 1.

22 For an explanation of my use of "subjectivity" and "subjectification" in relation to the Althusserian notion of interpellation, see Chapter 1.

23 See Teresa Brennan's *Exhausting Modernity* for an original and extremely lucid proposition of how modernity and the psychological economy of capitalism must be addressed as "the study of energetic and affective connections" (Brennan 2000: 10). Intriguingly, Brennan's account neglects the Marxist critique of psychoanalysis and of subjectivity developed by Wilhelm Reich in the early 1930s – a critique that first advanced an account of energetics in relationship to individual and social pathologies and that lies behind much of Deleuze and Guattari's critique of capitalism and its Oedipalization of representation in *Anti-Oedipus*. See Reich 1972, 1973 and Deleuze and Guattari 1983, *passim*.

24 For further discussion on the coming into being of choreography as neologism and technology of modern subjectivation, see Chapter 2.

25 For an exploration of this idea and the relation between the advent of choreography and the melancholic drive behind its understanding of absence, see Chapters 2 and 7.

26 As I suggested earlier, the question of ontology is central to performance studies. It is curious to see how a Hamlet emerges also in Schechner's identification of a deep ontological instability proper of performance, as if Hamlet was an inevitable event in performance's relationship to being: "All effective performances share this 'not-not not' quality: Olivier is not Hamlet, but also he is not not Hamlet: his performance is between a denial of being another (= I am me) and the denial of not being another

(= I am Hamlet)" (Schechner 1985: 123). It could be said that the whole of *The Last Performance* turns around this insight and this ambiguity.

27 Choreographer Suzanne Linke, along with Pina Bausch, is one of the main inventors of German Tanztheater.

28 In his lecture on *The Last Performance* at Tanzquartier Wien, March 2004, Bel narrates how at the opening of the piece in Brussels, audience members walked onto the stage, insulting the choreographer and the dancers, while confrontations erupted amongst audience members. In Berlin, in 1999, I witnessed some catcalls, and some demands for "Dance!" It's as if Bel's works are able to activate, with their quiet atmosphere, that historical role bourgeois dance audiences have taken for themselves since Nijinsky's *Sacré du printemps:* the role of the rioter.

4 Toppling dance: the making of space in Trisha Brown and La Ribot

1

> We should speak of two cuts through the world's substance; the longitudinal cut of painting, and the transversal cut of certain graphic productions. The longitudinal cut seems to be that of representation, of a certain way it encloses things; the transversal cut is symbolic; it encloses signs.
>
> (Benjamin 1996: 82)

2 For an in-depth critique of Pollock's project in its philosophical framing, esthetic innovations, and gender politics, see Amelia Jones (1998).

3 See also Schneider 1997: 38.

4 On the relation between colonialism, the empty territory and representation, see Carter 1996.

5 Laurence Louppe proposes an analogy of Brown's quadrigrams and Donald Judd's boxes. If indeed the form is similar, the intrusion of the linguistic and the mathematical in Brown's own formulation of the cube as compositional device places it closer to the ontological question of choreography's creation of its own space as an ongoing negotiation between language, space, and body. See Louppe 1994: 147.

6 On one occasion, at the Montpellier Dance Festival, Trisha Brown performed *It's a Draw/Live Feed* on a stage and before an audience. As of the writing of this chapter, it was the only occasion Brown had an audience before her. It is important to stress that I am confining my analysis exclusively to the performance in Philadelphia, due to the critical implications brought by the way this performance was mediated by the camera.

7 Regarding the function of the obtuse as that which in an image remains beyond meaning and proper visibility, see Roland Barthes "The Third Image" (Barthes 1985).

8

> We shall speak of a fully "perspectival" view of space [. . .] only when the entire picture has been transformed [. . .] into a 'window,' and when we are meant to believe we are looking through this window into a space.
>
> (Panofsky 1997: 27)

9 For a summary of such critiques see Jean-Noël Laurenti's essay "Feuillet's Thinking" (in Louppe 1994: 86–8).

10 For a critique of perspective in relationship to mobility and embodiment, see Weiss 1995.

11 On the question of women, dance and house arrest, see Derrida 1995.

12 The top of the drawing is the side that is parallel and nearest to the wall on which it is going to be hung.
13 For a historical analysis of the ideological and representational functions of the panorama, see Otterman 1997.
14 About the ontological distinction between "world" and "earth" see "The Origin of the Work of Art" (Heidegger 1993).
15 See also my essay "Still: On the Vibratile Microscopy of Dance" (in Brandstetter *et al.* 2000).
16

> I must, to begin with, insist on the following: in the scopic field, the gaze is outside, I am looked at, that is to say, I am a picture. This is the function that is found at the heart of the institution of the subject in the visible. What determines me, at the most profound level, in the visible, is the gaze that is outside.
>
> (Lacan 1981: 106)

17 "If, in order to create a sense of illusion, the scenic artist works in accordance with the laws of perspective, why should the *maître de ballet*, who is likewise an artist, or should be, transgress them?" (Noverre 1968: 45).
18 I am using in English "what-will-come" in the sense of the French "*l'avenir.*" What will come (*l'avenir*) is to be distinguished from the "future" as Jacques Derrida has already pointed out. One belongs to the always unforeseen unfolding; the other to the programmatic regimentation of efficient chronometry.

5 Stumbling dance: William Pope.L's crawls

1 For more on Heidegger's politics and on the politics of his philosophical project see *The Heidegger Controversy: A Critical Reader* (Wolin 1993).
2 For an excellent critical reassessment of Fanon's clinical and critical work, see Read 1996.
3 "Hence, better than a semiology, what Brecht leaves us with is a seismology" (Barthes 1989: 212).
4 For a discussion of modernity's intimate relation to colonialism, see Chapter 1.
5 See in particular the chapter "Grammar and Etymology of Being" (Heidegger 1987: 52–74). There, Heidegger writes how the Greek *parousia* (presence) is a "standing in itself or self-enclosed [. . .] For the Greeks, 'being' basically meant this standing presence" (1987: 61). See pp. 70–2 for how this standing is also an emerging into the light. Derrida deepens Heidegger's critique of metaphysics, reminding us that the entirety of Western metaphysics is predicated on a system of presence that secures its center. Derrida's notion of *différance* destabilizes the center, by introducing the fundamental mobility of deferring and deferment (Derrida
6 For a critical reading on the deep intersection between performance and philosophy in Piper's work, see Moten 2003: 233–54.
7 I refer the reader to the excellent documentary on Fanon by Isaac Julien: *Frantz Fanon: Black Skin, White Mask,* Great Britain 1996, Mark Nash, producer.
8 According to Laban's system of movement notation, the sagittal refers "to the forward-backward plane and any plane parallel thereto" (Hutchinson 1970: 497).
9 "An intoxication comes over the man who walks along and aimlessly through the streets. With each step, the walk takes on greater momentum" (Benjamin 1999: 417). Benjamin saw in the *flâneur* the activation of a dialectics between the individual and the crowd. However, the privilege of the *flâneur* is never quite indexed. Benjamin jots down the following note, which has resonances for the argument I will develop in a moment on the question of the ground of racism: "Asphalt was first used for sidewalks" (1999: 427). Thus the *flâneur's* intoxication and increasing momentum is

predicated on a flattening of the ground, already a colonial, if not the colonial gesture. See also, on the *flâneur*, Benjamin 1986b: 156–8.

10 These included Filipa Francisco, Sophiatou Kossoko, Eleonora Fabião, Meg Stuart, Lula Wanderley, Gina Ferreira, Harry Lewis, William Pope.L, and myself.

6 The melancholic dance of the postcolonial spectral: Vera Mantero summoning Josephine Baker

1 For a brief discussion of Martin's notions of mobilization and of his articulation of a politics for critical dance studies see Chapter 1.

2 Here, I am not only referring to the famous outlining of "the repetition-compulsion" Freud discusses in the final pages of his essay – that prefaces his later musings on the death drive in *Beyond the Pleasure Principle* – but also to Freud's description of his perambulations on the "deserted streets of a provincial town in Italy," as awakening in him an uncanny feeling (1958: 143): "the uncanny effect of epilepsy" due to its uncontrolled convulsions (1958: 151), the motions "of animated dolls, and automatons" (1958: 132), and, quite to the point of my argument the motions of "feet which dance by themselves" (1958: 151). Freud portrays all these examples of uncanny mobility as symbolic displacements of the appearance and motility in the scopic field of that which should be forever hidden and stilled: the mother's genitals (Freud 1958).

3 For a discussion of blackness as contagion see Browning (1998).

4 The "uncanny atmosphere" brought about by repetition "forces upon us the idea of something fateful and unescapable where otherwise we should have spoken of 'chance' only" (Freud 1958: 144).

5 For a discussion of Paul Carter's "politics of the ground" see Chapter 5. See also Carter 1996.

6 Article 2 of the Portuguese Colonial Act of 1930, the legislative document regulating the "Empire" that Salazar had approved even before the rectification of the new Constitution for his *Estado Novo* regime reads: "It is the *organic essence* of the Portuguese Nation to fulfill the historical mission of possessing and colonizing overseas domains and to civilize the indigenous populations" (Rosas and Brito 1996: 21, translation mine, emphasis added).

7 For a discussion of the implications of such ontological "discovery" see Chapter 1.

8 Hers is also a mythic figure in Portuguese folklore. The *dama dos pés de cabra* (*lady with goat's hooves*) is an enchanted seductress already marked as other – for this Lady is also a Moorish woman.

7 Conclusion: exhausting dance – to be done with the vanishing point

1 I discuss this dynamic in my essay "Inscribing Dance" (Lepecki 2004).

2 See Agamben 1993: 11–21.

3 See Chapter 4.

4 Phelan notes that "only rarely in this culture is the 'now' to which performance addresses its deepest questions valued. (This is why the now is supplemented and buttressed by the documenting camera, the video archive)" (1993: 146). But, according to Bergson, the question has to be reversed because the "now" – if it is indeed a temporal now – could never be reduced to an instant that passes by. The instant, as Bergson demonstrates, is a quantity, while time is a quality.

References and bibliography

Agamben, G. (1993) *Stanzas: Word and Phantasm in Western Culture*, Minneapolis, Minn.: University of Minnesota Press.

Althusser, L. (1994) "Ideology and Ideological State Apparatuses," in Zizek, S. (ed.) *Mapping Ideology*, New York: Verso, 93–140.

Arbeau, T. (1966) *Orchesography: A Treatise in the Form of a Dialogue Whereby All Manner of Persons May Easily Acquire and Practise the Honourable Exercise of Dancing*, New York: Dance Horizons.

Ariès, P. (1974) *Western Attitudes toward Death: From the Middle Ages to the Present*, Baltimore, Md.: Johns Hopkins University Press.

—— (1977) *L'Homme devant la mort*, Paris: Éditions du Seuil.

—— (1982) *The Hour of Our Death*, New York: Vintage Books.

Austin, J. L. (1980) *How to Do Things with Words*, New York and Oxford: Oxford University Press.

Bachelard, G. (1994) *The Poetics of Space*, Boston, Mass.: Beacon Press.

Badiou, A. and P. Hallward (2001) *Ethics: An Essay on the Understanding of Evil*, London and New York: Verso.

Banes, S. (1987) *Terpsichore in Sneakers*, Middletown, Conn.: Wesleyan University Press.

Banes, S. (1989) "*Terpsichore* Combat Continued," *The Drama Review*, 33, 4 (Winter), 17–18.

—— (1993) *Greenwich Village 1963: Avant-Garde Performance and the Effervescent Body*, Durham, NC and London: Duke University Press.

—— (1995) *Democracy's Body: Judson Dance Theater, 1962–1964*, Durham, NC and London, Duke University Press.

Banes, S. and M. Baryshnikov (2003) *Reinventing Dance in the 1960s: Everything Was Possible*, Madison, Wisc.: University of Wisconsin Press.

Banes, S. and S. Manning (1989) "Terpsichore in Combat Boots," *TDR*, 33, 1 (Spring) 13–16.

Banes, S. (1989) "Terpsichore Combat Continued, *TDR*, 33, 4 (Winter), 17–18.

Barker, F. (1995) *The Tremulous Private Body: Essays on Subjection*, Ann Arbor, Mich.: University of Michigan Press.

Barthes, R. (1985) *The Responsibility of Forms: Critical Essays on Music, Art, and Representation*, New York: Hill & Wang.

—— (1989) *The Rustle of Language*, Berkeley, Calif., University of California Press.

Bel, J. (1999) "I Am the (W)Hole between Their Two Apartments," *Ballett International/ Tanz Actuell Yearbook*, 36–37.

Benjamin, W. (1986a) "On Language as Such and on the Language of Man," in P. Demetz (ed.) *Reflections* New York: Schocken Books, 314–32.

—— (1986b) "Paris, Capital of the Nineteenth Century," in P. Demetz (ed.) *Reflections*. New York: Schocken Books, 146–62.

—— (1996) "Painting and the Graphic Arts," in M. Jennings (ed.) *Walter Benjamin: Selected Writings, 1913–1926*, Cambridge, Mass. and London: The Belknap Press of Harvard University Press, 82.

—— (1999) *The Arcades Project*, Cambridge, Mass. and London: The Belknap Press of Harvard University Press.

Berliner, B. (2002) *Ambivalent Desire: The Exotic Black Other in Jazz-Age France*, Amherst, Mass.: University of Massachusetts Press.

Bessire, M. (ed.) (2002) *William Pope.L: The Friendliest Black Artist in America*, Cambridge, Mass.: MIT Press.

Bhabha, H. (1994) *The Location of Culture*, London and New York: Routledge.

—— (2002) "On Mimicry and Man: The Ambivalence of Colonial Discourse," in P. Essed and D. T. Goldberg (eds) *Race Critical Theory*, Malden, Mass.: Blackwell.

Bois, Y.-A. and R. E. Krauss (1997) *Formless: A User's Guide*, New York: Zone Books.

Borer, A., J. Beuys and L. Schirmer (1996) *The Essential Joseph Beuys*, London, Thames & Hudson.

Bourdieu, P. (1991) *The Political Ontology of Martin Heidegger*, Stanford, Calif.: Stanford University Press.

Brandstetter, G., H. Völckers, B. Mau and A. Lepecki (2000) *Remembering the Body*, Ostfildern-Ruit: Hatje Cantz.

Brennan, T. (2000) *Exhausting Modernity: Grounds for a New Economy*, London and New York: Routledge.

Browning, B. (1998) *Infectious Rhythm: Metaphors of Contagion and the Spread of African Culture*, New York: Routledge.

Bruggen, C. van (1988) *Bruce Nauman*, New York: Rizzoli.

Burt, R. (1998) *Alien Bodies*, London and New York: Routledge.

Burton, R. (2001) *The Anatomy of Melancholy*, New York: The New York Review of Books.

Burt, R. (2003) "Memory, Repetition and Critical Intervention: The Politics of Historical Reference in Recent European Dance Performance," *Performance Research*, 8, 2 (June), 34–41.

Butler, J. (1993) *Bodies That Matter: On the Discursive Limits of "Sex,"* London and New York, Routledge.

—— (1997a) *The Psychic Life of Power: Theories in Subjection*, Stanford, Calif.: Stanford University Press.

—— (1997b) *Excitable Speech: A Politics of the Performative*, New York: Routledge.

Carr, C. (2002) "In the Discomfort Zone," in M. Bessire (ed.) *William Pope.L: The Friendliest Black Artist in America*, Cambridge, Mass.: MIT Press, 48–53.

Carr, D. (1986) *Time, Narrative, and History*, Bloomington, Ind.: Indiana University Press.

Carter, P. (1996) *The Lie of the Land*, Boston, Mass. and London: Faber & Faber.

Cheng, A. A. (2001) *The Melancholy of Race*, Oxford and New York: Oxford University Press.

Copeland, R. and M. Cohen (eds) (1983) *What Is Dance?* Oxford: Oxford University Press.

Corbin, A. (1986) *The Foul and the Fragrant: Odor and the French Social Imagination*, Cambridge, Mass., Harvard University Press.

Crimp, D. and L. Lawler (1993) *On the Museum's Ruins*, Cambridge, Mass.: MIT Press.

Cross, S. (2003) "Bruce Nauman: Theaters of Experience," in S. Cross (ed.) *Bruce Nauman: Theaters of Experience*, New York: Guggenheim Museum Publications, 13–21.

Courtine, J.-F. (1991) "Voice of Consciousness and Call of Being" in E. Cadava, P. Connor and J.-L. Nancy (eds) *Who Comes After the Subject?*, London and New York: Routledge, 79–93.

Cunningham, M. (1997) "Space, Time and Dance," in M. Harris (ed.) *Merce Cunningham: Fifty Years*, New York: Aperture.

Debord, G. (1994) *The Society of the Spectacle*, New York: Zone Books.

Delanty, G. (2000) *Modernity and Postmodernity: Knowledge, Power and the Self*, London: Sage.

Deleuze, G. (1988) *Bergsonism*, New York: Zone Books.

—— (1994) *Difference and Repetition*, New York: Columbia University Press.

—— (1995) *Negotiations*, New York: Columbia University Press.

—— (1997) *Essays Critical and Clinical*, Minneapolis, Minn.: University of Minnesota Press.

Deleuze, G. and F. Guattari (1983) *Anti-Oedipus*, Minneapolis, Minn.: University of Minnesota Press.

—— (1987) *A Thousand Plateaus: Capitalism and Schizophrenia*, London: Athlone Press.

—— (1994) *What Is Philosophy?* New York: Columbia University Press.

Derrida, J. (1978) *Writing and Difference*, Chicago, Ill.: University of Chicago Press.

—— (1981) "Economimesis," *Diacritics*, 11, 2–25.

—— (1986) *Margins of Philosophy*, Chicago, Ill.: University of Chicago Press.

—— (1987) *The Truth in Painting*, Chicago, Ill.: University of Chicago Press.

—— (1990) "Force of Law: The 'Mystical Foundation of Authority,'" *Cardozo Law Review*, 11, 919–1046.

—— (1994) *Specters of Marx: The State of the Debt, the Work of Mourning, and the New International*, New York: Routledge.

—— (1995) "Choreographies," in E. W. Goellner and J. S. Murphy (eds) *Bodies of the Text*, New Brunswick, NJ: Rutgers University Press.

Dexter, E. (2005) *Bruce Nauman: Raw Materials*, New York: Abrams.

Diamond, E. (1997) *Unmaking Mimesis*, London and New York: Routledge.

Didi-Huberman, G. (1998) *Phasmes: Essais sur l'apparition*, Paris: Les Éditions de Minuit.

Dupré, L. (1993) *Passage to Modernity: An Essay in the Hermeneutics of Nature and Culture*, London and New Haven, Conn.: Yale University Press.

Eng, D. L. and S. Han (2003) "A Dialogue on Racial Melancholia," in D. L. Eng and D. Kazanjian (eds) *Loss*, Berkeley, Calif. and London: University of California Press, 343–371.

Falvey, D. (2004) "Patron Sues over Show's 'Obscenity,'" *Irish Times*, 5.

Fanon, F. (1967) *Black Skin, White Masks*, New York: Grove Press.

Feldman, A. (1994) "From Desert Storm to Rodney King via ex-Yugoslavia: On Cultural Anesthesia," in N. Seremetakis (ed.) *The Senses Still: Perception and Memory as Material Culture in Modernity*, Chicago, Ill.: University of Chicago Press, pp. 87–107.

Ferguson, H. (2000) *Modernity and Subjectivity: Body, Soul, Spirit*, Charlottesville, Va. and London: University Press of Virginia.

Fernandes, C. (2002) *Pina Bausch and the Wuppertal Dance Theater: The Aesthetics of Repetition and Transformation*, New York: P. Lang.

Feuillet, R.-A. (1968) *Chorégraphie: Ou l'art de décrire la danse*, New York: Broude Bros.

Foster, S. L. (1996) *Choreography and Narrative: Ballet's Staging of Story and Desire*, Bloomington, Ind.: Indiana University Press.

Foucault, M. (1977) "Nietzsche, Genealogy, History," in D. F. Bouchard (ed.) *Language, Counter-Memory, Practice*, Ithaca, NY: Cornell University Press.

—— (1997) *Ethics: Subjectivity and Truth*, New York: The New Press.

Franko, M. (1986) *The Dancing Body in Renaissance Choreography*, Birmingham, Ala.: Summa Publications.

—— (1993) *Body as Text, Ideologies of the Baroque Body*, Oxford: Oxford University Press.

—— (1995) *Dancing Modernism / Performing Politics*, Bloomington, Ind.: Indiana University Press.

—— (2000) "Figural Inversions of Louis XIV's Dancing Body," in M. Franko and A. Richards (eds) *Acting on the Past*, Middletown, Conn.: Wesleyan University Press.

—— (2002) *The Work of Dance: Labor, Movement, and Identity in the 1930s*, Middletown, Conn.: Wesleyan University Press.

Freud, S. (1958) "The Uncanny," in B. Nelson (ed.) *On Creativity and the Unconscious*, New York: Harper & Row, 122–61.

—— (1991a) "Mourning and Melancholia," in P. Rieff (ed.) *General Psychological Theory*, New York: Simon & Schuster.

—— (1991b) "The Unconscious," in P. Rieff (ed.) *General Psychological Theory*, New York: Simon & Schuster.

Garafola, L. (ed.) (1997) *Rethinking the Sylph: New Perspectives on the Romantic Ballet*, Hanover, NH and London: University Press of New England for Wesleyan University Press.

Gil, J. (1998) *Metamorphoses of the Body*, Minneapolis, Minn.: University of Minnesota Press.
Goffman, E. (1959) *The Presentation of Self in Everyday Life*, New York: Doubleday.
Golden, T. (ed.) (1994) *Black Male: Representations of Masculinity in Contemporary American Art*, New York: Whitney Museum of American Art.
Gordon, A. (1997) *Ghostly Matters: Haunting and the Sociological Imagination*, Minneapolis, Minn.: University of Minnesota Press.
Graham, D. and E. de Bruyn (2004) "Sound Is Material," *Grey Room*, 17, 108–17.
Grosz, E. (1994) *Volatile Bodies: Toward a Corporeal Feminism*, Bloomington, Ind.: Indiana University Press.
Habermas, J. (1998) "Modernity – An Incomplete Project," in S. Hall (ed.) *The Anti-Aesthetic: Essays on Postmodern Culture*, New York: The New Press, 3–15.
Hall, S. (1996) "The After Life of Frantz Fanon: Why Fanon? Why Now? Why *Black Skin, White Masks*?" in A. Read (ed.) *The Fact Of Blackness*, Seattle, Wash.: Bay Press.
Heathfield, A. and H. Glendinning (2004) *Live: Art and Performance*, New York: Routledge.
Heidegger, M. (1987) *Introduction to Metaphysics*, London and New Haven, Conn.: Yale University Press.
—— (1993) *Basic Writings*, San Francisco, Calif.: Harper & Collins.
—— (1996) *Being and Time: A Translation of Sein und Zeit*, Albany, NY: SUNY Press.
Hintikka, J. (1958) "On Wittgenstein's 'Solipsism,'" *Mind*, 67, 88–91.
Hoghe, R. (1987) *Pina Bausch: Histoires de théâtre dansé*, Paris: L'Arche.
Holland, K. (2004) "Action against Dance Festival Fails," *Irish Times*, 34.
Hollier, D. (1992) *Against Architecture: The Writings of Georges Bataille*, Cambridge, Mass.: MIT Press.
Horkheimer, M. and T. W. Adorno (1997) *Dialectic of Enlightenment*, London and New York: Verso.
Hutchinson, A. (1970) *Labanotation*, New York: Theatre Arts Books.
Jameson, F. (2002) *A Singular Modernity: Essay on the Ontology of the Present*, New York: Verso.
Jones, A. (1998) *Body Art/Performing the Subject*, Minneapolis, Minn.: University of Minnesota Press.
Jowitt, D. (1988) *Time and the Dancing Image*, Berkeley, Calif.: University of California Press.
Kaprow, A. and J. Kelley (2003) *Essays on the Blurring of Art and Life*, Berkeley, Calif.: University of California Press.
Kisselgoff, A. (2000) "Partial to Balanchine, and a Lot of Built-In Down Time," *New York Times*, E6.
Krauss, R. E. (1981) *Passages in Modern Sculpture*, Cambridge, Mass.: MIT Press.
Kraynak, J. (2003) *Please Pay Attention Please: Bruce Nauman's Words*, Cambridge, Mass.: MIT Press.
Krell, D. F. (1988) "The Perfect Future: A Note on Heidegger and Derrida," in J. Sallis (ed.) *Deconstruction and Philosophy*, Chicago, Ill. and London: University of Chicago Press.
Kristeva, J. (1989) *Black Sun: Depression and Melancholia*, New York: Columbia University Press.
Lacan, J. (1981) *The Four Fundamental Concepts of Psycho-Analysis*, New York: Norton.
Laplanche, J. and J.-B. Pontalis (1973) *The Language of Psychoanalysis*, New York: W.W. Norton.
Laurenti, J.-N. (1994) "Feuillet's Thinking," in L. Louppe (ed.) *Traces of Dance: Drawings and Notations of Choreographers*. Paris: Editions Dis Voir.
Lefebvre, H. (1991) *The Production of Space*, Cambridge, Mass. and Oxford: Blackwell.
Lepecki, A. (2000) "Still: On the Vibratile Microscopy of Dance," in G. Brandstetter and H.Völckers (eds) *ReMembering the Body*, Ostfielder-Ruit: Hatje Cantz, 334–66.
Lepecki, A. (ed.) (2004) *Of the Presence of the Body: Essays on Dance and Performance Theory*, Middletown, Conn.: Wesleyan University Press.
Le Roy, X. (2002) "Self-Interview 27.11.2000," in K. Knoll and F. Malzacher (eds) *True Truth About the Nearly Real*, Frankfurt: Künstlerhaus Mousonturm, 45–56.

Le Roy, X., J. Burrows and F. Ruckert (2004) "Meeting of Minds," *Dance Theatre Journal*, 20, 9–13.

Limon, E. and P. Virilio (1995) "Paul Virilio and the Oblique," *Lusitania*, 174–84.

Lott, E. (1993) *Love and Theft: Blackface Minstrelsy and the American Working Class*, London and New York: Oxford University Press.

Louppe, L. (1994) *Traces of Dance: Drawings and Notations of Choreographers*, Paris: Éditions Dis Voir.

Lourenço, E. (1991) *O Labirinto da Saudade: Psicanálise Mítica do Destino Português*, Lisbon: Publicações Dom Quixote.

Mackenzie, J. (2000) *Perform or Else*, London and New York: Routledge.

Man, Paul de (1984) *The Rhetoric of Romanticism*, New York: Columbia University Press.

Manifesto for a European Performance Policy (2001) available online at http://www.meeting-one.info/manifesto.htm.

Manning, S. (1988) "Modernist Dogma and 'Post-Modern' Rhetoric: A Response to Sally Banes' Terpsichore in Sneakers," *TDR*, 32, 32–9.

—— (1993) *Ecstasy and the Demon: Feminism and Nationalism in the Dances of Mary Wigman*, Berkeley, Calif.: University of California Press.

—— (2004) *Modern Dance, Negro Dance: Race in Motion*, Minneapolis, Minn.: University of Minnesota Press.

Martin, J. (1972) *The Modern Dance*, New York: Dance Horizons.

Martin, R. (1998) *Critical Moves*, Durham, NC and London: Duke University Press.

Marx, K. and F. Engels (1969) *Selected Works*, Vol. I, Moscow: Progress Publishers.

Merleau-Ponty, M. (1968) *The Visible and the Invisible*, Evanston, Ill.: Northwestern University Press.

Mieli, P., M. Stafford and J. Houis (1999) *Being Human: The Technological Extensions of the Body*, New York: Agincourt/Marsilio.

Morgan, R. C. (ed.) (2002) *Bruce Nauman*, Baltimore, Md. and London: The Johns Hopkins University Press.

Moten, F. (2003) *In the Break: The Aesthetics of the Black Radical Tradition*, Minneapolis, Minn.: University of Minnesota Press.

Mounce, O. H. (1997) "Philosophy, Solipsism and Thought," *Philosophical Quarterly*, 47, 186 (January), 1–18.

Muñoz, J. E. (1999) *Disidentifications: Queers of Color and the Performance of Politics*, Minneapolis, Minn.: University of Minnesota Press.

Nancy, J.-L. (1993) *The Birth to Presence*, Stanford, Calif.: Stanford University Press.

Natansom, M. (1974) "Solipsism and Sonality," *New Literary History*, 5, 2 (Winter), 237–44.

Nauman, B., L. Castelli and S. Brundage (1994) *Bruce Nauman, 25 Years*, New York: Rizzoli.

Noverre, J.-G. (1968) *Letters on Dancing and Ballets*, New York: Dance Horizons.

Otterman, S. (1997) *The Panorama: History of a Mass Medium*, New York: Zone Books.

Panofsky, E. (1997) *Perspective as Symbolic Form*, New York: Zone Books.

Patton, P. and J. Derrida (2001) "A Discussion with Jacques Derrida," *Theory and Event*, 5, 1.

Phelan, P. (1993) *Unmarked: The Politics of Performance*, London and New York: Routledge.

—— (1995) "Thirteen Ways of Looking at Choreographing Writing," in S. L. Foster (ed.) *Choreographing History*, Bloomington, Ind.: Indiana University Press, 200–10.

—— (1997) *Mourning Sex: Performing Public Memories*, London and New York: Routledge.

Ploebst, H. (2001) *No Wind No Word: New Choreography in the Society of the Spectacle*, Munich: K. Kieser.

Rapaport, H. (1991) *Heidegger and Derrida: Reflections on Time and Language*, Lincoln, Nebr.: Nebraska University Press.

Read, A. (ed.) (1996) *The Fact of Blackness: Frantz Fanon and Visual Representation*, New York: Bay Press.

Reckitt, H. (2001) *Art and Feminism*, New York: Phaidon Press.

Rcich, W. (1972) *Character Analysis*, New York: Farrar, Straus & Giroux.

—— (1973) *The Function of the Orgasm: Sex-Economic Problems of Biological Energy*, New York: Noonday Press.

Rosas, F. and J. M. B. D. Brito (eds) (1996) *Dicionário De História Do Estado Novo*, Lisbon: Bertrand Editora.

Salazar-Condé, J. (2002) "On the Ground," *Ballett International*, October, 60–3.

Sallis, J. (1984) "Heidegger/Derrida-Presence," *Journal of Philosophy*, 81, 594–601.

Schechner, R. (1985) *Between Theater and Anthropology*, Philadelphia, Pa.: University of Pennsylvania Press.

Schilder, P. (1964) *The Image and Appearance of the Human Body: Studies in the Constructive Energies of the Psyche*, New York: Wiley.

Schneider, R. (1997) *The Explicit Body in Performance*, London and New York: Routledge.

—— (2005) "Solo, Solo, Solo," in G. Butt (ed.) *After Criticism: New Responses to Art and Performance*, London and Malden, Mass.: Blackwell, 23–47.

Schwartz, H. (1992) "Torque: The New Kinaesthetics," in J. Crary and S. Kwinter (eds) *Incorporations*, New York: Zone Books, 70–127.

Seremetakis, N. (ed.) (1994) *The Senses Still: Perception and Memory as Material Culture in Modernity*, Chicago, Ill.: University of Chicago Press.

Siegel, M. B. (1972) *At the Vanishing Point: A Critic Looks at Dance*, New York: Saturday Review Press.

—— (1992) "What Has Become of Postmodern Dance? Answers and Other Questions," *TDR*, 36, 1 (spring), 48–69.

Siegmund, G. (2003) "Strategies of Avoidance: Dance in the Age of the Mass Culture of the Body," *Performance Research*, 8, 82–90.

Siegmund, G. (2003) "Strategies of Avoidance: Dance in the Age of the Mass Culture of the Body," *Performance Research*, 8, 2 (June), 82–90.

Simon, J. (ed.) (1994) *Bruce Nauman: Exhibition Catalogue and Catalogue Raisonné*, Minneapolis, Minn.: Walker Art Center.

Sloterdijk, P. (1989) *Thinker on the Stage: Nietzsche's Materialism*, Minneapolis, Minn.: University of Minnesota Press.

—— (2000a) *L'Heure du crime et le temps de l'oeuvre d'art*, Paris: Calmann-Lévy.

—— (2000b) *La Mobilisation infinie*, Paris: Christian Bourgeois Editeurs.

Spångberg, M. (1999) "In the Quarry of the Modern Age," *Ballett International/Tanz Actuell Yearbook*, 40–2.

Taussig, M. (1993) *Mimesis and Alterity: A Particular History of the Senses*, London and New York: Routledge.

Taylor, D. (1997) *Disappearing Acts: Spectacles of Gender and Nationalism in Argentina's "Dirty War,"* Durham, NC: Duke University Press.

Teicher, H. (2002) *Trisha Brown: Dance and Art in Dialogue 1961–2001*, Andover, Mass.: Addison Gallery of American Art.

Thompson, C. (2004) "Afterbirth of a Nation: William Pope.L's Great White Way," *Women and Performance: A Journal of Feminist Theory*, 27, 14:1, 65–90.

Weiss, A. S. (1995) *Mirrors of Infinity: The French Formal Garden and 17th-Century Metaphysics*, New York: Princeton Architectural Press.

Wigley, M. (1995) *White Walls, Designer Dresses: The Fashioning of Modern Architecture*, Cambridge, Mass.: MIT Press.

Wittgenstein, L. (1961) *Tractatus Logico-Philosophicus*, London: Routledge & Kegan Paul.

Wolin, R. (1993) *The Heidegger Controversy: A Critical Reader*, Cambridge, Mass.: MIT Press.

Zarrilli, P. (2002) "The Metaphysical Studio," *TDR*, 46, 2 (Summer), 157–70.

Index